Treating Schizophrenia

Werner M. Mendel

Treating Schizophrenia

Jossey-Bass Publishers

San Francisco • London • 1989

TREATING SCHIZOPHRENIA
by Werner M. Mendel

Copyright © 1989 by: Jossey-Bass Inc., Publishers
                      350 Sansome Street
                      San Francisco, California 94104

&

Jossey-Bass Limited
28 Banner Street
London EC1Y 8QE

Library of Congress Cataloging-in-Publication Data

Mendel, Werner M. (Werner Max), (date)
  Treating schizophrenia.

  (The Jossey-Bass social and behavioral science
series)
  Bibliography: p.
  Includes index.
  1. Schizophrenia—Treatment. I. Title. II. Series.
[DNLM: 1. Schizophrenia—therapy. WM 203 M537t]
RC514.M434   1989   616.89′8206   88-46080
ISBN 1-55542-151-2

Manufactured in the United States of America

The paper in this book meets the guidelines for
permanence and durability of the Committee on
Production Guidelines for Book Longevity of the
Council on Library Resources.

JACKET DESIGN BY WILLI BAUM

FIRST EDITION

Code 8926

The Jossey-Bass
Social and Behavioral Science Series

Contents

ix

Part Two: The Treatment

Preface

Much has changed during my forty years of patient care and research in the field of psychiatry. As a result, we now have new diagnostic terms and medications and the severely mentally ill are living out their lives in the community rather than in the hospital. Still, many things are remarkably unchanged. For example, every few years, vocabularies of euphemisms are resurrected in connection with newly invented fads. New unproven theories are announced as "research breakthroughs." And where it counts most—that is, in benefits to patients afflicted with schizophrenia—there has been relatively little change.

The talking and listening therapy appropriate for individuals with minor problems in living also remains almost unchanged. Theories and the jargon change, but the treatment of patients remains the same. Current data on psychotherapy outcome show that psychotherapy helps some, does not help others, seems to get better results in the hands of "psychotherapeutic therapists," and gets worse results in the hands of "psychonoxious therapists"—that is, the clinically inept, the personally disorganized, and the poorly trained.

The psychopharmacological agents used for the treatment of major illnesses are better focused than they were in the past in that they do a superior job of suppressing symptoms with fewer side effects. But these agents have not cured schizophrenia to date. For the persistently severely mentally ill, particularly patients with a correct diagnosis of schizophrenia, there is little change in their lives, in the course of their illness, in their degree of dysfunction, or in the amount of satisfaction they derive from living. As a result of changing fashions in society, many chronically mentally ill individuals are now living in the community uncomfortably and in poor circumstances. Yet their lives are not dissimilar to their former lives in the large public psychiatric hospitals. Some patients work in sheltered workshops in the community rather than on farms and in "industries" in the large state hospitals. Unfortunately, we cannot demonstrate any improvement in their lives. All we can show is a new way of thinking about patients and illness, a new fashion in treatment, and an exchange in problems of living—from those of long institutionalization to those of the revolving door that leads into and out of the community. In the second part of this book I compare the well-documented life of an individual with schizo-phrenia in the 1920s (the case of Ellen West) with that of an individual with schizophrenia in 1989 (the case of Amelia East). When we make comparisons between patients of these different periods, we must be sure that we compare individuals with similar circumstances. There have always been excellent psychiatric hospitals and terrible psychiatric hospitals. Similarly, there have always been good community support systems and terrible com-munity support systems. These variables exist today as they did several hundred years ago.

American psychiatry, following in the footsteps of European psychiatry, has turned away from psychodynamics, psychoanalysis, psychotherapy, and relationship therapy to focus entirely on the pharmacological intervention. We have given up on the thorough understanding of the individual who lives his or her life with illness. We are now "scientific," by which we mean that we attempt to emulate the physical sciences by setting up experiments, holding variables constant, and using statistical techniques that test the proposed hypotheses. With this approach, the psychiatric literature has become increasingly complex, the patient has become further distanced from the clinician, and our techniques have been constantly stymied in the blind alleys of our basic ignorance about mental illness. In the process of becoming scientific, we have thrown out much of our valuable clinical knowledge and the clinician's skill.

Persistently mentally ill persons have great difficulty finding empathy, understanding, and support among clinicians and society. The present generation of clinicians is graduating from training programs that are no longer interested in teaching the skills necessary to listen to, talk with, or relate to patients. Of course, it is true that once we have discovered the "schizococcus" and have found the appropriate "schizocillin," then clinical skills and intervention can be limited to making the correct diagnosis and prescribing the appropriate medication. However, as of 1989, the clear, simple, and neat treatment of schizophrenia seems to be a long way off.

In the meantime, approximately 0.5 to 1 percent of the population suffers from an illness that we cannot cure, whose etiology we do not entirely understand, and that we treat with medications that do not work very well. We call this illness *schizophrenia*. The treatment is administered by physicians whose ardent hope for a "magic bullet" has incapacitated them as interested, concerned, and supportive clinicians who can help patients deal with incurable illness, immeasurable suffering, and frequently unimaginable distress.

Against this backdrop of our current knowledge, I present my observations of continuous contact with individuals living with schizophrenia. It is true that much of this material will be thought of as unscientific—that is, it is presented in case history form rather than in tables. It is also true that many critics will look at this material and say that these observations cannot be duplicated or checked by the scientific method. In fact, the only way to duplicate these observations is to live and work, as I did, for thirty-five years with 497 patients who have the correct diagnosis of schizophrenia. In spite of often-voiced criticism of the method of clinical experience, I firmly believe that a return to good clinical sense is essential if we are ever to solve the puzzle of schizophrenia. I do not see how an individual can do research in schizophrenia without knowing the course of the illness so that he or she can begin to evaluate what difference treatment intervention makes. After all, a difference that makes no difference is no difference.

The study on which this book is based is unique in that it reports on 497 patients who were observed over a period of thirty-five years, as I mentioned above. To my knowledge, there is no other study in the literature on a closely observed patient population group as large as this one. Furthermore, this patient group spent the majority of the time living in the community rather than in the hospital. This prevents confusing the effect of schizophrenia with the effect of chronic social isolation secondary to long-term hospitalization.

Purpose of the Book

Treating Schizophrenia is intended to work on three levels. First, it is a very specific guide to the understanding and treatment of schizophrenia. By reading this book, the student and young clinician in the fields of psychiatry, psychology, social work, and counseling will understand the course of the illness and the philosophy and technique of treatment. The young clinician will get this from the specific content of the book as well as the many case vignettes and the three detailed cases presented in Chapters Nine, Ten, and Seventeen. As well, patients and their families will gain much understanding and hope from this book, which describes what to expect and how to cope with schizophrenia.

Second, this book presents many new findings for the experienced and mature reader, clinician, and researcher about the course of schizophrenic illness. Even without treatment, patients get better as they get older. I hope to convince the senior clinician that it is still most important to *first* do no harm (*primum non nocere*). If the patient is not harmed by treatment, then as he or she gets older, the illness will abate and the patient can live a nearly normal life. I also hope to convey to the senior clinician a theoretical model for treatment interventions that makes sense in terms of our present knowledge of the illness.

A third purpose of the book is to demonstrate the phenomenological approach to the understanding and treatment of illness. I believe Thomas Sydenham, who said in 1680, "Throw away your books and go back to the bedside." This is still important advice in

1989. Clinical observation in conjunction with laboratory research will guide the way to solving the puzzle of schizophrenia so that we can abolish the illness.

Overview of the Contents

This book contains two parts. Part One comprises nine chapters on the course of the illness as derived from the direct observation of patients living with schizophrenia. Part Two begins with a case from the 1920s (Ellen West, Chapter Ten) and ends with a current case (Amelia East, Chapter Seventeen). It is hoped that readers can compare these two cases separated by almost seventy years and judge for themselves what difference modern treatment makes. These two cases are a fair comparison, as both patients were bright, verbal, and socially advantaged. And both patients received the best treatment available at the time.

Chapters Thirteen and Fourteen need to be read as a pair. They present my philosophical orientation in using psychoactive medications and are precisely up to date for 1989 and the beginning of the 1990s. However, medications change rapidly as we move from one generation of psychoactive drugs to another. New medications are constantly being developed that more specifically target symptoms and have fewer unwanted side effects. Long before the rest of the book is out of date, Chapter Fourteen will be obsolete. But even when the specific information in regard to medications is out of date, the philosophy about medication presented in the chapter will be useful. Even ten or fifteen years from now it will illustrate a helpful way of thinking about medication.

Acknowledgment

I would like to express my appreciation to the Rockefeller Foundation, which appointed me Scholar-in-Residence at its Bellagio, Italy, center, for providing the setting and time for me to write the first draft of this book.

Hastings, Nebraska   Werner M. Mendel
February 1989

TO DORIS:

The magic of love,
joy, freedom, and our old age!

The Author

Werner M. Mendel is clinical director at the Hastings Regional Center in Hastings, Nebraska, and clinical professor of psychiatry and behavioral sciences at the University of Nebraska School of Medicine and the Creighton University School of Medicine in Omaha, Nebraska. He is also professor emeritus of psychiatry and behavioral sciences at the University of Southern California School of Medicine in Los Angeles. He received his B.A. degree (1948) in psychology from the University of California, Los Angeles, his M.A. degree (1949) in psychology from Stanford University, and his M.D. degree (1953) from Stanford University School of Medicine. He took his specialty training in psychiatry at St. Elizabeth Hospital in Washington, D.C., and at the Menninger School of Psychiatry in Topeka, Kansas. He was certified in psychiatry in 1959, took his analytic training at the Southern California Psychoanalytic Institute, and was certified in psychoanalysis in 1968. Mendel was appointed a fellow of the American Psychiatric Association in 1964 and Scholar-in-Residence at the Rockefeller Foundation in Bellagio, Italy, in 1980. He received a bronze medal from the University of Helsinki, Finland, in 1980 and the Distinguished Service Award from Los Angeles County in 1986.

Mendel's main research activities have been in the field of schizophrenia and in the development of the theory and technique of supportive care. His books include *The Therapeutic Management of Psychological Illness* (1967, with G. A. Green), *The Psychiatric Consultation* (1967, with P. Solomon), *A Celebration of Laughter* (1970), *Supportive Care: Theory and Technique* (1975), and *Schizophrenia: The Experience and Its Treatment* (1976). He has also published in excess of 100 papers in various scientific journals.

Treating Schizophrenia

Part One: The Disease

1

Understanding Schizophrenia: The Natural History Approach

Schizophrenia is ubiquitous throughout all cultures and populations. It occurs in approximately 0.5 to 1 percent of the world
population, regardless of the level of technological development or
the particular values and strivings of a society. Considerable
evidence suggests that schizophrenia has occurred at approximately
the same rate for many centuries of recorded human history
(Foucault, 1965). Yet the actual picture of schizophrenia as it
emerges in different cultures and subcultures, in different social
classes, and, most important, in different individuals living in
unique settings varies tremendously. The picture is further complicated by treatment interventions. Such interventions are not only
determined by the needs of the patients and our understanding of
the illness to be treated. To a large extent they are also determined
by the needs of the societies in which the patients find themselves
and the requirements of those societies in response to illness,
particularly mental illness resulting in behavioral aberrations
(Jaspers, 1963). Thus, what schizophrenia looks like and how its
course runs over a period of three decades in the life of a human
being are tremendously altered by physical, social, psychological,
economic, and political factors.

Many times before, our observations have led us to the
conclusion that the course of schizophrenia and its effect on the

1

lives of individual patients can be understood only in the context of the total situation (Rutter, 1986). How various individuals live is in part determined by schizophrenia and in part by what else they are and what else they have. If they have a supporting family, a benevolent society, a lot of talent and personal assets, their lives will be very different from those who have the same schizophrenia but none of the supporting conditions.

Definition of Schizophrenia

Because diagnostic fashions change from time to time and from one part of the country to another, it is important to define the condition called schizophrenia for purposes of describing our patient population more accurately. Schizophrenia is a chronic mental illness characterized by exacerbations and remissions and consisting of major disabilities in the areas of thinking, feeling, and behavior (Bleuler, 1950). In the present state of our knowledge, we cannot make the diagnosis until the patient has had the illness for at least six months. The reason for this added provision is that during the acute episode, the acute exacerbation of schizophrenia cannot easily be distinguished from acute schizophreniform psychosis. We are close to developing better biological markers to distinguish the brief reactive psychosis from the acute exacerbation in the schizophrenic patient.

Schizophrenia is a chronic illness with a lifelong pattern of exacerbations and remissions, which is generally described as a mental illness. The major disability is that the patient suffers from three nuclear dysfunctions: failure to manage anxiety, failure to manage interpersonal relationships, and failure of historicity. How these specific disabilities resulting from the disease process affect the individual patient is to a large extent determined by the requirements the particular society, culture, social class, physical environment, and biology make on the individual. In some settings the disability caused by the schizophrenia is only minimally incapacitating, whereas in other settings the patient is so severely incapacitated as to require prolonged care, management of dependency, and support. It should be emphasized that the difference in the clinical picture is not so much a result of the difference in the course of the illness in various individuals as it is in the difference the disability makes in the life of each individual, resulting from his or her life situation. It is for this reason that in lieu of our having a specific treatment and cure for the illness, we find that the rehabilitation model is the most suitable for the treatment and care of schizophrenic patients. That model allows us to minimize the disabilities caused by the defect in individual patients by various social, psychological, and physiological adjustments of the patients to their environment.

The Natural History Approach

Toward the end of the nineteenth century, the natural history approach was the backbone of modern medicine. Famous clinicians (Schneider, 1959), many of whom gave their names to diseases, have in common the quality of being master observers of illness in human beings and superb describers. Their descriptions led to the new era of scientific medicine in which the experimental and scientific approach resulted in discovery of etiology of many illnesses and eventually to their cure and prevention. The manipulation of carefully controlled variables that yielded important answers to many of the biological problems plaguing humanity have become the basis of a phase of medicine generally called the scientific method (Shryock, 1947). Unfortunately, some human afflictions have not yielded their secrets to the scientific method characterized by measurement and experimentation in the production of illness. Schizophrenia is one of these conditions. Furthermore, some of the illnesses that seemed to yield their secrets to the biomedical approach have recently revealed new and widely conflicting interactions between genes, predisposition, environment, psychological factors, and sociological responses. In the headlong, enthusiastic forward rush of the success of experimental methods in medical science, we have forgotten the natural history approach. We have forgotten that science is concerned with observation, description, definition, and classification, and only then with measurement, experimentation, generalization, explanation, prediction, evaluation, and finally control.

This volume utilizes the natural history approach, drawing upon the direct and continuous observation of patients and illness over a period of more than three decades. In addition, it draws upon indirect observation through the collection of detailed histories by the observers over six decades of illness. Because we found it increasingly difficult to fit our theory based on measurement and experimentation with the nature of the condition and the patients we observed, we followed in the footsteps of Sydenham and went back to the bedside. This text reemphasizes the natural history of illness approach of modern medicine to provide a background from which to evaluate the patient, his or her illness, and the effectiveness of various treatment interventions.

At this point it is necessary to clarify the difference between scientific description and poetic description. This is in no way meant to detract from the superb literary descriptions of illness and treatment found in our language. Few descriptions of narcolepsy are superior in conveying the mental state than the one given by Dickens in his *Pickwick Papers*. The anecdotal approach of presenting case histories of individual patients has a long and honest tradition in medicine. It illustrates the illness for the clinician and allows us a considerable freedom of subjectivity. Certainly the masterful descriptions of individual cases (Jens, 1987), even when they include a great deal of poetry in their subjectivity, give us glimpses and insights that add to our understanding of the clinical picture. Yet the natural history approach is based on both longitudinal observation and multiple case summaries (Laing, 1965). The natural history must be based on a large enough number of individual cases to minimize the effect of variation caused by differences between patients, situations, and illness variables. Such a natural history is a summary or an average into which the course of most cases fall but allows for some description of the atypical cases as outside the limits of the usual norm of natural history.

As already noted, one individual human being with schizophrenia is as different from another human being with schizophrenia, as one physician is different from another, or as one writer is different from another (Burton, Lopez-Ibor, and Mendel, 1974). For this reason, I have strongly objected to calling people who live their lives with schizophrenia *schizophrenics* because the term blurs all of these differences and only allows us to focus on the sickness. Particularly in Western psychology, there has been a great deal of emphasis on individual differences. Such emphasis seems especially justified when we describe human beings who live with this illness. It is necessary to emphasize how each host responds differently and how each social, psychological, and familial system supports differently.

In the process of emphasizing individual differences, however, we must not lose sight of the contribution that similarities can make to our understanding. The natural history approach to an illness focuses on similarity as the basis for knowledge about the illness while at the same time allowing and recognizing individual differences. The similarities between human beings who live with schizophrenia allow us to understand the course of the illness, to pronounce prognoses, and to evaluate the effectiveness of treatment interventions as long as the observations of natural history are based on an adequately large sample of observed cases.

Steering a course between emphasis on individual differences and similarity of groups as a class can be difficult. Yet it is necessary. One can say that each individual human being is so unique that nothing we say about him or her has any validity for others. We can also be so preoccupied by our search for similarity that we finally see only what is the same, concluding that every human being, because he or she is conceived, born, matures, declines, and eventually dies, is exactly like every other human being, who necessarily goes through that process. Both of these approaches, even in their extremity, are of course correct and true. Yet both approaches, together and balanced, give us a more useful position for understanding (Hagstrom, 1965).

The Patient Population Under Study

The population that forms the basis of the following presentation of the natural history of schizophrenia is based on the observed lives of patients living with their illness in the community. More than 6,000 patients were the subjects of diagnostic study. They became the basis of our understanding of the signs and symptoms of schizophrenia and their ordering into the three nuclear disabilities, with a list of restitutional and consequential signs and symptoms. The patients ranged in age from sixteen to forty-six

years at the time they entered the study; this time of entry was called
the index crisis; that is, the time when each patient appeared with
serious clinical problems requiring either hospitalization or other
major interventions to resolve a crisis. Subsequent chapters will
show that this index crisis is not the first episode of disorganization
and symptoms occurring in this episodic illness. At the time of the
writing of this book, the patient population ranges in age from
twenty-four to seventy-one years. The population is 52 percent male
and 48 percent female. Thirty-seven percent of the patients came
into the study while presenting as a public patient in a public
hospital or public emergency room. Sixty-three percent represent
private patients; 5 percent of the population is black, 3 percent
Spanish surnamed, and 92 percent Caucasian (Table 1). Throughout the study, all of the 497 patients have spent the majority of their
lives outside the hospitals, although some had prolonged hospitalizations before coming into the study during the index crisis. The
average hospitalization while in the study was 8.5 days per year
(Table 2).

These descriptions of the particular patient group do not
represent a cross section of society; neither are they entirely representative of other populations of patients with schizophrenia found
in the literature (Bleuler, 1968, 1974, 1978; World Health Organization, 1957, 1979). Most of the long-term follow-up has been with
patients who have been hospitalized a great deal more than this
particular population, who have spent most of their time in the
community. Rather, this particular population represent patients
followed over more than three decades of clinical work in public
and private settings. Thus, the natural history is more or less
colored by that special circumstance of various treatment settings
(May, 1968) and treatment interventions that have followed in the
footsteps of deinstitutionalization (Meyerson and Herman, 1983).
Yet it must quickly be added that the history is, of course, influenced by the relationship with the patients' supporting resources,
which were part and parcel of the observation process. All of these
patients received long-term supportive care in varying degrees,
depending on the clinical condition during crisis. The interventions generally were massive during crisis, whereas during remission they were minimal, sometimes only symbolic. Nevertheless,

Table 1. Description of 497 Patients in Study.

Age range (1988)	24–71 years
Age median (1988)	39 years
Male	52%
Female	48%
Public sector patients	37%
Private patients	63%
Caucasian	92%
Black	5%
Spanish surname	3%
Place of entry into study	
Northern California	10%
Southern California	84%
Midwest U.S.A.	3%
Washington, D.C.	1%
Other	2%

Table 2. Length of Hospitalization.

Reporting Period	*1953–1988*
Range (During 35 years)	0–92 days/year
Average/year	8.5 days

continuous supportive care was available to all of these patients; being evaluated, described, and observed was, in itself, part of the supportive care program.

The 497 individuals in the study form the data base from which the material that appears here is drawn for the discussion of the natural history of schizophrenia as it was found in the western United States in the 1950s, 1960s, 1970s, and 1980s. The natural history is presented as a scientific contribution to the understanding of schizophrenia.

2

Age of Onset

In most studies that are concerned with the age of onset of schizophrenia, the data used to determine onset consist of the first hospitalization for psychiatric illness or the first frank psychiatric disorder identified as such by the patient or the family. Neither one of these events is a satisfactory basis for the study of the age of onset of schizophrenia. This must be deduced from a detailed history obtained from the patient, the family, the school, and any other significant environment.

Age of onset data that are based on the first admission to the hospital or first admission for psychiatric care are totally unreliable because each of these occurrences is in turn based on social, environmental, familial, economic, geographic, and behavioral factors. These tend to reflect attitudinal factors of society much more accurately than the actual onset of illness. In the hyperpsychological environment of upper-middle-class suburbs in Los Angeles, the child who has a minor temper tantrum or does not do as well in school as his parents think he ought to will be referred for psychiatric care. On the other hand, in nonmiddle-class, nonurban environments of the cotton-growing Imperial Valley (fifty miles away), an adolescent may have severe psychotic symptoms, including delusions and hallucinations, that are simply overlooked.

Life History

We must use the individual's own life history as control and as a technique of pinpointing the onset of the illness. This can be done by obtaining a detailed history from the patient and the family and the society with which the individual has had contact. This history must pay particular attention to levels of function in such easily measurable areas as school (grades, achievement, social function, athletic function, and so on), other organizations (Boy Scouts, Girl Scouts, church groups, special-interest groups, and so forth), family, and relationships with peers, authority figures, and support figures. It is from such historical observations in each case that one can spot a very specific time of onset of the illness that is characterized by a major change in conduct, response to the environment, and orderly developmental progression. Typically, the point of onset rarely involves physician intervention and is almost never associated with psychiatric care or even identified as the onset of a major psychiatric illness.

The time the patient first came to the attention of the inpatient or outpatient facility and thus entered our long-term study is, as already noted, called the index crisis. The crisis, for purposes of our description here as well as for the purpose of the study of the number of exacerbations per year, is related to the age of the patient. It is the circumstance in which the life of the individual is significantly interrupted enough to require a major intervention in the opinion of the patient, the family, the environment, or a mental health professional. Such major intervention might include initiation of treatment, hospitalization, medication (change in medication or increase in medication by at least 50 percent), or rediagnosis (from other illness to schizophrenia). The crisis might also be characterized as a major disruption in the patient's life, consisting of loss of ability to function to the extent of loss of job, loss of membership in a training program, loss of membership in a family as the result of being expelled or divorced, or loss of living circumstance (being expelled from an apartment or a house).

The crisis as defined by the patient, his or her environment, or the mental health professional who leads the patient into his or her first contact with a supportive care network that provides the observations for the study of the natural history of schizophrenia is the index crisis. Typically, in our study the index crisis was the third or fourth episode of exacerbation of the schizophrenic illness; it represented the thirtieth or fortieth episode for some individuals, depending on their age at the time they came into the study. Because at all times our crisis intervention and treatment activities were defined as part of the mental health network, the patient and the environment defined the crisis as frankly psychiatric. For this reason, the index crisis was always characterized by obvious psychiatric symptoms.

Time of First Episode

From the history, it appears that the first episode of illness typically occurs somewhere between the ages of twelve and nineteen, the most frequent time of onset being at the ages of seventeen and eighteen (Table 3). There is no gender difference for the age of onset. The history one obtains is that the individual was perfectly normal until the onset or first episode. Also, his or her normality and accomplishments in school or social organizations tend to be somewhat exaggerated by the family when compared with reality. This is so because the change in the ability to function is clearly noticed after the first acute episode and during the first remission; both the dysfunction and the prior function tend to be exaggerated by the observer. It is not an infrequent finding to hear that prior to the onset of the episode, the patient was a straight-*A* student but afterward was only able to get *C*'s. When we obtain the school

Table 3. Age of Onset (First Episode Age from History)
for 497 Patients.

Age	12	13	14	15	16	17	18	19
N	4	6	47	51	48	112	136	93
% of N	0.8	1.2	9.5	10.3	9.7	22.5	27.4	18.7

record, it turns out that the patient was really a *B* student. Then, during the first period of remission after the first episode, he or she was a *C* student. We have made the same observations in regard to social function, intellectual function, and changes in personality reported during the index crisis about the first crisis. Almost never, except retrospectively, is the first crisis—that is, the onset of schizophrenia—identified as a frankly psychiatric illness. In only one case did we ever witness a first crisis that also became the index crisis. This occurred because the patient's family was personally known to us and the youngster involved could be examined immediately.

Nature of First Episode

The nature of the first episode signaling the onset of the schizophrenic illness is such that it is often not diagnosed at all but simply seen in retrospect as a major change in the life of the individual (Binswanger, 1960). Typically, individuals are reported as being suddenly quite different. They may change by becoming withdrawn, quiet, very shy, or very outgoing. These changes in personality brought out during the first episode may result in certain environmental changes and in interpersonal responses that are often reported as the cause rather than the effect of crisis. For example, the patient may break off an intense relationship with a boyfriend or girlfriend, may resign or not be elected to school office, may have difficulty with authority figures in school or in the community, and may then associate with a different group of people. All of these events, which on careful study of the situation, even when the study is done restrospectively, are found to be the result of personality changes occurring in the patient during the first episode, are afterward reported to be the cause. Thus, when the patient is seen in the psychiatric facility during the index crisis, the parents may report that he was perfectly fine until he was rejected by a girlfriend at age sixteen, or that she had no difficulties at all until she was expelled from the school volleyball team. Careful history taking from both the patients and their families, and whenever possible from significant others who observed the patients at the time (aunts, uncles, close personal friends, teachers, coaches, and so on) demonstrates that the patients changed dramatically and then could no longer manage the interpersonal and environmental adaptation required to maintain themselves in their prior status with groups or individuals.

Table 4 summarizes the types of first episode experienced by our 497 patients. A number of them saw the first episode as a medical crisis. Common diagnoses included such vague ailments as mononucleosis, hepatitis, endocrine imbalances, growth spurts, and so forth. Needless to say, when we attempt to go back to specific medical findings, these diagnoses turn out to be impressionistic rather than proven by appropriate laboratory work. However, both the patient and the family frequently accepted the presence of the medical illness. Often the sequelae, during both remission and subsequent exacerbations, were seen as an extension of the medical problem that occurred during the first crisis. Helping interventions given during the first episode when diagnosed as medical were primarily carried out in the context of the medical model. Thus procedures of rest, diet, and hormonal supplements tended to be used by families and physicians. Because the first episode is relatively short-lived, the improvement seen in patients as they went into clinical remission was usually attributed to whatever was being done for them at the moment. This further confirmed to both the patients and their families the correctness of the medical diagnosis and the treatment intervention. The decreased ability to function during the first remission after the first episode could also be easily attributed to postsickness sequelae by both patient and family.

Another group of first episodes tended to be misidentified as primarily behavioral. Both the family and the environment reported major changes in the behavior of the patient. These were attributed either to a developmental phase the patient was going through (He

Table 4. Nature of First Episode.

	%	N
Medical	22	109
Behavioral	26	129
Environmental	13	65
Other	39	194
	100	497

was wonderful until he became an adolescent; then he developed exaggeration of all of his adolescent characteristics and became stubborn, difficult, and unmanageable) or to external factors. These might be reported as the changing requirements of society as the patient grew older. (Everyone was dating, but Jill was not ready for it, so she felt left out and different and couldn't get along with it.) Or the changes might be reported as behavioral changes secondary to growth patterns. (When Jane started her menses, she was not the same. She became wild and uncontrollable, whereas before she had been such a good girl.) The response of family and environment to these behaviorally understood and described first episodes of the illness ranged from punitive to indulgent, from biological to psychological. Some children were punished or were attempted to be regulated in the family, in the school, or in the community. Others were treated with medication (medication for hyperactivity syndromes, vitamins, megavitamin therapy, hormonal supplements) or psychological, individual, or group counseling. Much as with the first episodes of schizophrenic illness identified as medical, the behavioral episodes also responded to whatever was being done because the episode was self-limiting and would go into remission.

The third category of first episodes was described by families and patients as being primarily environmental. A variety of factors were usually identified, ranging from physical factors (At fifteen, John fell off his bike and has not been the same since.) to geographic factors (Susan was fine until we moved to New York City and she started high school. She couldn't cope with the new group of people and has not been the same since.) to social/environmental factors (Harry was fine until my husband and I separated when the boy was sixteen. After that he got in with the wrong crowd and has been in trouble ever since. He used to be such a fine boy and did so well in school.).

Although the three areas of medical, behavioral, and environmental factors of the first episode seem to cluster, a goodly number of histories simply present a major change in the continuity of the life of the patient. This is noticeable to both the patient and the family but is not tied to any one of the three specifics.

The average length of the initial episode was four weeks, with a reported range of one week to twenty-four weeks. However, the vast majority of onset episodes did not last more than four weeks (Table 5).

Never was the episode experienced either by the patient, the family, or the social group as catastrophic or as the onset of a long and chronic mental illness. Only in retrospect, as the patient and his or her family were repeatedly asked to give a history of the onset of the present illness, would the initial episode come into focus as the point at which the life of the individual changed in a major way. It is unfortunate that the little bit of testing data that was available accidentally on some patients, because they were tested during the initial episode as part of a child guidance clinic workup or school psychology effort, was not sophisticated enough or reliable enough for one to draw any conclusions. A considerable amount of data has been gathered by us and others to compare psychological test performances during exacerbation and in periods of remission. From this data one can perhaps extrapolate to the initial crisis. However, conclusions remain highly speculative and must necessarily be suspect.

Premorbid Personality

From our recognition and partial understanding of the initial crisis occurring at the time of the onset of clinical schizophrenia, it is only a short step to begin to think about the premorbid personality. We should preface such a discussion by saying that nothing about premorbid personality in those individuals who developed clinical schizophrenia is well enough understood to allow one to speculate with any degree of confidence. The clinical literature, particularly the older literature, abounds with anecdotal individual histories (Schwing, 1954). These histories tend to describe the premorbid child as particularly gifted, particularly bright, particularly good, particularly inquisitive and oppositional, and particularly successful (Vonnegut, 1974). As already mentioned, part of this may be distortion caused by the noticeable and acute change to a contrasting condition during and after the first crisis. Obviously, it would be of great value clinically as well as experimentally to identify the biological, psychological, and social factors

Table 5. Length of Onset Episode (from History).

Weeks	1	2	3	4	5	6	7	8	12	16	20	24+
N 497	12	23	81	201	56	49	18	18	31	3	3	2
% of N	2.4	4.6	16.3	40.4	11.4	9.9	3.6	3.6	6.2	0.6	0.6	0.4

(Waxler, 1974) that are common in the premorbid state of later clinically ill patients with schizophrenia.

At present, a number of psychological test clusters are reported to identify children who became schizophrenic. If these findings turn out to be valid and reliable, they will allow us to identify personality and biological factors associated with the already proven genetic predisposition to schizophrenia. We could also begin to identify the "schizophrenia carrier" and perhaps even identify environmental factors to be avoided by schizophrenia-prone people. However, all of this still is a long way from useful knowledge to be applied even potentially in the individual case. Nevertheless, some very recent research efforts are being made to explore these fascinating questions.

At the University of Wisconsin, a group of psychologists believe that they have identified a certain peculiarity in the mechanism of thinking of college students who later become clinically ill with schizophrenia. They are now in the process of setting up a prospective study to demonstrate their point (Chapman and Chapman, 1987). Another group of studies has attempted to show that even before the onset of clinical symptoms of schizophrenia the premorbid personality of a preschizophrenic child shows filtering mechanism defects in information processing. It is believed that there is some evidence that these children cannot distinguish between background and foreground, between important and unimportant; all information and all input are handled as equivalent. Related studies have been done on attention deficit in siblings of patients with schizophrenia. It is proposed that this deficit points to a finding of preschizophrenia. Related studies also attempt to explore attentional measures in children at high risk for schizophrenia on the basis of hereditary disposition. Attempts have been made to study childhood social competence premorbidly, and recently a series of studies have appeared, primarily in the European literature, showing that a period of "reactive depression" could be demonstrated before the onset of the first episode of schizophrenia. There is also a great deal of literature on the attempt to identify premorbid family and social situations, including the birth or death of significant others in the family, the birth position of the patient, the status of the patient in the family pattern. The papers comprising this literature, which are speculations on small patient populations, have not given us any confirmatory evidence on these subjects as yet.

Effects of the Environment

Both the recognition of and response to the initial episode of schizophrenic illness are markedly influenced by the patient's cultural, social, and familial environment. What the patient, the family, and the culture believe about schizophrenia influences the recognition of it and the treatment interventions proposed. What happens to patients when they finally do receive the diagnosis of schizophrenia is to a large extent determined by their environment. The picture of schizophrenia varies tremendously from social class to social class and from country to country (Andrews, Vaughn, Harvey, and Andrews, 1986). We must therefore be reminded that the individuals forming the basis of this study were mostly middle-class, Caucasian, western American individuals who had their index crisis sometime between 1954 and 1980. Yet when we look at populations of patients in totally different settings, such as the Moscow urban area of the Soviet Union and the rural area of the People's Republic of China, there is enough similarity to allow us to come up with a consistent picture of a natural history of schizophrenia. The premorbid biology, sociology, or psychology has not been adequately defined.

In the composite picture of our typical patient, the first onset of symptoms usually appears in the form of a crisis at about age sixteen. The initial episode usually lasts four weeks. Most frequently it is not diagnosed as a mental or psychiatric illness; rather, it is seen as a major change in the patient's life. It is attributed to either a medical problem, an environmental problem, or a change in the patient's behavior. There is no significant difference in the time of onset between males and females. After the initial crisis, there is a period of remission followed by periods of exacerbation and remissions of varying lengths that last throughout the patient's life.

3

Undulating Pattern
of the Illness

Although the nineteenth century psychiatric literature talks about the natural history of schizophrenia as showing a relentless downhill course without periods of exacerbation and remission, I have not seen such a case in the thousands of cases I have observed, consulted on, and treated over the last four decades. I would add that this includes cases observed before the common usage of psychotropic medication and includes some 20 cases of the 497 who never were on psychotropic medication, either because of personal idiosyncrasy or history of excessive side effects to medication. The undulating life picture of exacerbations followed by remissions followed by exacerbations is so much a part of every case in which I have observed human beings living with schizophrenia that I believe it must become part of the definition of the illness. Schizophrenia is an illness characterized by an undulating clinical course. There is a great deal of individual variation from patient to patient and from exacerbation to remission. Some remissions are of excellent quality, so much so that clinically the patient may look "well," whereas other remissions are only partial, and some of the major stigmata of the schizophrenic illness remain clearly demonstrable.

Once the initial episode described in Chapter Two (which is usually not identified clearly as the onset of schizophrenic illness except in retrospect) has run its course, it is usually followed by a period of excellent remission. That is, no frank stigmata of psychosis are easily demonstrated during the first remission. However, it is usually noted that the patient does not return to the level of intellectual, emotional, or interpersonal functioning he or she had attained prior to the first exacerbation. Often it is only during this first remission that the initial suspicion arises that there is something seriously wrong with the individual and that in fact a psychiatric disorder may be present. One of the findings that appears to be helpful in making a differential diagnosis between schizophrenia and affective psychotic episodes is the observation that affective patients tend to return to a level of function similar to that which they had prior to their exacerbation, whereas schizophrenic patients tend not to do so.

The first remission is of variable length. In some cases, it may last for several months, even a year. In other cases, it is followed by another exacerbation within a few weeks. Because the first exacerbation is often not identified as psychiatric and indeed the first remission quite frequently does not lead to a psychiatric diagnosis, it is difficult to speculate what if anything is done or not done during the remission that prolongs or shortens it, or what if anything precipitates exacerbation and crisis. Because the patient's level of functioning after the first exacerbation and during the first remission is somewhat more limited than it was previously, obviously his or her coping mechanisms are less able to deal with the requirement of challenge and stress. Usually the first episode occurs during the period of adolescence when the patient's world is one of change, stress, and storm. It is easy to find in each case social, sexual, political, economic, or familial stresses with which the patient had great difficulty in coping and which are incorrectly called responsible for the next exacerbation. Although such conclusions are not warranted, it is true that the individual who has schizophrenia has decreased coping capacity, and therefore many of the normal storms and stresses of adolescence are beyond his or her emotional means. It is not true that these stressful situations can be identified as causative of exacerbation. It is our conclusion, derived from the natural history approach, that the sequence and cause of exacerbation and remission cannot be clearly related to either stress or treatment or the patient's circumstance. Rather, it seems to be an independent pattern of undulation related to the patient's age and the nature of the illness. That is not to say that treatment interventions of a biological, psychological, or social nature do not make a difference in the life of the patient. They do; but they do not seem to make a difference in the number of exacerbations and remissions or in the sequence of crisis and calm.

Exacerbation

We have defined the exacerbation as a period of the patient's life when functioning disorganizes to the extent that major changes are required in his or her status. These deteriorating functions include the intellectual, emotional, and interpersonal. For the purpose of gathering our statistics from the observed population, we have decided to call an episode an exacerbation when a patient experiences such major changes as being terminated from a job that he or she could previously handle, being terminated from a relationship (divorce, expelled from the parental home, abandoned by a close friend), being terminated from a training program or school, being so socially disorganized as to require hospitalization, being picked up by local police authorities for aberrant behavior, or requiring a marked change of medication (a major change in the medication used, including at least doubling of dosage) to control the major psychotic symptoms.

The exacerbation often results in crisis (Caplan, 1965). That is, as a result of increasing signs and symptoms of psychosis that cause disorganization in the patient's life, he or she loses job, family ties, friends, behavior organization, or the ability to care for himself or herself. Because the pattern of regular exacerbations is the nature of the schizophrenic illness and cannot be prevented, the purpose of treatment becomes the prevention of crisis. As the patient enters a period of exacerbation, competent and timely treatment can intervene to prevent a crisis resulting from that exacerbation (Feurlein, 1983). A crisis is a disorganization of the patient's life.

Remission

The period of remission is defined as the time during which the patient does not show florid psychotic symptoms and can manage to function in the social milieu in which he or she lives. By no means are most remissions complete. There is the observation that as the periods of exacerbation and remission continue, there is some noticeable decrease in overall function in later remissions as compared to earlier ones. This seems to occur only in the first five years of illness. The observations of the sequence of exacerbation and remission in the natural history of schizophrenia are complicated by the fact that treatment interventions tend to "teach" the patient and thus alter the clinical picture. In the days when patients would remain in the hospital throughout much of their life, they showed not only the effect of schizophrenia but also the effect of prolonged exposure to the isolation of the hospital environment. However, none of the 497 patients in our group experienced prolonged hospitalization. They spent almost all of their life outside of the hospital and in the community. Thus, perhaps they form a better basis for observing and describing the natural history than did the older populations who had prolonged periods of social isolation. (See Table 2.)

Characteristics of the Undulating Pattern

As patients get older, they tend to have fewer exacerbations per year. While in their twenties, they may have six exacerbations per year; in their thirties, three; in their forties, one or two. They tend to have no further exacerbations after the age of fifty (Table 6). This observation is based on the historical material obtained from our patient group. It is borne out by our direct observation of patients while we provided supportive care over a period of more than three decades.

Table 6. Number of Exacerbations per Year from History and Direct Observation.

Age	15–20	20–25	25–30	30–35	35–40	40–45	45–50	50+
Average	5	6	5	4	2	1	fewer than 1	fewer than 1
Range	1–8	7–10	3–10	1–8	1–8	0–6	0–3	0–1

By observing our patient population for a long period and through many exacerbations leading to the undulating picture of exacerbation and remission, we found that the pattern of disorganization occurring at the beginning of the exacerbation is fairly specific for the individual patient but not at all specific for the course of the illness. The patient who disorganizes and is about to go into a new exacerbation may show signs of intellectual, social, biological, or behavioral disorganization and dysfunction in various combinations. However, the interesting and clinically useful observation is that for the individual patient there emerges a pattern of signs and symptoms of disorganization that is consistent throughout the individual's lifetime. (See Chapter Sixteen.) In order to make this observation, there must be three or four periods of the patient's coming out of remission and going into exacerbation to establish the pattern. Once it has been established, both the patient and the clinician can use the pattern to monitor the patient's progress and to be alerted early to the oncoming exacerbation; this allows for treatment interventions that abort the exacerbation early enough to prevent some of the major disorganization in the patient's life and crisis. The pattern of changes may include psychological factors such as changes in thought pattern, the occurrence of obsessive patterns, or changes in dream patterns. On the other hand, it may include changes in behavior, including alterations in eating patterns, sleeping patterns, and patterns of attention and irritability. It may also include changes in biological state as seen with the appearance of specific physiological symptoms, including pain, and changes in cardiovascular and gastrointestinal function. Also seen are changes in interpersonal patterns as noticed by the patient and the people living with him or her. These changes may be in any direction, including increased irritability, increased calmness, increased tolerance of stress, and decreased tolerance of stress. This observation on the consistency of the signs and symptoms for each patient as he or she moves from remission to exacerbation once the illness has been fairly well established is an observation we have not seen in the literature. Yet the observation was implied in some of the case reports of psychoanalytically informed supportive psychotherapy of patients with schizophrenia in the 1940s and 1950s (Bessell and Mazzanti, 1959; Hoch and Polantin, 1949; Parfitt, 1956; Sechehaye, 1951).

Usually, by the time patients have experienced their third exacerbation, their symptoms during that period are so clearly and grossly psychotic that the diagnosis of schizophrenia is made and they fulfill the criteria of a multitude of diagnostic systems, including Bleuler, Schneider, Feighner, DSMIIIR, and the MMPI, as well as our approach to diagnosis. During the intervention, patients are officially labeled as psychiatric patients and begin their life careers in patienthood. They must then cope with all of the social and psychological consequences of being defined as a psychiatric patient. Once patients have been defined as psychiatrically ill and diagnosed as having schizophrenia, the treatment intervention begins. Whether the intervention is psychopharmacological, psychotherapeutic, or of a social rehabilitation nature or a combination of all of these, it will determine the picture of the clinical state during subsequent remissions and exacerbations. Yet quite independent of the type or quality of the treatment intervention, the undulating clinical picture of exacerbation and remission continues in regular rhythm.

During the first decade of the illness, the length of crisis and exacerbation and the length of remission remain fairly steady. That is, exacerbations tend to last from a few days to a few weeks, whereas remissions last from a few weeks to a few months. The quality of the remissions, while showing some early decline, remains steady after the first few episodes unless the patient has been specifically injured in his or her ability to function by some of the treatment interventions. The quality of the exacerbations also remains fairly steady, although the severity and the length of symptoms can be somewhat altered by treatment. Certainly it is possible now to reduce the pain and agony of the frank psychotic episodes by the appropriate use of a supportive psychotherapeutic relationship and a psychopharmacological agent. Nonetheless, as the patient gets older, there is a change in the pattern of exacerbations and remissions that seems quite independent of treatment. The older patient tends to have shorter exacerbations with less severe frank psychiatric symptoms and the periods of remission are lengthened until finally, after the age of fifty, the patient stays in more or less continuous remission with no further episodes of acute exacerbation.

One might then ask that if indeed schizophrenia is an illness characterized by an undulating pattern of exacerbations and remissions, and if indeed our observation is correct—after the age of fifty the patient tends to no longer experience exacerbations but rather stays in a continuous state of remission—then is it not true that perhaps the schizophrenia is no longer present in the older patient, that he or she has been cured by age? Our observations indicate that the answer must be a clear negative. Detailed observation and description of the older schizophrenic patient during the period of prolonged remissions show that the undulating pattern continues. Although overall the patient remains in remission clinically and does not display any major or florid psychotic symptoms, in fact there is a continued periodicity in observable and measureable functions during this older age. These fluctuations do not go so far as to show periods of clinical exacerbation and remission, but they go far enough that both the observant patient and the observant clinician can recognize the pattern. In the older literature, the patient has been called "burned out" in the description of this phase. It seems, however, that it is the illness that tends to burn out. (See Chapter Eight.)

I must add an interesting observation that derives from the natural history approach to the study of schizophrenia. From the description of our 497 patients in Chapter One, it is evident that many of them had their index hospitalization after many years of illness. Once they became part of this observational group and received long-term supportive care, their exacerbations and remissions were available for direct observation. However, we also took great care in obtaining detailed history about the illness prior to the index hospitalization. Thus we were able to compare those of our patients who received supportive care during the early years of their illness with those of our patients who had their index hospitalization later and who did not receive continued supportive care in the early years of illness.

Although such comparison is seriously flawed from the point of view of scientific design, because we were comparing direct observation with variable and often probably unreliable historical data, we could not help but notice that there was no major difference between the two groups in terms of the number of exacerbations and remissions per year. What did seem to be different between the two groups was the consequence of the exacerbations in terms of a patient's developing crisis and in terms of the patient's life. That is, because of our supportive care system and treatment philosophy, our patients did not spend long periods of time in the hospital with each exacerbation, whereas those who were treated outside of our system and had their prior episodes treated by a variety of approaches through the public and private sectors tended to spend a great deal more time in hospitals. Although there was no change in the number of exacerbations per year, there was a great deal of difference in the quality of life and the social and vocational levels of function of individuals in the two groups. As a result of the difference in the length of hospital treatment, this observation becomes the basis of an extremely important conclusion that I will further elaborate in the chapter on the difference treatment makes. But even at this point, there is evidence that illness once it is established takes its own course. This seems to be true even though this course may be altered by a variety of treatment approaches, by the society in which the patient finds himself or herself, and by the response of that society to the patient's illness.

It has been of considerable interest to compare the pattern of exacerbations and remissions, including the number of exacerbations per year occurring in patients with this illness, in a variety of different socially structured societies. It is true that in those societies where the intellectual, interpersonal, and emotional responses required of a member are less demanding (as, for example, in Sudan) (Beck, 1978; Böök, 1953; Böök, Wetterberg, and Modrzewska, 1978; Kulhara and Wig, 1978; Stevenson, 1979; Tooth, 1950; Waxler, 1979; Wijesinghe, Dissanayake, and Dassanayake, 1975) or where the vocational and educational choices are less determined by individual assertiveness than in others, patients with the disabilities of thinking, feeling, will, and interpersonal relationships caused by schizophrenia are functionally less incapacitated than are patients in our Western, highly individualistic and technological social structure. But aside from that, the incidence of schizophrenia and the general course of schizophrenia are remark-ably similar in all societies throughout the world.

In drawing a composite picture of a typical patient, let us show that the patient had the onset of his first exacerbation at age seventeen; the exacerbation lasted four weeks, and it was misdiag-nosed as a minor medical ailment. The exacerbation was followed by a period of two months of remission. During that remission, his parents noted that he was not nearly as friendly and outgoing as he had been. Also, his teachers sent home notes saying that he was not performing up to his capacity. At the same time, his girlfriend, with whom he had been going steady for over a year, dropped him in favor of another. She did this because he no longer seemed to respond to her need for attention and seemed much less interested.

Within a few days, our composite patient began hearing voices that seemed to be repeating his own thoughts. He became suspicious of his surroundings and developed some beginning ideas that the food at home was poisoned by arsenic vapors pervading the house. He stopped eating, began behaving strangely, and uttered strange sayings that were incomprehensible to his parents. He stayed away from school, spent all day in front of a mirror drawing peculiar pictures on his skin.

At that point, the family took him to a psychiatrist, who examined him, made the presumptive diagnosis of schizophrenia, and had him hospitalized. The patient remained in the hospital for a period of six weeks, during which he received psychotropic medication and was also given a battery of psychological tests that confirmed the diagnosis of schizophrenia. He left the hospital to return to his home while continuing the medication and seeing the psychiatrist once a week. His adjustment was extremely poor at home, his parents were embarrassed by his state, and he was unable to fit in with prior expectations of his life situation. Intermittently, he experienced auditory hallucinations. The psychiatrist referred the patient to a well-trained psychiatric social worker who specialized in psychotherapeutic treatment of schizophrenia. In her sessions, she discovered that it would be better for the patient to leave his home, and he was placed in a "halfway house," where he lived with other patients while attending "continuation school."

After approximately two months in the halfway house, the patient developed severe psychotic symptoms, including the delusion that he was the Messiah and auditory hallucinations calling him Christ and also telling him that he was to be crucified. He was rehospitalized and his medication was increased. The patient remained in the hospital for a period of two months. After this, his third exacerbation in the first year of his illness, he was placed in a group residence called a "board and care home." There he continued with his medication and began a program of psychosocial rehabilitation.

4

Patient in Remission, in Exacerbation, and in Crisis

It is essential that the treating clinician be thoroughly familiar with schizophrenia during its periods of exacerbation and periods of remission. The clinician must know the patient's disabilities as well as abilities in both of these phases. Moreover, treatment must be based on a thorough understanding of each patient's function, limitations, and possibilities.

During exacerbation it is necessary to understand in detail the abilities and disabilities of a particular patient. Not knowing these details will lead to mismanagement and the precipitation of a crisis that causes much pain, suffering, and hardship to both the patient and the society in which he or she lives. Preventing the development of crisis in the patient experiencing exacerbation is one of the major functions of supportive care and will make a great deal of difference in the quality of life of the schizophrenic patient.

Except for the first or sometimes even the second acute episode, which represents a point of exacerbation in the chronic undulating illness and which tends to produce a psychosocial crisis often requiring medical, social, or psychological intervention, such regularly occurring points in the illness tend to appear frankly psychiatric, demonstrating clear and gross psychotic symptoms. The patient begins his or her career as a psychiatric patient, receives a psychiatric diagnosis, and begins psychiatric treatment.

It is equally important to remember that even in periods of remission, patients have serious disabilities caused by their schizophrenia. By underestimating these disabilities a clinician may push patients beyond their emotional means and precipitate a crisis. On the other hand, by underestimating patients' *abilities* during remission a clinician may keep patients from fulfilling their capacities to maximize their function and pleasure in life.

It may be helpful to take a moment to define more precisely some of the terms used thus far. In describing the chronic course of schizophrenia, we have focused on the undulating nature of the illness, characterized by periods of exacerbation and remission.

Exacerbation

Periods of exacerbation consist of a clear appearance of major psychiatric symptoms, including the demonstration of thought process disorder, affective dysfunction, and behavioral disorganization. The appearance of these psychiatric symptoms during the period of exacerbation often results in a crisis if the patient's behavior cannot be tolerated by the people and organizations which live with and around him or her. It is during exacerbation that the diagnosis of schizophrenia is usually made. If one looks at various diagnostic schemes proposed by Bleuler, Schneider, Feighner, the New Haven Schizophrenia Scale, and others, one notes that they are dependent on the findings of psychotic symptoms during the period of exacerbation (Mellor, 1970). However, there are serious problems with making a diagnosis of schizophrenia using only the information and observations obtained during the exacerbation or resulting crisis. The major psychotic symptoms are frequently indistinguishable from those of other psychotic illnesses. We will discuss this problem further in Chapter Seven.

The signs and symptoms of the exacerbation are dramatic. They vary from patient to patient, but they tend to be fairly specific for the individual patient from one episode to another. Yet even here, there are variations. In part this accounts for the different types of schizophrenic diagnoses the patient may carry throughout his or her career. If one looks through old hospital records and compares one hospitalization with another, it is clear that this difference in diagnosis of the type of schizophrenia represents a difference in predominance of symptoms. One time the patient is primarily paranoid, another time mostly silly, and a third time mostly affective.

The signs and symptoms exhibited during the exacerbation fall into the categories of thinking, perception, feeling, and behavior. The difficulty in thinking is exemplified by thought process disorder, generally called loose associations, in which the logical thinking and the usual secondary process (adult cause and effect connection) is not present. It is this defect in the mechanism of thinking that becomes the basis of the process of delusional thinking. The content of the delusions, however, is the result of the experience and dynamics of the patient and the society in which he or she lives. The patient also shows major difficulties with perception both in the consensually validated surrounding world of reality and in his or her own internal physiological and psychological processes. These defects in perception result in the gross symptoms of hallucinations and during the time of the exacerbation usually include auditory hallucinations. However, on occasion, though rarely, there may be visual, tactile, olfactory, and kinesthetic hallucinations in descending order of frequency. Thus, secondary to the disorder of thinking and the disorder of perception, the patient develops delusions and hallucinations. As a consequence of these disorders, although occasionally independent of them, the patient may develop disorders of affect.

Whatever else one may say in describing patients during the exacerbation, any clinician who has spent much time with these patients is impressed with the pain and suffering that they experience (Binswanger, 1960). Much of the pain is secondary to the delusions and hallucinations, but a great deal of it is quite independent of them. Often the patient in her extremity of suffering may present a behavioral response to her affect that makes her appear flat and/or inappropriate. Yet as one continues to observe this state, it becomes clear that the patient suffers from a fluctuating and mercurial affect that buffets, jabs, and pokes her while it makes her life a living hell. During such periods of suffering the suicidal risk is increased because some patients choose termination of life to escape the unbearable pain. Properly used, psychotropic medications (see Chapters Thirteen and Fourteen) can be helpful during this period in reducing the pain to make life somewhat more bearable. Reminding both the patient and ourselves that the exacerbation is a passing phase and self-limited is anxiety binding and helpful. Sometimes this is the only lifeline the patient can hold onto during her suffering (Fromm-Reichman, 1939).

The fourth area of dysfunction apparent during the exacerbation is the disorganization of behavior. This area is particularly troublesome to family and society and often results in the strongest response by others. If the patient is simply suffering, misthinking, and misperceiving but not behaving bizarrely, therapeutic interventions tend to be less rigorous. Once the patient behaves bizarrely in the community, society tends to respond with whatever treatment methods are available to remove the patient from sight.

A high level of painful and disorganizing free-floating anxiety is a major symptom of most exacerbations. This high level of anxiety easily leads to further disorganization of thinking, feeling, and behavior. It must be treated environmentally, psychotherapeutically, and psychopharmacologically. Removing the patient from making decisions is the preferred environmental treatment. Supportive psychotherapy in a strong therapeutic alliance is the interpersonal approach of choice. (See Chapter Eleven.) Anxiolytics offer a very useful chemotherapeutic approach.

The particular diagnosis of the type of schizophrenia made during the exacerbation tends to focus on the major symptom. Thus, if a disorder is primarily in the area of behavior, the patient is thought to belong to the catatonic type. If the patient is primarily disordered in her thinking and shows persecutory delusions, grandiose delusions, delusions of jealousy, and hallucinations with persecutory and grandiose content, then she is diagnosed as the paranoid type. If she primarily shows problems of affect, she was formerly called hebephrenic or schizoaffective but under the new system of classification is called the disorganized type. If there is a mixture of all of these signs and symptoms during the episode, as there usually is, the patient is called the undifferentiated type.

The length of the episode of exacerbation varies from a few days to several weeks. The clinical picture is markedly influenced by the treatment intervention. If the episode is treated in a hospital, the length of hospitalization will determine, to some extent, the length of the episode. Often the length of hospitalization is not related to the clinical state of the patient but rather to extraneous factors, including such items as the length of time it takes to organize the posthospital discharge plan, the amount of hospital insurance the patient has, and the type of crisis treatment she receives.

There is considerable difference of opinion among clinicians as to the best method of treatment during the crisis. Because this is not a chapter on treatment, the various bits of evidence for a variety of points of view will not be discussed here. But it is important to point out that the natural history of the patient is altered in terms of the length of the exacerbation by the particular treatment process used. If the patient is left relatively to her own devices, the length of exacerbation tends to decrease with age, just as frequency of the exacerbation decreases. Because this observation flies in the face of observations made in the older literature, where the statement is frequently found that "as the patient gets older the exacerbations last longer," it would be nice if we had data to confirm our observation. Unfortunately, we do not because the length of treatment during the exacerbation, and therefore the exacerbation itself, was strongly influenced by our clinical orientation. Our thirty-five years of experience demonstrates that to *do the least that does the job* and gets the exacerbation over with as quickly as possible is the preferred course of treatment!

Our patients have particularly short exacerbations and crises. We feel confident in our observation of the population we have treated for thirty-five years. We have noted that shorter hospitalizations and very brief treatment of the exacerbation and crisis are best. Not only do the exacerbations become less severe, often crisis can be prevented, but there is also considerable evidence that the quality of the subsequent remission is much better (Mendel, 1966).

During the exacerbation, psychological testing shows a clear demonstration of the disorganization and disorder of thinking, perception, feeling, and behavior. Patients perform poorly on intelligence tests, are bizarre in their Rorschach responses, give disorganized stories on the TAT, and show no evidence of organicity on the Bender or the Reitan. They do show high and statistically significant curves on the MMPI, particularly on the schizophrenia scale, the paranoia scale, the anxiety scale, and the XYZ scale. Also very useful are the Draw-A-Person tests, which give good projection of distortions of self-image, and the picture assembly, which provides insight into the core conflicts. Cognitive level testing, either by the Allen Lacing Technique (Allen, 1988) or the Scratch-Pad Assembly, gives accurate information about the level of dysfunction resulting from information-processing difficulty. Daily cognitive level testing is useful in making treatment and discharge decisions, as is the TPR (temperature, pulse, and respiration charting) in following the course of an infectious illness.

Here is a rather typical exacerbation of one of our 497 patients. His name is Jack Latham. He was diagnosed as having schizophrenia at age twenty-two, when he had his first psychiatric hospitalization. Our history revealed that he had actually changed in major ways at age sixteen during his high school career. The first episode could be clearly pinpointed; it presented as a behavioral episode.

By the time Jack had the exacerbation to be described here, he was twenty-nine years old. He had had regular exacerbations and remissions but only required hospitalization about once every three years, when an exacerbation would go far enough to result in crisis. Just prior to this exacerbation he had been living by himself in the community, had been able to maintain a job as a stockbroker in a local firm, and had a number of satisfied customers. He was making a very good living. He spent an inordinate amount of time going to seminars and courses about stocks. He went to work earlier and stayed later than anyone else did, and he also did much charting and graphing. Even in an industry where everyone works very hard and is highly competitive, his amount of work was noted to be excessive. Neither Jack's colleagues nor his boss nor his customers knew he was mentally ill. They saw him as peculiar, but some thought of him as an eccentric genius because he had been able to obtain good results for his investors as the result of a particularly friendly market. Jack's social life consisted of his membership in a model railroad club, which met once a week. He participated actively, focusing primarily on the model railroads rather than on interpersonal relationships. He was also a member of a local gym, where he engaged in body building. He exercised by himself and had little social interaction with other clients or instructors, even though the opportunity to do so was offered to him regularly. All of this time he was maintained on varying doses of neuroleptics.

During the past year Jack received supportive care primarily by telephone because I was living 1,500 miles away. He managed to see me in person once every three months by taking a trip to my new location. We usually spent an hour together discussing his life and reconfirming that he was still in need of neuroleptics. Intermittently, we also dealt with small problems like sleep disturbances and increasing anxiety when on two occasions he became somewhat overinvolved with a rather aggressive lady friend. In between these appointments he would call me about once a month, and we would chat for a few minutes on the phone. Essentially, he used the phone to check that I was still alive, still available for supportive care. I had encouraged him to make contact with a local colleague of mine, but he was not interested because he found he could get enough support from me even from such a distance.

When the stock market suddenly collapsed and Jack was no longer able to please his customers and his colleagues, he was overwhelmed. He found it necessary to make a large number of margin calls for his customers, all of whom were unhappy and some of whom blamed him for bad investment advice. He himself lost a considerable amount of money, although his losses were only paper losses. He could not handle the stress of being considered a failure by some of his customers and no longer being the fair-haired boy in the office.

He developed high levels of anxiety, called me several times a day, and began showing signs of increasing disorganization on the phone. He took excessive amounts of anxiolytics and started going to a bar and drinking heavily, which he had never done before. He reported that he was hearing voices calling him homosexual and a thief. I increased his dosage of neuroleptic. (He had been on Stelazine 10 mg h.s. Now I gave him 10 mg t.i.d.) He continued to call me every few hours and became very frightened that I would rehospitalize him. I suggested that he come to see me. I told him that if he felt insecure about the trip he could bring along his sister who was two years older so that he would feel more secure.

He came to see me without his sister. After a two-hour appointment with me, in which we reviewed his present difficulty, he took a room at a local motel. I suggested he call his office immediately and tell them that he needed a two-week sick leave and that someone else needed to take over his customers. I also suggested that he get a guest membership in a local health club and continue to exercise vigorously twice a day. We saw each other every day for four days. He needed no further increase in medication, and he began to calm down. The voices disappeared.

Jack felt that he could no longer tolerate working as a stockbroker and certainly could not go back to his own office. Even though I tried to dissuade him, he sent a letter of resignation to his brokerage firm, giving ill health as the reason. We spent several more days talking about his future. He was feeling much better and noticed that once he was off the "hot seat" in the brokerage firm his psychosis abated. After a few more days he decided to return to Los Angeles and sign up for a course in paralegal work, in which he had previously expressed considerable interest.

Jack returned to Los Angeles, and he did sign up for a paralegal course. At the time of this writing, he is back to getting supportive care via telephone and rare visits. His medication has again been decreased to 10 mg h.s. It is interesting to note that in this patient, an exacerbation occurred at about the same time that the stock market crash caused increasing social pressure. A very detailed history I took from Jack showed that although the drop in the stock market was the event that would have precipitated a crisis if I had not intervened, in fact he showed signs and symptoms of exacerbation approximately six weeks before the stock market crash. It is easy to erroneously believe that the pressure of events caused the exacerbation. This was not the case. The patient was experiencing exacerbation, and therefore his coping mechanisms were impaired so that when the stock market crash occurred, he could not handle the complicated interpersonal relationships with his clients or his own anxiety, and he developed frank psychotic symptoms. These could easily have led to hospitalization and total disruption of his life. He used the lifeline of supportive care to rescue himself from a situation beyond his emotional means.

Remission

Periods of remission tend to get longer and longer as the patient ages if the course of the illness and the patient have not been influenced by periods of inappropriately prolonged hospitalization or inappropriate pharmacological intervention. Once the patient passes the age of fifty, the remissions tend to be more or less permanent, although within the remission, both clinical observation and psychological testing will reveal fluctuations.

In the early part of the illness, that is, during the first and second halves of the second decade, many patients show a decreased ability to function from remission to remission. This decline in function has already been described as occurring in the first remission and perhaps extending to the fourth or fifth remission. It should also be noted that in some patients this decline does not occur. However, I have seen no patients who carried a confirmed diagnosis of schizophrenia whose level of function after the acute exacerbation return to the level or state prior to the first episode. If this does occur, the diagnosis is usually incorrect and the patient eventually turns out to be suffering from an affective psychotic disorder that was misdiagnosed as schizophrenia.

In periods of remission the patient is by no means totally asymptomatic. Although the more florid signs and symptoms are not present, significant disorder of thinking, perception, affect, and behavior may persist. However, during a period of remission such disorder does not cause major disruption in the patient's life. Thus, during remission there is a range of symptom severity. In the best remission, the patient is totally asymptomatic and to the inexperienced clinician appears to have no evidence of schizophrenia. This condition would be officially diagnosed as schizophrenia, residual type. On the other hand, if during the remission, some delusions or hallucinations, affective blunting, inappropriateness, or stereotyped or obsessional behavior remained, the diagnosis would tend to be schizophrenia, chronic, undifferentiated type.

The question should be raised whether patients are in fact not having schizophrenia during a period of remission when they are totally without symptoms. Perhaps they are cured and only later have a new attack of schizophrenia. Such a view has been proposed on a few occasions by clinicians who are primarily concerned with crisis intervention and cross-sectional samples of patients with schizophrenic illness (Valliant, 1964). However, this view cannot be supported by any clinician who has worked with patients with schizophrenia over a prolonged period of time. In no way can those who have witnessed the natural history of schizophrenia over the lifetime of patients support such a view. The persistent and totally unaltered defect patients have in managing anxiety, in handling interpersonal relationships, and in being able to use historicity is clearly seen and demonstrated during both remission and exacerbation throughout their lifetime. (This is described in detail in Werner M. Mendel, *Schizophrenia: The Experience and Its Treatment,* 1976, Jossey-Bass, San Francisco.)

From a clinical observational vantage point, one would say that even during remission, even during the prolonged and so-called final remission of the older patient, there remains a clearly discernible brittleness that manifests itself in limited adaptive and coping capacities, particularly in response to interpersonal stress. Patients also tend to continue to be easily disorganized when experiencing relatively increased levels of anxiety that would not be disorganizing to the nonschizophrenically ill person. It must be added that these patients tend to improve when faced with a serious physiologic threat of physical illness. A number of our patients have become seriously physically ill, requiring major surgery or having catastrophic diagnoses (aortic aneurysm, carcinoma, meningioma, and so forth). Yet they did not experience exacerbation of the schizophrenic illness while they were physically ill. In fact, we have observed two cases in which the appearance of a life-threatening physical illness seemed to abort the exacerbation of the psychiatric illness immediately. We have no explanation for this finding except to reject the hasty conclusion drawn by some that this demonstrates the volitional control of psychotic symptoms. The answer to this puzzle is certainly much more complicated than that.

Upon psychological testing during a remission, patients appear quite different in their performance than they were during the exacerbation. Generally, their scores on intelligence tests (WAIS) improve markedly (up to thirty points), coming nearer their level of potential. The improvement is particularly noticeable in the area of performance, and the scatter between verbal and performance scores decreases. The tests for organicity, including the Bender and the Reitan, continue to be negative. The MMPI shows marked changes in the direction of returning to a more normal profile. The schizophrenia scale is reduced to a near normal level. The paranoia scale tends to be reduced to the near normal, and the anxiety level goes way down. This instrument shows the most dramatic changes, in our experience. Performance on the Thematic Apperception Tests also improves dramatically. Patients' stories become organized, appropriate, and though they do not show a great deal of creativity or elaboration, are adequate.

The Rorschach most clearly shows continued psychopathology. Although patients generally tend to give more responses than they did during the period of exacerbation and the content of their responses is somewhat less bizarre, the idiosyncrasy of their thought processes remains clearly evident. Because of some specialized techniques in scoring the Rorschach, it appears to be the best instrument of the readily available psychological tests for the diagnosis of schizophrenia in patients during remission. The cognitive level tests improve remarkably as the patient goes into remission, usually lagging several days behind symptom improvement.

In recent years there has been considerable progress in the refining of psychopharmacological agents for the relief of patients suffering from schizophrenia (McEvoy, Howe, and Hogarty, 1984). Obviously none of these agents are curative, and some patients do not do well clinically with these medications. However, one finding in regard to medication that is clearly impressionistic at this point has considerable potential value for the diagnosis of schizophrenia. We have noticed for many years now that the response of nonschizophrenic individuals to the same dosage of chlorpromazine is much greater than the response of patients who have schizophrenia. We discovered this because we insisted that our various trainees and residents who were going to use this medication on patients take one dose themselves. While an oral dose of 100 mg of chlorpromazine has relatively little sedative or antipsychotic effect on the patient with schizophrenia during both exacerbation and remission, such a dose is severely incapacitating for the healthy person.

We have seen our young residents unable to function for one or two days after one dose of 100 mg of chlorpromazine. We are only beginning to have the laboratory tools available to check serum levels and red blood cell levels of chlorpromazine and some of its metabolites. Thus it is much too early to speculate on the explanation of this fascinating clinical observation. However, it does appear likely, merely on the basis of this clinical observation, that one might use a response to an oral test dose of chlorpromazine as a potential diagnostic test.

Here is an example of the difficulties patients may get into while in remission if the clinician is not alert. Renae Doran is a forty-seven-year-old divorced Caucasian female who was in supportive care with me for approximately thirty years. She came to our study in acute exacerbation when the police brought her to the county hospital in a grossly psychotic state. History revealed an onset of schizophrenia at approximately age thirteen when many things had changed her life. She had responded well to our crisis intervention and was discharged from the hospital in good remission after twenty-four days. In subsequent years she managed to graduate from college, take a master's degree in physical education, and obtain a permanent teaching position in a local high school. Over the years she had one other hospitalization for a period of six days when she disorganized at age thirty-one. At that time she was recently married and after two months decided to have the marriage annulled. She felt she could not handle marriage, and her husband could not handle her exacerbations. At one time she was maintained on a low dosage of neuroleptic, but for the past ten years she had not required any medication. Her aftercare consisted of a once-a-month half-hour visit to my office, where we reviewed the reality of her life and spent much time giving her permission not to try to do more than she felt she could do. She was well liked at school, had received appropriate pay increases over the years, and did some socializing with other teachers after hours. In her personal life she was somewhat withdrawn, and many of her friends and members of her family thought of her as a typical "spinster schoolteacher." Yet she was able to work regularly, to enjoy her various physical activities, including golf and swimming, and to relate at least somewhat to her family. On several occasions she was asked to coach a team at school, but each time, with the support of her therapist, she was able to decline the offer because she felt she could not handle the interpersonal tensions involved. She was able to handle regular physical education classes very comfortably.

When I retired from practice and was about to set sail for a five-year circumnavigation, I referred her for supportive care to a young colleague who thoroughly understood the basic principles of this approach. The three of us had two joint sessions to make the transition, and the patient began seeing her new psychiatrist approximately three months before I departed.

When I returned to the United States five years later, I was contacted by this patient's eighty-three-year-old mother, who went to considerable lengths to find me. She told me that her daughter had not done well during my absence, had spent a considerable amount of time (nine months) in a hospital, and had resigned from her teaching position. To the mother, she seemed overmedicated. The mother asked me to see the patient as soon as I could.

I called my colleague, who confessed to me that he had made some serious mistakes in handling the patient and that the patient had experienced a great deal of disruption in her life. He had been seeing her in supportive care for approximately six months when he decided the patient was doing so well that I had probably been wrong in my diagnosis. He conveyed this message to her and suggested that she should have new psychological testing to see whether indeed she had schizophrenia or some more easily treatable condition such as a neurotic disorder. He sent her to an inexperienced psychologist who found no evidence of schizophrenia but rather made the diagnosis of a chronic anxiety neurosis in a basically hysterical personality. On the basis of this test information my colleague suggested to the patient that she engage in intensive insight-oriented psychotherapy with him on a three-times-a-week basis. In the therapy he focused on her sexual inhibitions and interpersonal conflicts, using aggressive confrontations as his major strategy. He noticed some disorganization in her but thought that this was based on her hysterical personality.

After approximately four months of therapy the patient developed a psychotic disorganization, including a delusional system and auditory hallucinations. She believed herself to be an angel of God who had been sent to earth to reform humanity. Because these particular symptoms had a hysterical flavor, my colleague decided to place her in a private hospital for a short period of time so she could reorganize. He assumed that she was experiencing a transference psychosis. However, the hospitalization went very badly; the patient was given large doses of neuroleptics to which she did not respond well, and no reason for discharge was found. She was finally discharged after nine months when her hospitalization insurance ran out. My colleague attempted to provide supportive care after hospitalization, but the patient would not accept this. She wanted insight-oriented psychotherapy, feeling this was the way to go. She could no longer accept her interpersonal limitations and the difficulties with her anxiety management, which previously she had known as being part and parcel of her chronic illness. Eventually, she left my colleague and was seen by the same psychologist, who again misdiagnosed her and attempted insight-oriented psychotherapy. The downward spiral in her life continued to the point that she resigned from teaching, lived increasingly like a recluse, and was essentially nonfunctional after a serious suicide attempt.

What happened in this case is that the clinician did not understand that the patient still had schizophrenia when she was in excellent remission and functioning well. With insight-oriented psychotherapy he attacked her defenses and shattered her adjustment. He raised demands and hopes in her which were beyond her emotional means. Unfortunately, it was very difficult for her afterward to accept supportive care.

I no longer lived in the area, and the patient did not have enough of a positive transference to me to start a long distance supportive care relationship. I referred her to a local social worker who was an expert in supportive care. With him, she was able to develop a supporting relationship, and according to my latest information she is again stabilized and doing fairly well, although not yet working regularly. This case is a sad illustration of how important it is for the clinician to make the correct diagnosis and to act on that diagnosis in his or her therapeutic approach. The disorganization and downhill course this patient experienced was entirely the result of incorrect treatment.

Returning to our composite picture of a typical patient from the previous chapter, the patient is now in the board and care home, after his third exacerbation, having his third remission. He is still in the first years of his illness. He has no frank psychiatric symptoms. His state is characterized by a general amotivationality and poor judgment in his interpersonal relationships. This is being dealt with in an organized psychosocial rehabilitation program in which he is given only as much responsibility as he can handle (Mendel, 1968b). His living circumstance, his socialization, and his prevocational training are being directed by his therapist, who also provides the appropriate level of psychotropic medication on which he seems to function best. The goal of treatment now is to normalize his life as much as possible and to help equip him to use the usual resources of support found in any community and not particularly related to the mental health system. (See Chapter Fifteen.) Ten weeks after he has been in the program, there is some reappearance of paranoid delusions and some hallucinations. At that time the patient's medication is increased, an anxiolytic agent is added, and his program is slowed somewhat to make the threat of part-time employment less frightening to him. The amount of structure in his program is slightly increased. After approximately two weeks the frankly psychotic symptoms again disappear, and over the next month the medication is again decreased to the prior level. Thus, the fourth exacerbation has been the shortest (less than two weeks). It was entirely handled in the community and without interruption of his life circumstances so that the exacerbation did not result in a crisis.

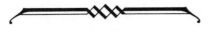

5

Role of Treatment in
the Course of the Illness

This chapter presents a point of view about the role of treatment in the natural history of schizophrenia. Treatment and various treatment procedures are discussed in terms of their influence (Mosher and Keith, 1979) on the natural history of the illness and on the life of the patient with the illness. As noted earlier, the treatment outcome of any approach must be judged against the background of natural history, particularly in the case of an illness that is characterized by periods of exacerbation and remission and has a natural course of decreasing symptomotology with age. It is clear that not only does the natural course of the illness in the life of the patient influence treatment outcome, but treatment approaches themselves, whether psychological, sociological, or pharmacological, influence the outcome of the illness. A careful history approach is necessary not only to make a diagnosis (discussed in Chapter Seven) but also to understand where the patient is with his or her life vis-à-vis the natural history and the influence of treatment.

   Treatment as it is used in this chapter does not refer only to interventions that are planned for the patient's benefit, such as increasing comfort, decreasing pain, increasing function, and decreasing disabilities. It also refers to treatment of the patient by society, family, peers, and culture, in short, by his or her environment. All of these factors make extremely important contributions to the clinical picture and the natural history. How the environment and the patient feel about illness, about mental illness, about dysfunction, about psychiatric symptoms, and about psychiatric treatment makes a great deal of difference not only to the patient and his or her family but also to the course of the illness. Thus, *where* patients have schizophrenia makes a great deal of difference as to how disabled they are by it, how they feel about themselves and their illness, how their friends and families feel about them and their illness, how they respond to the illness, including the pain and agony and dysfunction, and how they respond to treatment. Even though the difficulties of thinking and feeling and perception and behavior are observed throughout the course of the illness, the content of each of these areas of dysfunction is very much influenced by the concerns of the particular society in which patients live. The content of paranoid delusions, for example, was very different in the 1950s, when it tended to concern itself with McCarthyism and Communists in the United States, than it was in the 1970s, when the content tended to be related to nuclear radiation and pollution, and in the 1980s, when the content of delusions changed to economic concerns.

In different cultures, subcultures, and social settings the response to illness and psychiatric symptoms as well as the amount of disability caused by them varies a great deal. When we compare a rural setting and its traditionally agricultural life with an urban setting in a highly competitive and intensely interpersonal environment of an American city, there are major differences. These differences may be so great that the course of the illness almost appears to be altered. In the urban setting, the disabilities caused by the signs and symptoms of schizophrenia that eventually result in the amotivationality and the interpersonal ineffectiveness and clumsiness tend to make the patient so ineffective that his or her independent function is seriously compromised. The picture is further complicated by the absence in the American urban setting of a naturally occurring family or neighbor support network to assist the patient in functioning. Added to this is the general level of tension, the lack of physical space, and the high level of competition that characterize much of the urban environment. Under these circumstances, patients who are highly incapacitated in those very areas in which a competent level of function is required, that is, in the areas of anxiety management and interpersonal skills and the ability to learn from life's experience (historicity), have a much harder time. Similar patients with the same course of illness, the same diagnosis of schizophrenia, the same signs and symptoms of gross psychosis during exacerbation, and precisely the same disabilities during periods of remission, have a much better life and are much less incapacitated by their disabilities if they live in the peasant society of Ceylon or in the rural setting of Nigeria or India (Hollingshead and Redlich, 1958; Parsons, 1953, 1958).

Certainly society and social system make a great deal of difference. We have had the opportunity to observe patients who suffer from schizophrenia in a setting where a social support system is not specifically created by the mental health establishment but rather as a result of the political and economic structure of society, as for example in the People's Republic of China, the Soviet Union, and other socialist countries. In these settings there are ready-made peer groups, peer support systems, and peer-pressure systems into which schizophrenic patients fit as the result of their citizenship, their work assignment, their living assignment, and their membership and action in political groups rather than as a result of their having schizophrenia. If the whole system is essentially a sheltered workshop and if every citizen spends a considerable portion of each day in meetings and group activities, then the disabilities caused by the illness of schizophrenia are much less of a problem to patients than they would be in the urban, competitive, individualistic society found in the industrial cities of the United States. Thus, urban versus rural, socialist versus capitalist, industrial versus nonindustrial are examples of different societal structures that make a great difference in the life of a patient with schizophrenia. The natural history of the disease is altered by the amount and kind of disability caused by the nuclear defects of schizophrenia in the life of the individual that is lived in a particular society.

Specifically, those portions of the natural history that are altered by treatment and societal attitudes include (1) the length of the exacerbation, (2) the life disruption caused by the exacerbation, (3) the ability to achieve function and comfort during remission, (4) the difficulties caused by the secondary or side effects of treatment interventions, which are separate from difficulties and disabilities caused by schizophrenia, and (5) the content of the delusions, hallucinations, and paranoid perception.

Not altered are (1) the number of exacerbations per year, (2) the total length of the illness, (3) the decreasing severity of signs and symptoms during the exacerbation with age, and (4) the increasing length of remission and increasing quality of remission with age after the third decade of the patient's life.

The 497 patient lives we have observed have been lived in western United States technological urban settings. We found that what was expected of a patient by his or her family and subculture determined how the environment responded to the patient's illness and to the defects and disabilities caused by that illness. This of course is also expressed in the patient's own opinion of himself or herself and in essence determines how disabling the illness is and how painful the disabilities are for him or her. This is quite apart from the pain and chaos and disorganization caused by specific psychiatric symptoms.

A more detailed look at specific effects of planned treatment interventions shows the importance of expectancy. This is evident regardless of the model of treatment approach, be it medical, learning, social manipulation, or rehabilitation. All human beings respond to what is expected of them (Minkowski, 1933). This is particularly true for patients who are disorganized or chaotic in their self-concept, who are racked with pain and agony, whose interpersonal skills are impoverished, and whose anxiety level is so impairing that they are constantly overwhelmed by free-floating anxiety. These patients tend to require cues as to how they should think, feel, perceive, and behave. If a treatment setting implies the expectancy that the patients are totally incapacitated and can do nothing, that they have an illness with a relentless downhill course, and that they are hopelessly crazy, then their behavior, attitudes, thoughts, feelings, and perceptions will be molded by this expectancy (Stuart, 1980).

It is easily observed that one of the things that occurs in the usual mental health setting, be it a psychiatric hospital or clinic, is that patients learn how to be crazy. They learn what kinds of symptoms are expected of them and in what kind of behavior they must engage to receive attention and care. This learning process, which is the result of many treatment transactions in mental health treatment settings, tends to color and alter the patients' ability to function in society.

The sociology literature has discussed the downward drift observed in the schizophrenic patient's life. The individual patient, as a result of his impairment in social and vocational function, changes in social and financial status so that he is likely to move to a lower socioeconomic class. For example, a patient who comes from upper-middle-class parents and expectancy cannot function at that level and becomes an unskilled workman, lives on a very limited income, and associates with lower-middle-class people. Thus he has experienced downward social drift. If he marries, he tends to marry down, and if he establishes a family, he will be living a lower-middle-class life in contrast to his upper-middle-class parents. A similar downward drift is seen in female patients, whose social class tends to be more determined by their husbands, even today in spite of the emphasis on women's rights and female independence. Because of interpersonal disabilities, female patients tend to be involved with and marry men of a lower class than the class of their parents.

Functional disabilities in the vocational and interpersonal sphere that occur in patients of middle-class families in the urban American culture often tend to be hidden behind political and social causes. Patients reify their disabilities in the many political and social fringe movements available. These groups tend to attract schizophrenic patients. Various subcultures of right- and left-wing political extremes and experimental living arrangements have disproportionate numbers of patients who are correctly diagnosed as having schizophrenia. Patients who are expelled from their own society because their symptoms are intolerable to that society tend then to find a society that is more accepting. This in no way alters the course of the illness or the seriousness of their pain and dysfunction. It may, however, alter their life course to the extent that they have fewer difficulties as a result of their illness-caused defects and disabilities.

American middle-class society, which is upward-striving,

and the urban technologically proficient culture value independence, creativity, ambition, and aggressiveness. Such a society is not user friendly to the life of a person with schizophrenia. The personality characteristics secondary to impairment of schizophrenia are particularly disabling. These attitudes of the culture not only color society's response to patients but also the patients' response to themselves and to the goals of treatment. For example, psychiatry, which is a branch of medicine, finds itself somewhat more involved as an advocate for society than is usual in other branches of medicine.

Every physician intends to alleviate suffering and dysfunction just as a psychiatrist intends to do. It is also true that every physician has some general responsibility for society, as for example in the treatment and reporting of infectious disease. This public health aspect of medicine is somewhat more emphasized in the function of psychiatry. Besides caring for patients and alleviating their distress and dysfunction, the psychiatrist has also accepted a considerable responsibility for protecting society from mentally ill patients and their behavior. Thus more than any other physician, the psychiatrist is caught between the needs of the individual patient and the needs of society. Often the psychiatrist is more an agent of society than he or she wishes to be.

This special medical attitude of psychiatry colors the treatment of individual patients. For example, how heavily the psychiatrist medicates a patient and therefore risks some of the unwelcomed side effects of medication depends not only on the patient's discomfort and wishes but also on society's ability to tolerate the patient and his or her aberrant behavior in their midst, and what demand society makes to have that behavior suppressed. Because the use of medication, including the complications associated with that use (pseudo-Parkinsonism, depression, tardive dyskinesia, and so on), will affect the patient's ability to reconstitute after the exacerbation and ability to function during the remission, it appears that these social factors influence medical treatment and therefore the course of the patient with his or her illness (Greinspoon, Ewalt, and Shader, 1968).

If the social structure is such that society cannot tolerate patients with schizophrenic symptoms in their midst and insist on hospitalizing and thus sequestering patients, then such treatment

will alter the course of patients' lives. It has been demonstrated over
many years and in many countries that prolonged or continuous
hospitalization in a state of isolation from the mainstream of society
is severely incapacitating and interferes with the usual remission
process. Thus even though neither medication nor hospitalization
nor for that matter psychotherapy alters the basic process of
schizophrenia, it does markedly alter the course of patients' lives
when the secondary effects of treatment exaggerate disability and
dysfunction.

From the long-term study of individual patients with
schizophrenia, it has become clear that the specific symptom choice
(this is not a conscious choice) a patient makes is seriously influenced by the culture and society in which the patient lives. Literally, the fashion of going crazy changes from time to time and
culture to culture. When we first began observing patients with
schizophrenia, psychotic symptoms of movement such as catatonic
stupor and catatonic excitement were much more frequently seen
than they are today. Similarly, late symptoms of pseudodementia,
including hebephrenia, were much more frequently observed then.
Today these symptoms are much rarer, and in fact so much rarer
that the diagnosis of hebephrenic schizophrenia has been dropped
from the diagnostic statistical manual of 1980 and replaced by the
category "disorganized schizophrenia." On the other hand,
paranoid symptoms of schizophrenia were much more frequently
seen in the 1970s than they were in the 1950s. Moreover, the content
of paranoia has markedly changed and is very topically related to
the concerns of society at the time the patient first develops his or
her paranoid organizational response to the distress, discomfort,
and disorganization of the period of exacerbation of a psychotic
illness.

Religious content for delusions and hallucinations can exist
only in those patients for whom religion, religiosity, and religious
content are part of the culture and structure of their lives. If on the
other hand, the culture is concerned with government, international
relations, threat of war, overwhelming technology, and taxes, then
the content of delusions is related to those factors. Where formerly
the paranoid patients were in private communication with, watched
by, or had thoughts inserted by the devil, God, the pope, or priests,

today these same functions are performed by the FBI, the Communists, the Internal Revenue Service, or corporate headquarters. The amount of discomfort of delusions and hallucinatory symptoms has not changed. Nor has the course of the natural history of schizophrenia. But the content of delusions and hallucinations changes and is certainly a product of the culture and society.

Summary

In looking at the natural history of any illness, one must take into account not only the illness but the host and the environment in which the host for the illness must function. In this chapter we have focused on the environment, including the social, cultural, familial, economic, political, and treatment aspects that influence the course of the life of the individual who has schizophrenia. These factors do not alter the illness itself. There is no evidence from any of the comparative studies in a variety of cultures to indicate that the incidence of schizophrenia varies in different societies or cultures. It always appears to be the same, about 0.5 to 1 percent. There is also no evidence that there is any difference in the course of the illness itself, that is, in the pattern of remission and exacerbation, in the time of onset, in the age of the most disruptive crises, and the much later age of longer remissions and less chaotic exacerbations. However, what is different is the amount of disability caused by the defects of the illness and the response of the culture and society to these particular disabilities. Factors that are part of the culture, society, nationality, family, and treatment program do influence the life of the patient noticeably. It is very important that any kind of treatment program for schizophrenia be thoroughly based within the context of the particular society in which the patient has to live with schizophrenia. All of the areas of human function, including work, leisure, and interpersonal relationships, are strongly affected by the disabilities of schizophrenia. The attitudes toward work, leisure, and interpersonal relationships are also very much influenced by the culture.

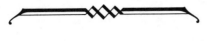

6

Factors Affecting Prognosis

The term *prognosis* is usually applied to the prediction of outcome of an illness in a particular patient. We here are concerned with observing, describing, and understanding differences in the course of illness among different patients. Are there differences, so to speak, in the virulence of certain schizophrenias, or are the differences entirely in the host? Are differences in the course of schizophrenia predictable or entirely fortuitous?

General clinical wisdom (Strauss and Carpenter, 1974a) has led to the ability to make some prediction about the probable outcome in the individual case. Clinical observations, when checked against the data of our study of 497 patients, are at least partially confirmed. However, we must be very careful both in the knowledge based on clinical wisdom and in the evaluation of our data to clearly differentiate that part of prognosis which is attributable to the course of the illness and that part which is attributable to the differences between people who have schizophrenia. Part of the outcome is clearly attributable to some of the factors mentioned in Chapter Five, such as the attitudes of society, culture, and family and the secondary problems caused by them and by treatment interventions.

In the literature of the latter part of the nineteenth century, the illness we now call schizophrenia (since Bleuler in 1908) was called dementia praecox. The name itself implied a necessary downhill course showing marked intellectual deterioration and a great drop in cognitive function as part and parcel of the diagnosis. Over the past century we have learned that a great deal of what was thought to be a relentlessly progressive and inevitably downhill course of the illness, in fact, is secondary to the very prolonged social isolation (often five or six decades) from family and normal society in the special subculture of the asylum. The progressive deterioration was thought to be so much a part of the diagnosis of schizophrenia that when an occasional case appeared in the literature that had a very different outcome (as for example, some of Freud's famous early analytic cases, which clearly fit the diagnosis of schizophrenia), a different diagnosis was made. Even though the literature at the turn of the century described the outcome of schizophrenia as invariably poor, and even though in retrospect we know that much of this poor outcome is related to factors consisting primarily of the result of treatment, we also see the influence of society. Today, too, the prognosis of the individual living in the urban Western technological setting is quite different from the prognosis of the individual living in a rural, nontechnological, and family-oriented society with strong social networks.

Aside from the effect of social and cultural factors in which the patient experiences his or her life with illness, there is also the matter of diagnostic subgroups. I am not concerned with the technique of confirming the diagnosis or the categorizing of various individuals with schizophrenia into useful and consistent groups. Rather, in the natural history approach I feel that schizophrenia is an illness with a consistent set of signs and symptoms, a predictable course with a closely identifiable set of defects and disabilities. When we see an individual case in which the natural history is so aberrant from the usual natural history of schizophrenia as to be beyond the bounds of variation from the norm, we must necessarily wonder whether the diagnosis has been correctly applied or whether our descriptions are so broad as to make the diagnostic category of schizophrenia meaningless. The matter of diagnosis will be discussed in much more detail in Chapter Seven. It is sufficient here to reiterate that when we correct our observations for social and cultural factors, for individual differences between people, and for the effect of the treatment transactions themselves, then a consistent prognostic picture emerges in the natural history that is not so diverse as to make one believe that this category is all-inclusive and therefore meaningless.

In the observations of my particular patient population, I was somewhat aided in that this population came from a homogeneous cultural and societal background and was exposed to a fairly consistent set of treatment interventions at least for that portion of the illness during which they were under my direct observation. Thus I was able to neutralize the social and cultural factors as well as those factors caused by differences in treatment intervention in their effect on prognosis. What was left were the observations based primarily on the natural history of the illness as modified only by individual differences among patients.

There certainly are some differences in prognosis between the diagnostic subgroups of schizophrenia. The more limited and precise use of the diagnosis of schizophrenia, which is exemplified by the most recent revisions in the diagnostic and statistical manual (Tischler, 1987), excludes those categories of subgroups that have not fit the usual pattern of the natural history. In those categories remaining in the general diagnosis of schizophrenia, there is some prognostic variation (Taylor, 1972). However, because the diagnostic subgroups are based primarily on the description of the major psychotic symptoms during the acute episode when the diagnosis is made and because these signs and symptoms observed and described are based on many factors, including premorbid personality, social and cultural factors, and acuteness of onset, then we may simply be involved in the circular argument that good prognosis causes good prognosis and that poor prognosis causes poor prognosis.

When we talk about prognosis from a history point of view, we must define our terms (Ciompi, 1980). If we talk about prognosis being good if the individual is totally without the illness, that is, if no remaining defect, signs and symptoms, or disabilities can be found, then the prognosis is never good. Not one single case in the 497 I have observed over an extended period has ever gotten totally over his or her schizophrenia to the extent that I could no longer detect the presence of the disease. Here I must add, however, that

I have been tight in the use of our diagnosis so that I excluded those individuals who are more correctly placed in the category of schizophreniform disorder or brief reactive psychosis. Those are generally individuals who have an entirely different history of illness and a different outcome. With these cases, there is one episode of acute psychosis without further evidence of psychosis and no prolonged disability or defects during the period of the continuous remission.

If on the other hand, good prognosis is based on the ability of the patient to live outside of the hospital setting, then the prognosis for each one of the 497 patients is superb (Lassenius, Ottosson, and Rapp, 1973). Not one of them has lived his or her life in the hospital or spent any extensive periods of time in the hospital while under my observation and care for thirty-five years. However, neither one of these extreme points of view regarding prognosis is really useful (Chase and Silverman, 1941). Rather, our understanding of prognosis must be based on the patient's lack of discomfort and distress and lack of disability and dysfunction and on the patient's successful and independent management of life, including the ability to relate, to work and to enjoy and function in the culture and society. On this basis I would say that generally the prognosis for the observed patient population has been good, and as the patients get older it improves. Although all of the patients remain limited in certain ways and maintain demonstrable nuclear disabilities and perhaps even biological markers (see Chapter Seven on diagnosis), most of them do function more and more normally, with increased comfort and with few episodes of exacerbation.

The literature of prognosis of the last forty years seems to have come full circle (Strauss and Carpenter, 1974b). In the 1940s, Polantin and Hoch (1947) described premorbid personality as one of the major factors influencing prognosis for the patient with schizophrenia. They found that the individual who had better intelligence, better social skills, better adaptive capacities, and a better record of having functioned in a society with other people prior to the onset of schizophrenia generally had a better prognosis for the outcome of schizophrenic illness. The emphasis by Polantin and Hoch was on differences in prognosis of the individual patient based on differences between individual human beings rather than on differences of the particular type of schizophrenia.

The literature of the 1950s and 1960s on prognosis and schizophrenia tended to focus more on differences in the disease itself. Great attempts were made to differentiate between reactive and process schizophrenia, particularly in the European literature. Although the observations leading to the attempts at clinical differentiation between types of schizophrenia were based on the same observations that had earlier led to emphasizing premorbid personality, the definite idea arose that poor outcome schizophrenia was really a different illness than good outcome schizophrenia. As we began doing comparative studies leading to better and more consistent application of the diagnosis, as for example in the Anglo-American study (Edwards, 1972), we slowly recognized that we were talking about differences in the host, that is, in premorbid personality.

The literature of the 1970s emphasized the objective results of premorbid personality (Fowler, 1972). We became interested in describing premorbid personality in such terms as whether the patients had been able to get married, whether they had been able to complete school, whether they had held a job, whether they were able to focus consistently enough to develop in a career or profession prior to being ill with the first episode. There was also an attempt to observe and describe how patients bounced back from the early episodes and how closely their function returned to their original premorbid state. All of these, of course, were ways of bringing premorbid personality into the picture as the major cause of difference in the course of illness (Harding, Zubin, and Strauss, 1987), that is, the prognosis for the life of the individual human being with schizophrenia.

After thirty-five years, we have more or less returned to the view that the most important factor in determining the course of a particular case of schizophrenia is the host, that is, the premorbid personality of the patient. The host's response to the schizophrenic illness is really determined by what else the patient is and has in assets and liabilities besides his or her schizophrenia. This is very similar to findings in physical illness. For example, in bacteriological disease, prognosis depends on the host's susceptibility, resistance, nutritional state, emotional state, genetic background, immunological response patterns, and coexisting infections. A very similar multifactoral approach helps us to understand and explain differences in prognosis in the history of schizophrenia among individuals. The patient who is intelligent, has better developed adaptive capacities, is better educated, has a better childhood history leading to greater resilience during adolescence, has special talents or special good looks or special interpersonal skills will have a very different life with schizophrenia than the individual who has very limited intelligence, has had a deprived and chaotic childhood, has never developed coping skills, and is without any talent or is physically unattractive.

It should be added that another host factor that has been implicated in the outcome in the clinical picture of schizophrenia is the factor of power and position. The individual who comes from a well-situated family, who has money and influence, and thus power, has a very different life with his or her schizophrenia than the individual who has none of these external assets. These assets are neither properties of personality nor the result of cultural and social responses to illness. Yet they do make a major difference in prognosis.

A contribution of premorbid personality tends to be accentuated by membership in certain social and cultural groups. The patient whose premorbid personality is such that his values fit with the culture in which he must live, with or without his schizophrenia, tends to get along better than the one who is out-of-step and alien even premorbidly. This fact explains why the large public psychiatric hospitals in the United States, with 29 percent of their first admissions being diagnosed as schizophrenia, are filled with a disproportionate number of members of the racially, economically, politically, and socially disenfranchised portion of the population. It also explains why, generally speaking, society's treatment interventions for this patient population are quite different (much more emphasis on chemical intervention and hospital treatment) than they are for those patients who are part of the majority culture (middle-class and Caucasian), a culture that also provides the personnel for the planning and implementation of treatment programs.

The type of onset, including the amount of the precipitating stress, has been observed to be related to prognosis in the individual case. This observation was confirmed in my own patient population. The more sudden the onset of the first episode of exacerbation, the better the prognosis for the life of the patient. This observation continues throughout the history of the illness—in that each time the prognosis for rapid resolution of crisis and rapid reintegration to a state of remission is better—if the onset of the particular episode of exacerbation is more acute.

In obtaining such data from history, we must be very careful to clearly differentiate observed clinical facts from errors of recollection. Many times family members report a very sudden change or acute onset several years after an episode has occurred, when in fact other information from other observers shows that the onset was very gradual, barely noticeable. What the family members are reporting is the sudden realization or insight that the patient is ill, which does not necessarily correspond to acute onset. Acuteness of onset can also be related to the types of symptoms in the individual episode. The more disorganized the individual is, usually the more sudden was the onset of the episode. If the particular episode of exacerbation had a very gradual onset, the patient is able to respond to his or her pain and misery with the development of coping mechanisms, albeit very pathological coping mechanisms. However, the direct result of this observation of onset rapidity is a difference in prognosis. The slow onset of a well-organized system of paranoid delusions results in poor prognosis. The chaotic disorganization resulting in confusion and wildly fluctuating and diffuse paranoia leads to good prognosis.

The prognostic observations were confirmed from my patient population by direct observation of the onset of exacerbations. Those patients who over periods of several weeks disorganized from a previous level of good remission into a state of exacerbation took longer to get out of the resulting crisis and generally had a poorer prognosis. Those individuals who in a matter of one or two days disorganized from a good remission had a much better prognosis, both for quickness of recovery from the exacerbation and for quality of remission following their particular exacerbation. However, there is a great deal of variation between patients as well as between episodes. Yet generally those patients who tended to have a more insidious onset of the initial episode and a more insidious onset of the subsequent episodes tended to have a poorer prognosis for comfort and successful functioning even in their fourth and fifth decades of life.

Attempts have been made to relate prognosis to severity of precipitating stress. It is said that the more severe the precipitating stress, the better the prognosis, and conversely the less evident the precipitating stress, the worse the prognosis. Within the limitations of any generality, this observation is correct.

Patients in whom a fairly substantial environmental situation of precipitating stress could be determined tended to have a better prognosis than those individuals in whom such a precipitating stress could not be identified. However, as we view the history of the individual and his or her life with schizophrenia, it emerges that the relationship of prognosis to severity of precipitating stress probably is simply another measure of premorbid personality. Individuals who have a good premorbid personality and function well socially and intellectually prior to the onset of their illness will often require a more clearly identifiable stressful situation to precipitate the actual clinical illness. Similarly, individuals who have been ill with schizophrenia for a long time but who manage to function fairly well during their remissions and are brought into crisis only as a result of a fairly clearly identifiable interpersonal or environmental stress are also the individuals who had a better premorbid personality and more intellectual, social, and adaptive skills with which to function. Individuals who have crises that are totally unrelated to any identifiable demand on their coping mechanisms tend to be people who have fewer resources and a more limited ability to live their lives.

Summary

It appears that all of the foregoing observations in regard to prognosis in schizophrenia relate to host response. When care is taken to be precise in the diagnosis of schizophrenia, when the premorbid personality is carefully assessed and reported, when the differences in clinical picture are corrected for factors of social, cultural, and intellectual function and background, when the course of the illness is separated from the consequences of treatment, and when the factors of precipitating stress and schizophrenia subgroup diagnosis are correctly seen as another aspect of premorbid personality, there remains no evidence whatsoever that there are differences in virulence of the disease process itself. From a natural history point of view there is no evidence for different types of schizophrenia having a difference in prognosis and a difference in course. The differences in clinical response seem to be entirely the result of host factors elaborated in this chapter.

7

Questions About Diagnosis and Diagnostic Subgroups

This chapter is devoted to a discussion of the validity of the DSMIIIR diagnostic category of schizophrenic disorder and its diagnostic subgroups from the natural history perspective. In addition, it attempts to assess the usefulness of diagnostic subgrouping.

Schizophrenic Disorder

Much has been written about the diagnosis of schizophrenia (Feighner and others, 1972). Those diagnostic systems based on the mental status examination or present state examination that attempt to group patients on the basis of findings in a cross-sectional examination tend to have much interdiagnostician unreliability. This observation has been recognized in DSMIIIR by the insistence that the diagnosis of schizophrenia cannot be made without at least a six-month history of illness. Furthermore, the term *chronic schizophrenia* has been removed from the diagnostic categories because schizophrenia by definition is a chronic illness. There must be evidence of deterioration from prior levels of function in such areas as work, social relations, and self-care even while the patient is in remission, and there must be evidence of intermittent exacerbations, including the major symptoms of psychotic disorganization (Cancro, 1973).

Nuclear Disabilities of Schizophrenia. The defects that have been seen in all cases of schizophrenia, both in my population of 497 patients and the thousands of others examined, consist of the simultaneous and persistent presence of defective anxiety management, impaired interpersonal relationships, and failure of historicity. Each one of these disabilities can occur in a multitude of psychiatric disorders. But the simultaneous occurrence of all three of them seems to be seen only in schizophrenia. The presence of these defects can be confirmed during both the period of exacerbation and the period of remission. It can also be confirmed by the relatively prolonged remissions toward the later portions of the patient's life, when he or she is no longer experiencing periods of acute exacerbation.

The ineffective and expensive anxiety management results in the patient's having high levels of free-floating anxiety that then secondarily bring about the major signs and symptoms of psychotic disorder and disorganization. The persistent defects in managing interpersonal relationships result in clumsy and disastrous interpersonal misadventures that secondarily result in such psychotic signs as autism, withdrawal, impaired self-esteem, and so forth. The failure of historicity experienced by these patients refers to the observation that they are unable to make judgments and decisions on the basis of their own lived history as though they had a memory defect or learning difficulty, neither one of which they actually have.

These three nuclear defects are found consistently throughout a patient's life during periods of exacerbation and remission. The defects can be demonstrated by skilled history taking and mental status examination as well as psychological tests. (See Table 7.) It is reasonable to assume that specific biological markers that can be correlated with the presence of these three nuclear defects will be identified in the near future.

Natural History Perspective. From a natural history point of view, schizophrenia is a chronic psychobiological illness characterized by an undulating pattern of exacerbations and remissions. The first symptoms of the illness appear usually as a fairly mild acute episode sometime between the ages of twelve and eighteen. This

Table 7. Clusters of Signs and Symptoms of Schizophrenia.

Nuclear Disabilities	Consequential Symptoms	Restitutive Symptoms
Failure of anxiety management	1. Tiredness and exhaustion 2. Loose associations 3. Communication difficulty caused by lack of discernible logic 4. Fragile adjustment 5. Affective lability 6. Failure to learn from experience 7. Confusion 8. Disorganized behavior 9. Amotivationality, ambivalence, ambitendency 10. Impaired reality contact	1. Panneurosis 2. Ritualistic behavior 3. Idiosyncratic thought processes 4. Suicide 5. Delusions 6. Hallucinations 7. Affective indifference and inappropriateness 8. Reduced functional intelligence 9. Reduced functional learning 10. Involvement with drugs and alcohol 11. Feeling of being out of control or in control of someone else
Failure of interpersonal transactions	1. Impaired self-boundaries 2. Feelings of emptiness and nothingness 3. Impaired flow of time 4. Impaired reality contact 5. Low self-esteem	1. Withdrawal 2. Autism, impaired reality contact 3. Megalomania 4. Delusions of grandeur 5. Paranoid symptoms 6. Hypochondriasis 7. Bizarre behavior 8. Hopelessness 9. Polymorphous sexual perversion 10. Difficulty in separating thoughts and events
Failure of historicity	1. Feelings of emptiness and nothingness 2. Impaired self-esteem 3. No past, no future 4. No flow of time 5. No sense of person 6. No continuity of person 7. Ambivalence and ambitendency 8. Failure to have "learned" from experience 9. Fragility of therapeutic relationship, which needs constant nourishment	1. Filling life witn nongoal-oriented activity 2. Enslavement in the present moment of action 3. Unwillingness to plan or commit to action 4. Living at the periphery of life 5. Disconnecting the personal world from the surrounding world

episode is not often recognized and is misdiagnosed. The pattern of exacerbations and remissions varies from patient to patient but appears to be age-related. As the patient gets older, the number of exacerbations decreases until finally at approximately age fifty the acute phase of the illness tends to disappear. There is a characteristic diminution of function in such areas as social relations, self-care, and work, from the premorbid personality to subsequent periods of remission. This includes some diminution from earlier remissions to later remissions until the patient's function tends to stabilize. In later years of the patient's life history, as the number of acute exacerbations decreases, there appears to be some general increase in the level of function during remissions, perhaps only as a reflection of the fewer numbers of disorganizations per year.

During the acute exacerbations, the patient experiences major disorganization, including disorder of thinking, feeling, perception, and behavior. He or she often shows gross psychotic symptoms, including delusions and hallucinations as well as changes in behavior secondary to these. During the periods of remission, some more subtle disorders of thinking, feeling, perception, and behavior may persist. However, during these remissions, the basic defect in the patient's ability to manage anxiety, to manage interpersonal relationships, and to use his or her own personally lived history as a basis for making judgments and decisions (historicity) is clearly recognizable and demonstrable on clinical examination and psychological testing (Mendel, 1964).

This is the diagnosis of schizophrenia as developed from the natural history approach. Although there is considerable individual variation from patient to patient, as indeed there is among all human beings, there is also a great deal of consistency. This consistency is enough to present a very clear picture that allows us to observe the similarities and to make a diagnosis (Mendel and Rapport, 1969). From such diagnostic statements we can also begin to make evaluations of effectiveness of treatment interventions.

Subgroups of Schizophrenia

In the official diagnostic classification found in DSMIIIR, the number of subgroups of schizophrenia has been reduced and the descriptions of subgroups are much more closely reflective of the natural history and clinical observations than was true of previous diagnostic systems, which were based on conceptual and theoretical models (Cooper, 1960). In the DSMIIIR classification, the subgroups of schizophrenia that can be diagnosed and coded include the catatonic, paranoid, disorganized, undifferentiated, and residual types. Absent from the subgroups are the formerly designated hebephrenic, simple, and schizo-affective types. These deletions make excellent clinical sense and are entirely in line with my observations of the natural history of the illness.

I discovered some years ago (Mendel, 1975a) that schizo-affective schizophrenia if observed for at least three years resolves itself into either schizophrenia or affective psychosis. The simple and hebephrenic subcategories tend on observation to be so dispersed with other symptoms that they more appropriately fit into either the disorganized or undifferentiated subgroup. Furthermore, the abolition of the diagnosis of childhood schizophrenia gives recognition to the clinical observation that the course and outcome of that condition was very different from the illness we call schizophrenia. Similarly, the diagnosis of acute schizophrenia has been appropriately abolished because approximately 25 percent of cases previously diagnosed as such have a history of no undulating course of illness and no further psychotic episodes. Under the new classification, such episodes are now called schizophreniform disorder or brief reactive psychosis. Such a classification takes into account the natural history as the basis for making the diagnosis.

Using the natural history approach, to make meaningful and useful subtype diagnoses, we need data on several acute episodes of exacerbation. In those patients where behavioral symptoms predominate, including catatonic stupor, catatonic negativism, catatonic rigidity, catatonic excitement, and catatonic posturing (DSMIIIR) and remain the major symptoms in each episode throughout the patient's life, we are justified in making the diagnosis of schizophrenic disorder, catatonic type. Similarly, if the patient's major and outstanding disorder is in the area of perception and thinking, characterized by the presence during each episode throughout the individual's lifetime of either persecutory delusions or grandiose delusions, preoccupation with jealousy or hallucinations with persecutory or grandiose content, we are justified from a natural history point of view in making the diagnosis of schizophrenic disorder, paranoid type (Tausk, [1933] 1946).

A third differentiated subcategory of schizophrenic disorder is the disorganized type. It is characterized by the persistent picture during the acute exacerbations throughout the individual's lifetime demonstrating the major psychotic symptoms that are secondary to disorder of thinking and feeling, including frequent incoherence, blunting, and silly and inappropriate affect in the absence of a systematized delusional presentation. There are a few patients who present such a picture throughout their lifetimes.

The fourth subgroup, the undifferentiated type, is the subgroup that includes a majority of the patients in my clinical group (see Table 8). These patients show a wide variety of major psychotic symptoms during the acute exacerbations. They further demonstrate that at various times in their life history one group or another of the major psychotic symptoms may predominate; that is, in one exacerbation the symptoms may primarily show disorders of perception, whereas in another they primarily show disorders of behavior.

The final subgroup designated in the diagnostic manual is referred to as the residual type and describes the patient between acute periods of exacerbation, when he or she is in partial or complete remission from the major psychotic symptoms. From the natural

Table 8. Diagnostic Subtype of Schizophrenia for the 497 Patients in Study.

Diagnostic Subgroup	Percentage of Population
Catatonic	16
Paranoid	8
Disorganized	0.4
Undifferentiated	75.6
Residual	0*

*The diagnosis was made during the index crisis. The diagnosis of residual schizophrenia requires that the patient have a history of acute schizophrenia but be asymptomatic at the time the diagnosis is made. However, during the index crisis, by definition the patient is not asymptomatic.

history point of view, this subtype makes no sense because it simply describes a particular state of the patient during repeated episodes of remission. In other words, the diagnosis of residual type can be made on everyone who lives with schizophrenia, depending on when the examination leading to the diagnosis is made (Merskey, 1972).

Thus, from a natural history point of view of the diagnostic subgroups (Ödegaard, 1963) of the general diagnosis of schizophrenic disorder, it makes sense that subgroups be differentiated on the basis of signs and symptoms throughout the life of the individual patient and that they be stable diagnostic categories throughout the natural history of the patient with this illness.

Usefulness of Diagnostic Subgrouping

We need to assess the usefulness of categorizing subgroups of schizophrenia (Spitzer and Fleiss, 1974). Does the life history of the patient who falls into the subgroup catatonic schizophrenia differ markedly from the patient who falls into the paranoid or undifferentiated category? Is this difference greater between groups than would normally be expected simply on the basis of individual variation between patients? Are there clusters of natural history that fall into such subgroups?

The answer to all of these questions is a qualified yes. The vast majority of patients with schizophrenia, including as already noted my group of 497, fall into the category of undifferentiated type. That is, they have a life course characterized by variability of major psychotic symptoms during the acute episode throughout their life histories (Winokur, 1974). A few patients from my observed population fall into the category of catatonic type, paranoid type, and disorganized type and do demonstrate some differences in the natural history that are clinically significant.

Let me restate the findings that are not different between the subtypes. There is no difference in the undulating pattern of exacerbations and remissions in the various subtypes. There is no difference in frequency of exacerbation; nor is there any difference in the age-relatedness of frequency of exacerbations. On the other hand, the differences between the subtypes can occur in the length of exacerbation, the storminess of exacerbation, the level of function during remission, and age of onset.

Length of Exacerbations. The length of exacerbations after the first three episodes is significantly shorter for patients who have a predominating picture of catatonic symptoms throughout life. It is shorter than that for the larger undifferentiated group and that for the disorganized group. It is difficult to compare length of exacerbations for the paranoid group because the periods of exacerbation are very difficult to define since crises in this group are usually precipitated by social response to symptoms rather than specific exacerbations of signs and symptoms.

Storminess of Exacerbations. Patients in the catatonic subgroup generally have stormier exacerbations, that is, more severe psychiatric symptoms requiring more intervention on the part of society and the treating agencies, than do the other subgroups. This is a general impression that has not been quantified so we cannot present it in any other way than this clinical description.

The disorganized type tends to have longer exacerbations that are generally less stormy than the undifferentiated type. However, this difference may simply be the result of the fact that the signs and symptoms of the former are less bothersome to the environment than to the patient and therefore are more easily tolerated in the community and require less intervention. In fact, it may be that the signs and symptoms are every bit as painful, and therefore stormy, to the disorganized type as are those of the catatonic type, the only difference being in the environmental response. It is also possible that part of my finding of longer episodes for the disorganized type is related to greater difficulty in observation because of the less disruptive and acute nature of the symptoms.

Because paranoid patients tend to get into great difficulty with legal and social systems of the environment during the exacerbation, they tend to be recognized as ill. However, depending on how long it takes them to get into difficulty with their symptoms, the actual exacerbation may antedate the social response by many days. For this reason, data on length of exacerbation for paranoid patients are highly unreliable. Similarly, observations on storminess of the acute episode is unreliable because this depends almost entirely on the response of society. The patient who writes a threatening letter to the president of the United States may not be clinically any sicker than one who threatens to sue Coca-Cola, but certainly she will be responded to very differently. She will quickly be identified by the Secret Service, hospitalized, and diagnosed as suffering from schizophrenia, paranoid type. The other patient, who is involved with the Coca-Cola Company, may not be recognized as being severely mentally ill for many weeks while she makes the rounds of lawyers and newspaper editors.

Level of Function. The literature contains a number of attempts to relate the level of function between exacerbations to the subtype of schizophrenia. Our observation shows no such relationship. However, we do note a relationship between acuteness of onset of exacerbation and postexacerbation level of function: the more sudden the onset of exacerbation, the better the level of function after the episode; and the more insidious the onset of the exacerbation, the less acute the episode and the greater the impairment in the following remission. This observation is independent of the subtype of schizophrenia except for the fact that certain subtypes tend to demonstrate a more acute course. Catatonic schizophrenia tends to be the most acute while disorganized schizophrenia usually demonstrates the least acute onset of exacerbation.

Age of Onset. Generally, the catatonic, disorganized, and undifferentiated subtypes have their onset about the same time, namely, in the second half of the second decade of life. My observations on the patient population in our study are consistent with these findings. It is also generally observed and believed that the paranoid subtype has later onset, that is, in the middle of the second decade of life. A note of caution is in order before we take this difference too seriously.

In paranoid patients, onset of illness is difficult to pinpoint. Because these patients tend to be secretive, tend to be guarded in their interactions with others, and tend not to show major signs and symptoms of psychiatric disorganization above and beyond the paranoid system, it is often difficult to tell when an individual episode begins, how long it lasts, and when the onset of the illness occurs. Most of the time paranoid patients do not come to the attention of medical authorities until relatively late. They usually get into difficulties with their peers and are seen as irritable and unpleasant to be with; subsequently, they are viewed as difficult people in society, often experienced as difficult neighbors, difficult customers, or difficult employees. Frequently, their early run-ins are with authority figures and the law, particularly if they tend to be actively litigious. Only as their behavior becomes more extreme do they tend to be recognized as mentally ill and then diagnosed as suffering from schizophrenic disorder, paranoid type. It is my impression that the relatively late onset in the natural history of paranoid schizophrenia may simply be a reflection of the difficulty in recognizing the signs and symptoms of the illness earlier. When a detailed history is available, including a considerable amount of observer information from peers, family members, and authority figures in camp, school, the workplace, and the community, it has been my experience that even in the subcategory of paranoid schizophrenia, the onset of the illness dates to the second half of the second decade of life. The following case illustrates the point.

Walter Thompson was a patient I met quite early in my career while I was a resident at St. Elizabeth's Hospital in Washington, D.C. When I first saw Walter he was sixty-five years old and had been retired from the army approximately six months. He had been divorced many years before, and his three children were grown up and scattered around the country. He kept a relationship with them, though it was somewhat stilted. He had had no contact with his former wife for some twenty-five years. At the time of his discharge, he was a master sergeant in the army, assigned to West Point to be in charge of the stable and the ceremonial mules. His retirement coincided with the retirement of the mules.

Walter had joined the army at age eighteen and had slowly worked his way up through the ranks. Apparently, he was an excellent soldier but also a very tough supervisor. He knew the system well and seemed to know whose authority he had to accept and to whom he was the authority. He enjoyed the highly structured army life and had very little life outside of it. When he retired, he bought a small tract house in a Virginia suburb of Washington, D.C. It was newly built, and he busied himself with landscaping. He became involved in controversy with three neighbors with whom he shared borders in the backyard. Eventually, despite many arguments, his neighbors decided to build a cement block fence in the backyard. Walter very carefully measured his lot and found that one of the neighbors had built the fence so that it extended three inches onto his property. He went to the police and the county assessor and hired a lawyer to try to deal with this. When he received no help, he placed sticks of dynamite under the wall and blew it up. When neighbors called the police, Walter seemed quite irrational. He talked about the neighbors' being Communists and was taken to the admitting room of St. Elizabeth's Hospital.

During the ensuing thirteen years, I got to know Walter well. He spent only a short time at St. Elizabeth's, but subsequently I followed him as an outpatient. He seemed to form a good therapeutic alliance, and at no time did he incorporate me into his paranoid system. As I became more experienced and got to know him better, I discovered that Walter had been paranoid since high school. He told many anecdotes that, although less extreme than blowing up a neighbor's fence, clearly demonstrated his ongoing paranoia. His general suspiciousness and litigiousness were frequently displayed throughout his life, even in the army, where he often felt people were discriminating against and taking advantage of him. However, the army had treated him well, and apparently army life allowed for considerable paranoia.

Walter seemed to have the usual number of exacerbations and remissions throughout life, though they rarely led to a crisis in which intervention was necessary. Crisis prior to his index crisis (at age sixty-five) had been handled in a civil or legal way and had never involved psychiatric care or medication. During his hospitalization he was given neuroleptics for a short period of time but they were of little help. (In those days only Reserpine was available as a neuroleptic.) In later years Walter never needed rehospitalization and never took any medication. He assumed the role of a rather eccentric old tiger, and many of his acquaintances excused his level of paranoia and irritability as being the result of more than forty-five years in the army. With minimal supportive care he was able to maintain that posture until his death at age seventy-eight.

Atypical Cases. A very small group of patients (in our sample, 2 out of 497) represent a different kind of clinical picture than the rest. They primarily show delusions of a grandiose nature; their changes in mood, activity, thinking, and perception are secondary to well-organized systems of thought and attitude. These particular patients do not show as clear a picture of undulation between periods of exacerbation and remission as most others do, although there is some cyclical tendency in the changes in severity of the signs and symptoms. However, these patients also do not clearly fit into the paranoid category because they do not show paranoia yet do show the three basic nuclear defects of function.

The two cases in our study must be classified as having a form of schizophrenia that is atypical of and different from the other subtypes of schizophrenic disorder. This group of two patients is so small that clinically it is relatively unimportant and may simply represent extremes of individual variation in natural histories of cases of schizophrenia.

Conclusion

The natural history of the group of 497 patients observed for approximately three and a half decades confirms the validity of the diagnostic category of schizophrenic disorder. Patients who are diagnosed have a predictable life history. The life histories of the various subtypes do not vary remarkably from the majority group diagnosed as schizophrenic disorder, undifferentiated type. There is variation between individual patients who live with schizophrenia, but this variation is no greater than it is in the general population; that is, one patient with schizophrenia is no more like another patient with schizophrenia than one patient with gallbladder disease is like another patient with gallbladder disease. However, in terms of the natural history, schizophrenia is entirely different and clearly distinguishable from gallbladder disease. Thus the natural history approach both confirms the validity of diagnosis of schizophrenia and at the same time is the best clinical tool for making the diagnosis in the individual case.

8

The Aging
Schizophrenic Patient

We have accumulated information about schizophrenic patients in their fourth, fifth, and sixth decades of life (See Table 6). The observations made on this group of patients is of particular interest because the American literature contains very little information about older patients. Moreover, the information that is available tends to be about patients who spent long periods of time in the hospital. The particular patients in our study are unique in that they have lived most of their lives continuously out of the hospital and in the community. Consequently, the clinical picture and the natural history of their illness are not contaminated or altered by the behavioral and social sequelae of long-term hospitalization.

In one study providing general screening of 1,500 individuals over age sixty in a Soviet city, investigators found that 1.6 percent had schizophrenia (Molchanova, 1975). However, only 0.6 percent were found to require active treatment of any kind. Although the incidence of schizophrenia in most populations throughout the world when corrected for diagnostic differences is generally 1 percent, the prevalence in that population tends to be higher because schizophrenia is a chronic, nonfatal illness. The fact that this study demonstrated that two-thirds of the cases were inactive after age sixty and only one-third were active to any degree at all seems to be in line with my observation of a decrease in acute exacerbations as patients age. (See Chapter Three.) Another study conducted in the Soviet Union of 751 patients with schizophrenia whose onset occurred in adolescence but who were studied as older patients showed that eventually 80 percent of patients were able to live in the community and that 40 percent were able to work in ordinary jobs. Fifty percent showed total remission. Yet another Russian study (Sukhovski, 1976) presented follow-up data on 146 patients with schizophrenia and showed that in late age the exacerbations or attacks ceased. The author observed that even in those patients who developed involutional and senility symptoms, there was no increase in the number of schizophrenic exacerbations. A general descriptive paper (Bridge, Cannon, and Wyatt, 1978) alludes to the decreased symptomotology in the older patient with schizophrenic disorder.

These recent Russian studies on the aging populations of schizophrenic patients living in the community are consistent with my findings on the observed population. In older patients a general state of remission appears to be continuous, and there are no gross psychotic symptoms (Cutting, 1983). Yet the three basic defects of schizophrenia persist and can be demonstrated in that long final remission. An undulating pattern remains, with patients having better weeks and worse weeks, although it never gets to the point of exacerbation with the presence of gross clinical psychotic symptoms.

How can we understand this change? Is it related only to the natural history of the illness itself, that is, a change in the "virulence" of the disease? Or is this change related to changes in the host, including psychological and physiological changes? Or is it the result of a changing social situation in which the patient finds himself or herself as a middle-aged or older member of society? The first proposal we dismiss very quickly by stating that we have absolutely no information because we have no way of observing the disease process outside of the host or of following the disease process other than by host response. Anything we might say without such information would be pure science fiction. Only when the exact biological cause of the illness has been discovered and can be studied outside the host will we have the answer. At this time the obvious observable change in the clinical picture of the older patient must be understood and explained in terms of the other two factors: host response and sociocultural changes.

Some considerable data are available to show that as patients age, their physiology changes. Clinically, this can be observed in the difference in patients' responses to psychopharmacological agents. I found that as patients age, they tend to require lower doses of psychopharmacological agents and an ever increasing number get along better without any psychotropic medication. This is true even for patients who could not get along without medication when they were younger. Over the years of observing patients, I have found that approximately 10 percent at any one time get along better without medication than with it. At all times 4 percent do much better without any medication. However, beginning with the fourth decade, an increasing number of patients who could previously never get along without medication, get along better without it. (See Table 9.) This continues in the older patients (Shapiro and Shader, 1979).

I obtained my data from the practice of placing each patient on an annual drug holiday. I did not do this in order to prevent tardive dyskinesia because I did not know about that condition in the early years; I simply developed it as a technique of assessing how much and whether a patient needed medication. Usually, the patient would experience some exacerbation and discomfort and difficulty during the drug holiday and then would be placed back on medication at a dosage that did the best job for him or her. It was always my policy that the least dose that did the job was the best way of medicating the patient. However, I often found that older patients not only avoided an exacerbation during the drug holiday but continued to do well, sometimes even better than before. Thereafter I would place the patients on medication once a year for a short period of time to see what difference it would make. Usually, the older patients would get worse with the medication, and I would then discontinue it again.

These findings not only indicate that a patient's need for medication must be reassessed on a regular basis throughout his or her life but also that his or her physiology, including the response to psychotropic drugs and to illness, changes. There is clear evidence for changes in the host's response with aging. Psycholog-

Table 9. Percent of Patients *Not* on Medication Six Months per Year (1979).

Age	12-15	15-20	20-25	25-30	30-35	35-40	45-50	50-55	55-60	60-65	65-70	70+
%	85	5	4	11	18	15	37	60	79	87	90	100

Note: 1979 represents a typical year. There was very little variation from the percentages over the past two decades.

ical changes also occur with age, including in some the development of organic central nervous system difficulties. Such changes also occur in some aging patients with schizophrenic disorder.

The condition of tardive dyskinesia, which occurs in patients who have been using neuroleptic medications for some time, tends to involve the older patient population. In our population of 497, there were two cases of tardive dyskinesia, both occurring after the age of forty. For these two patients, the condition was partially reversed over a period of two years by slowly decreasing doses of psychotropic drugs that had perhaps caused the condition in the first place. Tardive dyskinesia is difficult to differentiate from spontaneous dyskinesia, which occurs in aging populations.

We can understand some of the changes in the clinical picture of schizophrenia patients on the basis of the social and cultural changes that occur for older people in our society. The functions in which schizophrenic patients have particular difficulty because of their problems with historicity, interpersonal relationships, and anxiety management and their secondary difficulties with amotivationality as well as impaired self-esteem become less important for older people. The areas in which society expects less as patients get older include sexual function, vocational function, relationship with family, social pressure to be independent, and the need to deal in society with assertiveness and aggressiveness. (Perhaps the "juices" flow more slowly.) Probably the most important factor, however, is society's changed expectations for all older citizens. This seems to result in fewer demands and fewer pressures for function and therefore in fewer failures. For this reason, as schizophrenic patients get older, they become less different from the general population. They are more like everyone else their age, and their disabilities are more acceptable to society.

As patients get older, however, they have to deal with new demands from their psychosocial environment. They may be somewhat more prepared to cope with such demands in part because life is now less disrupted by periodic psychotic exacerbations. On the other hand, the patients' basic defects remain apparent and incapacitating even during the prolonged remission of older age. Patients' observable "brittleness," which refers to the minimal amount of stress they can handle and the limited coping capacity they have available, remains a problem. Yet it does appear that our patient population generally finds it easier to handle some of the demands of becoming older. Many of these patients have maintained a dependency role with aging parents long beyond what is usual for the general population. Still, as they get older, these patients do seem to be able to adjust to the death of significant others in their lives, others who have responded to their dependency need over many years. During times of severe physical illness, including life-threatening illness, older patients seem to cope remarkably well, even to the extent of appearing psychiatrically clinically improved. I have had the opportunity of seeing several of my long-term patients die of serious illness. Of eight patients, all except one handled their own illness and death as well as any human being could, without showing any complications due to their schizophrenia in the management of the terminal state. The one exception developed an acute exacerbation of severe psychotic symptoms on discovering his terminal carcinoma.

Summary

From the literature and from my own observation of the patient population it seems clear that as patients get older they have fewer exacerbations and longer remissions. When they are past fifty, they tend to have a continuous remission without any evidence of frank and gross psychotic symptoms. Patients also tend to be more comfortable and more functional as they get older, perhaps in part responding to the differences in their own physiology and to the differences in cultural-societal expectations for them. Moreover, older patients tend to require less medication or no medication at all. They usually handle the problems of being older much more ably than they handled the problems of being younger. Thus it appears that older patients have a much improved prognosis for being asymptomatic and for improving the quality of their lives.

The statistics on reproduction, suicide, and longevity in the literature of schizophrenia are unconvincing. It has generally been said that schizophrenically disordered patients procreate less frequently than the general population. Yet a recent study disputes this fact and claims that there is no significant difference (Bleuler, 1978). Other studies show that the suicide rate among patients with schizophrenia is higher than that of the general population (Bleuler, 1978). Yet in my group of 497 patients we have had only three suicides in thirty-five years. (This may be due to the supportive care that the patients receive, to an artifact in the selection of the cases, or to good luck. But it does make us question both the data in the literature and our own observations.) There is evidence in the literature that even when corrected for suicide and accidental deaths, there is excessive mortality in patients with schizophrenia and affective disorders (Tsuang and Woolson, 1978). This has not been confirmed by my own observations. The natural history of schizophrenia based on longitudinal observation of patients does not lead us to believe that there is any evidence for either increased or decreased life expectancy associated with the presence of schizophrenia.

9

The Typical Patient: Composite Case

From a review of the natural history-oriented literature of schizophrenia and from the continuous observation of 497 patients, it is now possible to use the natural history approach to draw a composite picture of a typical patient, the course of the illness, and the outcome.

The patient was first seen when he was seventeen years old and a high school senior. He was brought for consultation by his family, a middle-class, urban, professional family. The patient had "suddenly gone crazy" two weeks earlier while attending a high school dance. He had become incoherent, disrobed in public, and had to be restrained with the help of the police. He was taken to a local county hospital, where he was suspected of drug ingestion. However, a drug screen showed no evidence of drug ingestion. He remained in the hospital for a period of one week, during which he received appropriate doses of psychotropic medication, and his gross psychotic symptoms improved. His family took him out of the hospital and returned him home. They found him withdrawn and strangely different in his thinking. Upon the advice of the hospital staff the family brought him for further psychiatric evaluation and treatment.

On initial psychiatric examination, the patient was cooperative but appeared somewhat vague, stunned, and noncomprehending of his recent situation. He was precisely oriented in all spheres and showed no deficits in memory for remote, recent, or immediate events. His thinking was highly idiosyncratic. He recalled recently hearing voices telling him his thoughts; he was somewhat vague as to whether these voices were still with him. He had difficulty in maintaining his attention on the procedures of the mental status examination. He showed some evidence of believing that he had special religious experiences, with the associated delusion that he was chosen by God for a very special mission in life. This delusion was generally vague and poorly systematized. He appeared to be quite anxious about his situation and about unknown factors, and he demonstrated some ritualistic behavior consisting of a regular pattern of tapping his fingers, which he felt he was supposed to do as per the instruction of his voices. He recognized that something had changed in his life but had no insight into the fact that he was suffering from a mental illness. His judgment of his present situation was markedly impaired, as indeed it was about his present state examination items.

Family history revealed he was the only child of an upwardly mobile, middle-class family. His father was a successful engineer, who had great expectations that his son would follow some professional career. The father had three brothers, one of whom had been intermittently hospitalized for prolonged periods of time with a diagnosis of schizophrenia. The patient's mother was an only child; she had been a schoolteacher prior to her marriage, seemed to be a warm, concerned parent, and was terribly bewildered by her son's mental illness. She was firmly convinced that the illness was the result of his association with nondesirable elements in the public school he was attending, and she also believed that he had been exposed to street drugs. She maintained this conviction even though there was no evidence that the patient had been involved with drugs at any time. The mother reported a family history with the only positive finding of a maternal aunt who had been mentally ill but whose diagnosis was unknown.

A more detailed history of the patient revealed that he had had no particular difficulty or unusual circumstances before, during, or immediately after his birth. He was a healthy child who developed normally. In his latency years he was particularly successful in school, in peer groups, and in Cub Scouts. He responded well to his father's demands to excel, and he consistently performed at the top of his particular level. In his adolescence he became somewhat resistant and stubborn vis-à-vis his parents, who attributed this to a modern world and normal adolescent behavior. As a sixteen-year-old high school student, he ran for student body office (vice-president). During the campaign, he suddenly stated that he felt like quitting. He thought he would not be elected. However, his father insisted that he could not quit in the middle of his campaign, that he had an obligation to all the people who were working for him to become vice-president. At his father's firm insistence, he continued and was elected. During the inauguration ceremony at the end of his junior year, he acted in a very unusual and silly manner, which neither his friends nor his family could understand.

During the summer between his junior and senior years, when he turned seventeen, he did absolutely nothing, which was unusual for him. In previous summers he had held a number of jobs, making a good bit of money, which he used to support his car. He refused to go to work, spent a great deal of time in his room, and seemed to become personally much more slovenly. On returning to school in the fall for his senior year, he had academic difficulty for the first time. While previously he had been an *A* student, at the half-semester mark he received failure notices in chemistry and algebra. The family was shocked and concerned about his planned future in college and talked to the school counselor. The counselor saw the young man and suggested that he have a medical evaluation since he seemed to be generally not feeling well.

The family physician who had known the patient for many years examined him and thought he might be suffering from a subclinical viral hepatitis. He allowed the patient to remain at home for four weeks, part of the time at bed rest. No firm evidence was found from laboratory procedures to confirm the diagnosis, but slowly the patient seemed to feel better. When he returned to school, with a great deal of help from his family and teachers, he was able to complete the first semester successfully, though his grades were markedly lower than they had ever been before. He became increasingly seclusive, and many of his friends reported that he had changed in major ways. The parents suggested that the patient have psychotherapy, which he refused. Next came the episode that led to his hospitalization and the examination.

The patient then went back to school to complete his final semester. He had great difficulty concentrating, but with the help and goodwill of the school administration, he was allowed to graduate. He continued on neuroleptic medication. Approximately two months after the previous episode and immediately after his graduation from high school, the next acute exacerbation occurred. During the two months of his partial remission, he was seen once a week, during which time a comfortable therapeutic alliance was established and his medication was adjusted and supervised. He was eager for help because he was having great difficulty in trying to figure out what was happening to him. He was scared and feeling uncomfortable with his high level of free-floating anxiety.

As the acute exacerbations began, he noticed difficulty in going to sleep, an inability to eat, and a reappearance of loud voices calling him unpleasant names. The dosage of medication was increased, and he was seen for daily appointments. On the fifth day of the exacerbation, he became increasingly disturbed in the middle of the night and began throwing furniture out of his room onto the street. His frightened parents called both the police and the psychiatrist, who arrived at the same time. The patient was given an intravenous sedative, and a nursing assistant was assigned to stay with him. Within three weeks, the patient's exacerbation stopped and a good state of remission returned. However, both his parents and the psychiatrist noticed that his level of function had shown some general decline. Where previously he was neat, now he tended to be personally sloppy. While previously he had shown interest in the world around him, now he appeared much more withdrawn. He would spend hours walking through town alone and would reappear looking exhausted, with holes in his shoes and socks. On one occasion he apparently acted peculiarly in a public park and was picked up by the police, who called his parents to come and get him.

Within three months he experienced another acute exacerbation. This time he started screaming and yelling invectives at passersby at a busy intersection in the middle of town and was picked up by the police and taken to the local psychiatric emergency room. He was hospitalized for four weeks at the local state hospital, receiving increased doses of neuroleptic medication before being discharged back to his home. Upon his return home, supportive care and treatment were taken up once more, medication was decreased, and the family was given regular support to manage their discouragement and hopelessness about the young man's illness. They felt they could not continue to face the episodes of exacerbation and wanted to have him cured. They had read a great deal of the literature on megavitamins, psychoanalytic treatment associated with long-term hospitalization, and social milieu treatment in "safe" houses in the community operated by a group of English psychiatrists who believed that schizophrenia was not an illness. In spite of a great deal of advice to the contrary, the family used its financial resources to have the patient partake in each of these treatment programs over the next six years.

He spent the first year in a private psychiatric hospital at great expense, receiving megavitamin treatments. Subsequently, he was hospitalized in an Eastern private hospital for a period of two years. Here he received no medication at all but had daily psycho-analytic sessions, seven days per week. The next two years he split between a psychiatric hospital, where he was heavily medicated, and a community living center, where he received no medication and was encouraged to believe that his illness was not an illness but a problem that could be overcome by willpower.

After six years of these treatment attempts, and several hundred thousand dollars later, the patient returned home and was again seen by our group. He was now twenty-four years old. A detailed history of the prior six years showed that he had had approximately four exacerbations per year of his schizophrenic disorder. However, because he had been continuously institution-alized, these exacerbations had made little difference in his circumstances. Depending on which place he resided in, the exacerbations had been interpreted in terms of whatever was going on at the moment, that is, with changes in medication, new insights in psychotherapy, or special events in the patient-peer milieu. When we saw him again, he was in fairly good remission and, with support and relatively low doses of phenothiazine, appeared to be able to function, albeit at a limited level.

At this point he was placed in a psychiatric rehabilitation program called mainstreaming (See Chapter Sixteen). He was seen weekly for management of his medication and planning of his rehabilitation program and the setting of goals. He lived independently in an apartment in the community, and he had contact with rehabilitation technicians (catalysts) several hours each day to help him to learn to use community facilities for socializing and to begin his vocational evaluation, training, and employment.

Within five years, by the time he was twenty-nine and having approximately three to four exacerbations per year—none of which required hospitalization but all of which required massive intervention and changes in medication—he finished a degree in business school and obtained competitive employment with a bookkeeping firm. This particular job did not involve a great deal of interpersonal relationships or the need to engage in long-term relationships with other employees. He was part of an organization that supplied temporary bookkeeping help to other companies. Yet the job was permanent and regular. Such employment suited him particularly well. At this point, he was able to support himself and maintain a somewhat distant but superficially friendly relationship with his parents. His social activities consisted of belonging to a chess club, where he played twice a week, and taking courses at the local university extension division on general cultural subjects.

During his thirties he continued fairly comfortably in this life. He experienced an average of two exacerbations per year, none of which required hospitalization and all of which could be handled with increased attention. Over the years, he began to require smaller and smaller doses of neuroleptics, though he could never get along without any medication. He continued in his therapeutic alliance with his psychiatrist on a biweekly basis, during which supportive care was provided.

When he was forty years old his father died, an event that was not particularly upsetting to the patient. During the following two years, he had increased contact with his mother, who expected some emotional support from him, support that he was able to provide to some extent. He and his mother took a number of trips together, and he seemed to spend more time with her, visiting her two or three times a week for dinner.

By the time the patient was fifty, he had not experienced any major exacerbations for three years. He was still holding onto his bookkeeping work and seemed to be considered a generally reliable employee. He changed employers several times, but his position remained essentially the same. When he was fifty-two years old, his mother died quite suddenly, an event he seemed to tolerate fairly well. He inherited the family home, moved into it, and continued living there. He became interested in its upkeep and spent a great deal of time gardening and plumbing. He had no real friends, though he continued with his chess activities and occasionally socialized with the chess group. He continued to function at work and to be very able to take care of himself personally. He continued his relationship with the therapist, by now on a monthly basis. People who knew him casually thought of him as a very isolated person, a loner. They generally felt he must be suffering from loneliness. However, when colleagues at work or from the chess club made attempts to become friendly, the patient would reject them and withdraw further. People who had known him premorbidly in high school felt that he had changed completely, failed to fulfill his high promise, and something had gone wrong with him. The few cousins who knew him continued to show some interest in him, inviting him once a year to Sunday dinner, but they always found it painful to have him around and felt that it was also painful for him to be with them.

At age fifty-five the patient retired from his work. He sold his house and moved to a mountain vacation area approximately two hours from the city where he had lived all of his life. He bought a small rustic mountain home, opened a moderately successful shop selling local crafts, and displayed considerable interest in participating in community affairs. He helped form a local chess club, signed up to be a volunteer fire fighter, and helped organize and participated in a civic improvement drive. He had no further clinical exacerbations and during one of his annual drug holidays seemed to get along well without medication so that by now he continued without any medicine. Although people continued to see him as socially clumsy and generally shy, he was thought of as friendly, and indeed he seemed more interested in socializing. None of his new friends realized that he was psychiatrically ill, and he did not tell any of them of his previous psychiatric difficulties or history. His shyness and social clumsiness and his occasional need for short periods of withdrawal were viewed as normal variations rather than signs of mental illness by his new friends. He continued to see his psychiatrist, now once every six months, during which time he reported how his life situation was going. During these visits, he seemed more like a person visiting an old friend than having a psychiatric session.

At age fifty-eight he developed a pain in his left thigh, which on examination was diagnosed as a malignant bone tumor. Thorough examination showed evidence of metastases of the sarcoma, and he was confronted with the prognosis and the need to decide about amputation. In consultation with the psychiatrist and in a very clear and lucid state of mind, with relative calm, he decided to go ahead with surgery because he was enjoying life enough to want to be present as long as was practical. However, within six months he succumbed to the sarcoma. During the final six months of his life, he was fully aware of his prognosis and at times was in considerable pain. He had no difficulties with appropriate judgment and met death with a considerable amount of equanimity.

Part Two: The Treatment

10

The Case of Ellen West

This section of the book begins and ends with a case presentation. The first case is that of Ellen West, which is taken from the psychiatric literature as reported by the Swiss psychiatrist Ludwig Binswanger. His family operated a sanitarium in Switzerland, where he supervised treatment of this interesting patient. The section ends with a modern case, that of one of my patients from the population of 497. The two cases are separated by fifty years. Both cases are presented by using much of each patient's own words and the observation of various psychiatrists reporting the history of the illness.

The case of Ellen West was translated by me from the German, with considerable help from Joseph Lyons, Ph.D., who does not speak German but who was able to help put my translation into a much more comprehensible idiom. This case occurred long before the advent of psychotropic medication or modern techniques of community treatment. It also occurred in Switzerland, in a very conservative setting. In spite of the fact that it is an old-fashioned case and would be handled very differently today, with modern pharmacological and psychotherapeutic techniques, it does make an important contribution to our understanding of natural history, particularly because this patient provided, through her psychiatrist, a great deal of her own written material. Interesting also are the observations of this patient by various psychiatrists, including Dr. Emil Kraepelin and Dr. Eugen Bleuler, who developed the concept of schizophrenia approximately eighty years ago.

The Ellen West case is presented as an example of the phenomenological approach to the understanding of a life lived with schizophrenia. It lends itself particularly well to such an approach because the patient was verbal, bright, and talented. We have, thanks to Dr. Binswanger, many details describing the pain, suffering, and dread she experienced. The patient's writings and the meticulous description of the course of her life give us a clear picture of how life with schizophrenia is lived.

Many of my colleagues, when they first read this case, will disagree with the diagnosis. Kraepelin first diagnosed the patient as depressed. Jones believed her to be obsessive-compulsive. Bleuler knew her to be schizophrenic. Her first analyst saw her as obsessive-compulsive. Another analyst called her a manic-depressive. An internist thought she had an endocrine disorder. Another psychiatrist saw in her "pronounced hysterical traits" and believed she was suffering from anal eroticism. Binswanger knew she was schizophrenic. When I first read the case, I believed her to be a clear example of someone with an eating disorder. How can we understand such diversity of opinion among the world's experts?

A number of diseases have been called imitators. Before the availability of antibiotics, syphilis was known as "the great imitator." When syphilis became chronic, it imitated heart disease, skin disease, diseases of the central nervous system, including paranoia associated with paresis, flu (fever of unknown origin), and other conditions. Today we have Lyme disease. It, too, is caused by a spirochaete and is frequently misdiagnosed. Lyme disease imitates rheumatoid arthritis, influenza, and a number of other febrile diseases. Schizophrenia is also a great imitator. Chapter Two, Table 4, describes the misdiagnoses made for the first episode of schizophrenia in our 497 patients. In the older literature, one finds a great deal of discussion of the symptom of panneurosis as an early sign of schizophrenia. The symptom refers to the observation that many different neurotic symptoms can all be present in a patient at the same time or at various times throughout the illness. The neurotic symptoms do not bind the anxiety as they do for the nonschizophrenic patient. Ellen West had depression, hysteria, high levels of free-floating anxiety, suicidal ideation, eating disorder, obsessive-compulsive symptoms and manic episodes, substance abuse, and altered neurostress syndrome all at the same time.

In a study of polysurgical addicts (patients who had five surgeries or more, each for valid but vague complaints resulting in exploratory procedures) carried out at USC-LA County Medical Center, 75 percent were found to be suffering from schizophrenia. Their physical complaints were in fact somatic delusions. In a study of very fat patients who went to a special clinic (to be eligible the patient had to weigh at least 300 pounds), it was found that 45 percent suffered from schizophrenia as their primary disorder. These observations show what a great imitator schizophrenia is. Certainly Ellen demonstrated a multiplicity of signs and symptoms, each of which could be seen as a separate disease. However, when the picture is put together, it is clear that she was living her life with schizophrenia. She met the DSMIIIR criteria as well as our criteria (see Chapter Seven) of having the three nuclear defects that are pathognomic of the disease called schizophrenia.

Today Ellen would be treated very differently. She would not have been treated psychoanalytically. We know now that for patients with schizophrenia this technique is not helpful; in fact it is harmful. Rather, she would have been treated with supportive care (see Chapter Eleven). At various times in her life she would have also been treated with medication. When she was depressed, she would have received antidepressants. When she was exceedingly anxious, she would have been treated with anxiolytics, and when she was delusional she would have been treated with neuroleptics. She would have spent very little time in the hospital to prevent the regression and dependency that occurred. The focus would have been on rehabilitation, family support, and supportive care.

When you read this case and also the case of Amelia East (Chapter Seventeen), be a phenomenologist. Let yourself experience these two people, their suffering, their life-styles, and their coping mechanisms. Discover their disabilities and defects but also their strengths and their humanity. See how they are like you and yet how they are different. Recognize how life with schizophrenia proceeds and you will learn a great deal about the illness of schizophrenia.

CASE HISTORY OF ELLEN WEST[1]
Recorded by Ludwig Binswanger
Translated by Werner M. Mendel

Heredity

Ellen West, a non-Swiss, is the only daughter of a Jewish father for whom her love and veneration knows no bounds. She has a dark-haired brother four years older than she, who resembles his father, and a younger brother, who is blond. Whereas the older one "has no nerves" and is very well adjusted and cheerful, the younger brother is "a bundle of nerves" and is a soft womanish aesthete. At seventeen he was in a psychiatric clinic for some weeks for treatment of a mental ailment with suicidal ideas, and even after his recovery he remained easily excitable. He is married.

The sixty-six-year-old father is described as an externally very self-controlled, rather stiffly formal, very reserved, willful man of action; internally, however, he is very soft and sensitive and suffering from nocturnal depressions and states of fear accompanied by self-reproaches, "as if a wave of fear closed over his head." He sleeps poorly and is often under the pressure of fear when he gets up in the morning.

A sister of the father became mentally ill on her wedding day. Of the father's five brothers, one shot himself before the age of thirty (details are lacking), a second likewise committed suicide during a period of melancholy, and a third is severely ascetic, gets up very early, and eats nothing before noon because this makes one lazy. Two brothers fell ill with dementia arteriosclerosis, and later each died of a stroke. The father's father is said to have been a very strict autocrat, the father's mother, on the other hand, to have had a gentle, always conciliatory nature; she had "quiet weeks" during which she spoke not a word and sat motionless. All this is said to have increased as she aged. The mother of this woman—that is, the patient's great-grandmother on her father's side—is said to have been severely manic-depressive. She came from a family that

[1] "Der Fall Ellen West," *Swiss Archives for Neurology and Psychiatry*, 1944, Vol. 53, 255–277.

produced many outstandingly capable men but also many psychotics, one of whom I have treated personally (an eminent scholar).

The mother of Ellen West, likewise of Jewish descent, is said to be a very soft, kindly, suggestible, nervous woman, who underwent a depression for three years during the time of her engagement. The mother's father died young. The mother's mother was especially vigorous, healthy, and gay; she died at eighty-five of dementia senilis. There were five siblings of the mother, somewhat nervous, short, physically delicate; but all lived a long life; one died of tuberculosis of the larynx.

Course of Illness

Normal birth. At nine months Ellen refused milk and was therefore fed meat broth; nor could she ever tolerate milk in later years. On the other hand, she liked to eat meat, less well certain vegetables, and not at all some sweet desserts; if these were forced upon her, a tremendous resistance set in. She later confessed that even as a child she had passionately loved sweets so this was clearly not a case of an "aversion" but probably an early act of renunciation. [Unfortunately, in spite of two periods of psychoanalytic treatment in later years, we are completely in the dark about her early childhood; she no longer knows much about the first ten years of her life.]

According to her own statements and those of her parents, Ellen was a very lively but headstrong and violent child. It is said that she often defied an order of her parents for hours and did not carry it out even then. Once she was shown a bird's nest, but she insisted that it was not a bird's nest and nothing would make her change her mind. Even as a child, she said she had days when everything seemed empty to her, and she suffered from a pressure that she herself did not understand. After attending kindergarten she went to school in her first home from her eighth to her tenth year. At ten she moved with her family to Europe, where except for some trips across the ocean, she remained till her death. In Europe, she attended a school for girls. She was a good student, liked going to school, and was very ambitious; she would weep for hours if she did not rank first in her favorite subjects. She did not want to stay away from school when the doctor ordered it, fearing to fall behind the class or to miss something. Her favorite subjects were German and history; she was not as good at arithmetic. At this time she was of a lively temperament but still self-willed. She had already chosen as her life motto "aut Caesar aut nihil!" (Either Caesar or nothing!) Up to her sixteenth year her games were boyish. She preferred to wear trousers. From babyhood on Ellen West had been a thumb sucker; at age sixteen she suddenly gave that up, along with her boyish games, at the onset of an infatuation that lasted two years. In a poem written in her seventeenth year, however, she still expressed the ardent desire to be a boy, for then she would be "a soldier, fear no foe, and die joyously, sword in hand."

Other poems from this period already reveal a marked variability of mood: Now her heart beats with exultant joy, now the sky is darkened, the winds blow weirdly, and the ship of her life sails on unguided, not knowing whither to direct its keel.

In another poem from the following year, the wind is rushing about her ears, and she wants it to cool her burning brow; when she runs against it blindly, careless of custom or propriety, it is as if she were stepping out of a confining tomb, as if she were flying through the air in an uncontrollable urge to freedom, and as if she must achieve something great and mighty; then her gaze falls back into the world again and this saying comes to her mind: "Man, in small things make your world." She cries to her soul, "Fight on."

Age Seventeen. Ellen considers herself called to achieve something special; she reads much, occupies herself intensively with social problems, feels deeply the contrast between her own social position and that of the "masses," and draws up plans for improvement of the latter. At the same age (seventeen), following the reading of Niels Lyhne[2], she changes from a deeply religious person (despite the intentionally nonreligious upbringing her

[2]Niels Lyhne is both the title and central character of a famous Scandinavian novel by J. P. Jacobsen (1847–1885), published in 1880. Its stark and melancholy realist, religious nihilism and moving plot (concerning a disillusioned idealist) combined to give it a tremendous appeal to restless European youth at the turn of the century.

father gave her) to a complete atheist. In no respect does she care about the judgment of the world.

Still other poems from her seventeenth year are available. In one, entitled "Kiss Me Dead," the sun sinks into the ocean like a ball of fire, a dripping mist drops over sea and beach, and a pain comes over her. "Is there no rescue any more?" She calls upon the cold, grim "Sea-King" to come to her, take her into his arms in ardent love-lust, and kiss her to death.

In another poem, entitled "I Hate You," she sings of a boy, supremely beautiful, whom she now hates because of his victorious smile just as intensely as she had formerly loved him.

In a third one, "Tired," gray damp evening mists well up around her and stretch out their arms toward her cold, long-deceased heart, while the trees shake their heads in disconsolate gloom, singing an old, mournful song, and no bird lets its late song be heard, no light appears in the sky; her head is empty, her heart is afraid.

Age Eighteen. In diary entries from her eighteenth year she praises the blessing of work:

What would we be without work, what would become of us? I think they would soon have to enlarge the cemeteries for those who went to death of their own accord. Work is the opiate for suffering and grief. . . . When all the joints of the world threaten to fall apart, when the light of our happiness is extinguished and our pleasure in life lies wilting, only one thing saves us from madness: work. Then we throw ourselves into a sea of duties as into Lethe, and the uproar of its waves drown out the death-knell pealing in our heart. . . . When the day is done with its haste and unrest, and we sit by the window in the growing twilight, the book will fall from our hand, we stare into the distance, into the setting sun, and old pictures rise up before us. The old plans and hopes, none of which have been realized, the boundless barrenness of the world and our infinite minuteness stand before our tired soul. Then the old question crowds to our lips, "What for—why all this? Why do we strive and live, forgotten after a short span of time, only to molder in the cold earth?" . . . At such a time spring up quickly, and good for you if there is a call for you, and work with both hands, until the shapes of the night disappear. O work, you are indeed the blessing of our life!

She would like to gain fame—great, undying fame; after hundreds of years her name should still ring out on the lips of humankind. Then she would not have lived in vain. She cries to herself:

Oh, smother the murmuring voices with work! Fill up your life with duties. I will not think so much—my last address shall not be the madhouse! And when you have worked and toiled, what have you accomplished? What prevails around us and below us is still so much of boundless distress! There they are dancing in a brightly lighted hall, and outside the door a poor woman is starving to death. Starving! Not a crust of bread comes to her from the table of plenty. Did you observe how the fine gentleman, while speaking, slowly crushed the dainty bread in his hand? And outside in the cold a woman cried out for a dry crust! And what's the use of brooding on it? Don't I do the same?

In the same year the diary praises with the greatest enthusiasm everything new and beautiful that she experiences in Paris on a trip with her parents. A new little sentimental love affair develops. At the same time the wish now arises in her to be delicate and ethereal, as are the girlfriends whom she selects. Even now her poems continue to show the contradictoriness of her mood. One sings of sunshine and the smiling spring, of radiant blue skies over a free, wide land of pleasure and blissfulness; in another she wishes that the greening and blooming of the springtime world, the murmuring and rustling of the woods, might be her dirge; in a third the only longing left to her eyes is that for the darkness, "where the glaring sun of life does not shine": "If you still rule behind clouds, Father, then I beseech thee, take me back to thee!"

Age Nineteen. Through clouds and darkness the light of life breaks through again and again. A journey with her parents across the ocean, occurring during her nineteenth year, lives in her recollection "as the happiest and most harmless time" of her life. In a poem of this year, floods of light and "golden hands" rest upon grainfields, villages, and valleys, and only the mountains stand in darkness. And yet on this trip Ellen can never be alone, that is, away from her parents. Although she has a very good time while on visit to friends, she begs her parents to call her back to them. Returning to Europe, she begins to ride horses and soon becomes very skilled at it, no horse being too dangerous for her; she vies with experienced riders in jumping competitions. Like everything she does, she cultivates riding "with excessive intensity," indeed, as if it were her exclusive task in life.

Age Twenty. Ellen's twentieth year is full of happiness, yearning, and hopes. From her poems stream radiant joy of life—indeed, wild ecstasy of life. The sun stands high, spring gales "roar through the world," so how can one lag behind, lock oneself "into the tomb of a house"? Through her veins the blood "races and roars," youthful zest bursts her breast asunder; she stretches her strong young body, for the fresh marrow of life shall not stale, the ardent yearning for a wild joy shall not dry up, "pining away bit by bit." The earth is too stale and still, "I long for a storm that is shrill." "Oh, if 'He' would come now," now when every fiber of her is quivering so that she can hardly sit still to write, now, when she is "so completely cured in body and soul," when no sacrifice would be too great for her.

> He must be tall, and strong, and have a soul as pure and unblemished as the morning light! He must not play life nor dream it, but live it, in all its seriousness and all its pleasure. He must be able to be happy, to enjoy me and my children, and to take joy in sunshine and work. Then I would give him all my love and all my strength.

In the same year she makes her second trip overseas, to nurse her older brother, who is very sick. She takes pleasure in eating and drinking. This is the last time she can eat unconcernedly. At this point she becomes engaged to a romantic foreigner, but at her father's wish breaks the engagement. On the return trip she stops in Sicily and does some writing on a paper entitled "On the Woman's Calling". Here, according to her diary, she loves passionately, her pulse hammers out to her fingertips, and the world belongs to her, for she has sun, wind, and beauty all to herself. Her god is the god of life and of joy, of strength and hope; she is filled with a consuming thirst to learn, and she has already had a glimpse of the "secret of the universe."

The first weeks in Sicily are the last of her happiness in life. Already the diary is again reporting the shadows of doubt and dread; Ellen feels herself small and wholly forsaken in a world she cannot understand. To be sure, she is glad "to be far from the cramping influences of home." The pinions of her soul are growing, but this growth does not take place without pains and convulsions; indeed, in the midst of her loveliest, most exuberant moments, fear and trembling appear again. Pityingly, she looks down upon all her fine ideas and plans and closes her diary with the burning wish that they might one day transform themselves into deeds instead of merely useless words.

Along with this, however, something new emerges now, a definite dread, namely, a dread of getting fat. At the beginning of her stay in Sicily, Ellen still displays an enormous appetite. As a result she gets so fat that her girlfriends begin to tease her about it. At once she begins to mortify herself by fasting and taking immoderate hikes. This is taken so far that when her companions stop at some pretty spot Ellen keeps circling about them. She no longer eats sweets or other fattening things and skips supper altogether. When she goes home in the spring, everyone is horrified by how bad she looks.

Age Twenty-One. In the summer after her return to Italy her mood is markedly "depressive." She is constantly tormented by the idea that she is getting too fat, and therefore she is forever taking long walks. She takes up her diary again, complaining that she has no home anywhere, not even with her family, that she does not find the activity she is seeking, that she has no peace, that she feels a veritable torment when she sits still, that every nerve in her quivers, and that in general her body shares in all the stirrings of her soul:

"My inner self is so closely connected with my body that the two form a unity and together constitute my 'I,' my unlogical, nervous, individual 'I.'" She feels herself to be absolutely worthless and useless and is in dread of everything, of the dark and of the sun, of stillness and of noise. She feels herself on the lowest rung of the ladder that leads to the light, degraded to a cowardly, wretched creature: "I despise myself!"

In a poem, grim distress sits at her grave, ashen pale—sits and stares, does not flinch or budge; the birds grow mute and flee, the flowers wilt before its ice-cold breath. Now death no longer appears to her as terrible; death is not a man with a scythe but "a glorious woman, white asters in her dark hair, large eyes, dream-deep and gray." The only thing that still lures her is dying: "Such a delicious stretching out and dozing off. Then it's over. No more getting up and dreary working and planning. Back of every word I really hide a yawn."

In the fall of the same year Ellen gradually comes out of her depression. But along with her newly awakening joy of life and the urge to action, her paralyzing dread and despair continue. From her diary:

> I have not kept a diary for a long time, but today I must again take my notebook in hand; for in me there is such a turmoil and ferment that I must open a safety valve to avoid bursting out in wild excesses. It is really sad that I must translate all this force and urge to action into unheard words instead of powerful deeds. It is a pity of my young life, a sin to waste my sound mind. For what purpose did nature give me health and ambition? Surely not to stifle it and hold it down and let it languish in the chains of humdrum living, but to serve wretched humanity. The iron chains of property and comfort, the chains of gratitude and consideration, and, strongest of all, the chains of love. Yes, it is they that hold me down, hold me back from a tempestuous revival, from the complete absorption in the world of struggle and sacrifice for which my whole soul is longing. O God, dread is driving me mad! Dread which is almost certainty! The consciousness that ultimately I shall lose everything: all courage, all rebelliousness, all drive for

doing; that it—my little world—will make me flabby and
fainthearted and beggarly, as they are themselves. . . . Live?
No vegetate! Do you actually preach making concessions? I
will make no concessions! You realize that the existing social
order is rotten, rotten down to the root, dirty and mean; but
you do nothing to overthrow it. But we have no right to close
our ears to the cry of misery, and to walk with closed eyes past
the victims of our system! I am twenty-one years old and am
supposed to be silent and grin like a puppet. I am no puppet.
I am a human being with red blood and a woman with
quivering heart. And I cannot breathe in this atmosphere of
hypocrisy and cowardice, and I mean to do something great
and must get a little closer to my idea, my proud ideal. Will
it cost tears? Oh, what shall I do, how shall I manage it? It
boils and pounds in me, it wants to burst the outer shell!
Freedom! Revolution! . . .

No, no, I am not talking claptrap. I am not thinking
of the liberation of the soil; I mean the real tangible liberation
of the people from the chains of their oppressors. Shall I
express it still more clearly? I want a revolution, a great
uprising to spread over the entire world and overthrow the
whole social order. I should like to forsake home and parents
like a Russian nihilist, to live among the poorest of the poor
and make propaganda for the great cause. Not for the love of
adventure! No, no! Call it unsatisfied urge to action if you
like, indomitable ambition. What has the name to do with it?
To me it is as if this boiling in my blood were something
better. Oh, I am choking in this petty, commonplace life.
Bloated self-satisfaction or egotistical greed, joyless submis-
siveness or crude indifference; those are the plants which
thrive in the sunshine of the commonplace. They grow and
proliferate, and like weeds they smother the flower of longing
which germinates among them. . . .

Everything in me trembles with dread, dread of the
adders of my everyday, which would coil about me with their
cold bodies and press the will to fight out of me. But my
exuberant force offers resistance. I shake them off, I must

shake them off. The morning must come after this siege of nightmares.

In her diary she continues to air her hatred of the luxury and good living that surround her. She bemoans her cowardice and weakness in not being able "to rise above the conditions," in letting herself at so early an age be made flabby.

In the fall of the same year Ellen begins preparing for college entrance examinations with the intention of studying political economy. She gets up at five, rides for three hours, then has private lessons and works all afternoon and evening until late at night, with the help of black coffee and cold showers.

Age Twenty-Two. The next spring makes Ellen melancholy. She cannot enjoy the awakening of spring, feels merely "how low she has sunk," not only from her previous ideal image but from that which formerly she really was. Formerly the world lay "open before her" and she wished to "conquer" it. Her feelings and sensations were "strong and vigorous." She loved and hated "with her whole soul." Now she makes concessions; she would have ridiculed anyone who had prophesied this to her. With every year she has "lost a little of her old strength."

Age Twenty-Three. In the fall of the same year—Ellen became twenty-three at the end of July—she breaks down. At the same time she has an unpleasant love affair with a riding teacher. In addition, she watches her body weight and reduces her food intake as soon as a weight gain threatens again. But now dread of getting fat is accompanied by an intensified longing for food, especially sweets, and this is strongest when she has been made tired and nervous by being with others. In the presence of others, eating affords her no satisfaction; only when alone may she enjoy it. As always since the beginning of her dread of getting fat, she suffers from the conflict between the dread of getting fat and the wish to be able to eat unconcernedly. Even now her old governess observes that this conflict is "the cloud over her life." Especially during vacations is she in a "depressive unrest"; this does not disappear until she has regular work and a fixed daily schedule. Her plan to take the college entrance examination is again given up. Instead, within a few weeks she passes the teachers' examination in order to audit courses at the university.

Age Twenty-Four. During the summer semester of her twenty-third and the winter semester of the beginning of her twenty-fourth year, she studies in the town of X. This period is one of the happiest of her life. In the summer a love relationship with a student develops. The diary breathes joy of life and sensuality. After the close of the winter semester, in a poem entitled "Spring Moods," she writes:

> I'd like to die just as the birdling does
> That splits his throat in highest jubilation
> And not to live as the worm on earth lives on,
> Becoming old and ugly, dull and dumb!
> No, feel for once how forces in me kindle,
> And wildly be consumed in my own fire.

Ellen is enthusiastic about studying and student life. She goes with others on long excursions to the mountains, and now too she cannot be alone; her old governess is constantly with her. Neither can she free herself of her "fixed idea." She avoids fattening foods and, because she feels that she is nevertheless getting too fat, she undertakes a reducing diet, with her physician's consent, in the fall of that year.

At the same time the affair with the student turns into an engagement. Her parents demand a temporary separation. In the spring Ellen goes to a seaside resort, and here once again an especially severe "depression" sets in (she is twenty-four and a half years old). She does everything to get just as thin as possible, takes long hikes, and daily doses of thirty-six to forty-eight thyroid tablets! Consumed by homesickness, she begs her parents to let her return. She arrives completely emaciated, with trembling limbs, and drags herself through the summer in physical torment but feels spiritually satisfied because she is thin. She has the feeling that she has found the key to her well-being. The engagement remains in effect.

Age Twenty-Five. In the autumn, at the beginning of her twenty-fifth year, Ellen takes her third trip overseas. There a physician makes the diagnosis of Basedow syndrome (Graves' disease or exopthalmic goiter) and prescribes complete rest in bed. She stays in bed six weeks, and this makes her gain weight very rapidly, for which reason she weeps all the time. On her return home the following spring she weighs 165 pounds. Shortly afterward the engagement is broken.

In May Ellen is in a sanatorium. In the summer she attends a school of gardening. She is in a depressive mood, but physically she makes a completely healthy impression. Because she soon loses interest in gardening, she leaves the school prematurely. Again, she has attempted to reduce her weight by much physical activity and scanty eating. In the fall her cousin, with whom she has been friends for many years, takes a special interest in her. Until the following spring they take long hikes together, often twenty to twenty-five miles in a day. Besides this, she engages eagerly in gymnastics, is active in a children's home, though without enjoying it much, and longs for a real vocation. Although the broken engagement with the student remains an "open wound," a love relationship with the cousin develops. The "fixed idea" has not disappeared, but it does not dominate her as it formerly did.

At this time she writes a poem, evidently aimed at her former fiancé, in which she asks herself if he ever loved her at all, if her body was "not beautiful enough" to bear him sons:

Woe's me, woe's me!
The earth bears grain,
But I
Am unfruitful,
Am a discarded shell,
Cracked, unusable,
Worthless husk.
Creator, Creator,
Take me back!
Create me a second time
And create me better!

Age Twenty-Six. In her twenty-sixth year a love of music awakens in Ellen. She and her cousin plan to marry. But for two more years she vacillates between him and the student, with whom she has resumed relations. Not until her twenty-eighth year, after another meeting with the student, does she break off with him. She marries her cousin. Prior to that she has taken several physical culture courses, traveled a great deal, and consulted several famous neurologists at the request of her parents and her cousin.

Age Twenty-Eight. She hopes after marrying her cousin to get rid of her "fixed idea," but this is not the case. At the wedding she weighs 160 pounds, and even on the honeymoon trip she diets; as a result she steadily loses weight. In the summer following the spring of her marriage her periods cease. The conflict between the "wish for harmless eating" and her dread of getting fat torments her constantly.

Age Twenty-Nine. In the fall, just after her twenty-ninth birthday, while on a hike with her husband in a lonely neighborhood, she has a severe vaginal hemorrhage, despite which she must continue to hike for several more hours. The physician does a curettage and finds a miscarriage; he states that a good diet is a prerequisite for the possibility of a new pregnancy. For an entire year Ellen is torn this way and that between the desire to have a child and the dread of getting fat (from adequate nourishment).

Age Thirty. In her thirtieth year Ellen is even more intensely active in social welfare. She takes the warmest human interest in the people committed to her care, with whom she keeps up personal relationships for years. At the same time she impoverishes her nourishment and systematically and gradually becomes a vegetarian. Even after a short siege of grippe she does not spare herself. A treatment in a spa prescribed by a third gynecologist is unsuccessful, especially because she increases the laxative dosage so much that she vomits every night. When she finds that she is steadily losing weight, she is very pleased.

Age Thirty-One. The winter of her thirty-first year brings with it a rapid decline in her strength. In spite of an occasional high fever, which she keeps secret, she goes out in the street in the hope of catching pneumonia. Her facial expression changes. Ellen looks old and haggard.

The following spring, during a hike with her husband, suddenly and with elemental force, the confession bursts from her that she is living her life only with a view to being able to remain thin, that she is subordinating every one of her actions to this end, and that this idea has gained a terrible power over her. She thinks she can numb herself by work, exchanges her volunteer work in the welfare agency for a paid position, which obligates her to seven hours of office work a day, and after some weeks, in June she breaks down.

In every free minute she writes recipes of delectable dishes, puddings, desserts, and the like in her cookbook. She demands that those around her eat much and well, while she denies herself everything. She develops great skill in not letting them know that she is eating almost nothing by filling her plate like everyone else and then secretly emptying the greater part of the food into her handbag. At every meal she sweats profusely.

Ellen now goes with her husband to a sanitorium for metabolic diseases and at first follows the orders of the doctor so that her weight increases from 99 to 110 pounds. After her husband leaves, however, she deceives the physician by dropping her food into her handbag and secretly carrying weights when she is weighed.

Age Thirty-Two. At the beginning of her thirty-second year Ellen's physical condition deteriorates still further. Her use of laxatives increases beyond measure. Every evening she takes sixty to seventy tablets of a vegetable laxative, with the result that she suffers tortured vomiting at night and violent diarrhea by day. Ellen becomes more and more debilitated, goes back to bed in the afternoon, and is terribly tortured by the feeling that "her instincts are stronger than her reason," that "all inner development, all real life has stopped," and that she is completely dominated by her "over-powering idea, long since recognized as senseless." Yet her mood is rather cheerful, and it affords her satisfaction that her friends worry about her.

At the age of thirty-two and a half Ellen undergoes her first psychoanalysis, with a young and sensitive analyst who is not completely committed to Freud. She regains hope, again attends lectures, the theater, and concerts, and goes on excursions. But she is extremely restless and again overdoes everything. During the times when her husband is absent her old nursemaid must stay with her. She soon regards the psychoanalysis as useless. Still, she feels the opinion of her analyst, that her main goal is "the subjugation of all other people," to be "marvelously correct and frighteningly true."

During the analysis feelings of dread become more frequent, and now there appears above all the bothersome obsession of constantly having to think about food. She describes her feelings of dread as "the specters which constantly jump at my throat." Good hours seem to her like a "flood tide," but then "low tide" swiftly sets in again.

In a letter to her husband Ellen now compares her ideal, exemplified by her former fiancé, the student, with the ideal of being thin:

At that time you [the husband] were the life which I was ready to accept and to give up my ideal [the student] for. But it was an artificially derived, forced resolve, not one ripened from within. For this reason it did not work. I again started to send him packages and to be full of opposition to you. And only much later, when I was ripe within, when I had looked my ideal in the face and realized, "I have made a mistake, this ideal is a fiction," then, and only then, could I say yes to you calmly and with assurance. Just so I must now be able to look at my ideal, this ideal of being thin, of being without a body, and to realize: "It is a fiction." Then I can say yes to life. Before I do that, everything is a fallacy, like that time in X [the university town]. But it is simpler to get into the train and ride to Y [where the rupture with the student took place] than to bring to the light of day what lay buried and hidden in me. As for the comparison of you with life, and of the student with my ideal, of course, it is a lame one; there is only a superficial analogy. My saying yes [to the husband after her visit with the

student in Y] was also not yet the right thing. I chose you—
but then I still did not really become your wife. The thought
of my secret ideal, by which I do not mean the student—for
that was something external—I mean my life's idea, still
dominates my thinking. And that is so difficult that today I
am again just as desperate as weeks ago. Poor ———— , always
I have to keep disappointing you! As for externals, I have not
yet taken medicine again. But that makes me constantly touch
my abdomen and eat with dread and uneasiness.

At another time Ellen writes her husband:

The only real improvement, which must come from within,
is not yet here; Nirvana in a figurative sense, "the extinction
of greed, hate, and delusion" has not yet been reached. Do you
know what I mean by this? The greed to realize my ideal; my
hatred with the surrounding world which wants to make this
impossible; the delusion which lies in my seeing this ideal as
something worthwhile.

To this is annexed the very characteristic outcry: "The
thought of pancakes is still for me the most horrible thought there
is." Moreover, meat and fat, she says, are so repugnant that the mere
thought of them nauseates her. For the rest, she now has (during
the analysis) the will to become fatter but not the wish. She describes
it as a fight between duty and desire in the Kantian sense. However,
as long as it remains that, she is not "redeemed" because this
categorical imperative, this "thou shalt," comes from the outside,
as it were, and therefore can do nothing against the tenacity of the
morbid urge that rules her.
    At the same time she feels her present state, just because she
is making an effort to take no laxatives, to be "more torturing than
all that I have gone through hitherto. I feel myself getting fatter, I
tremble with dread of this, I am living in a state of panic. . . . As
soon as I feel a pressure at my waist—I mean a pressure of my
waistband—my spirit sinks, and I get a depression as severe as
though it were a question of goodness knows what tragic affairs."
On the other hand, if she has a "good bowel movement" there is

a "kind of calm" in her and she feels at ease. In spite of this she feels "the entire time, every minute," how terribly her life is dominated by her "morbid idea."

Now that Ellen knows her husband has told her parents what is the matter with her, she feels a great longing for them, especially for her mother; she would like to lay her head on her breast and have a good cry. But this, she says, is a passing mood. Basically, she feels no desire at all to be at home. Indeed, she feels dread of "the grave and serious nature" of her father.

Age Thirty-Three. In August, soon after Ellen's thirty-third birthday, the analysis begun in February comes to an end. Upon his return, her husband finds her in a state of severe dread and agitation. Her food intake becomes quite irregular; Ellen skips entire meals to throw herself indiscriminately with all the greater greed upon any foods that may happen to be at hand. Each day she consumes several pounds of tomatoes and twenty oranges.

A three-week visit with her parents at first goes better than expected. Ellen is happy to be out of the hotel atmosphere, to be able to spend the evenings with her family, and to talk things out with her mother. From the second week on, however, the picture changes again. For days Ellen cannot get over weeping, dread, and agitation. She walks in tears through the streets of her hometown and suffers more than ever from her hunger, especially because at home she has to sit at the table with others who eat normally. She now despairs completely of her illness being curable and can hardly be calmed down anymore.

A physician does a blood count and finds "irregularities in the composition of the blood." He advises a consultation with an internist at the university clinic in X, where she earlier audited lectures and to which she returns at the beginning of October with her husband and her old nursemaid. The internist advises clinical treatment. Ellen cannot make up her mind to do it. Instead, she undergoes psychoanalytic treatment for the second time. The second analyst with whom she enters treatment is more orthodox than the first.

On October 6 her husband leaves her, at the request of the analyst but against his own wishes. On October 8, after having previously expressed suicidal ideas, Ellen attempts suicide by taking fifty-six tablets of Somnacetin, most of which, however, she vomits up during the night. The analyst ascribes no importance to this attempt and continues with the analysis. For the rest, Ellen is left to her own devices and walks aimlessly and tearfully through the streets. These and the following weeks until the middle of November are, according to her own account, "the most horrible of my life."

In her dreams, too, Ellen is incessantly concerned with eating. Her husband is with her from October 16 to 24 and again continuously after November 6.

From her diary, resumed upon the advice of the analyst, the following October comments are of special interest.

October 19. I don't think that the dread of becoming fat is the real obsessive neurosis, but the constant desire for food. The pleasure of eating must have been the primary thing. Dread of becoming fat served as a brake. Now that I see the pleasure of eating as the real obsessive idea, it has pounced upon me like a wild beast. I am defenselessly at its mercy. It pursues me constantly and is driving me to despair.

What is the meaning of this terrible feeling of emptiness—the horrible feeling of dissatisfaction which takes hold after each meal? My heart sinks, I feel it bodily; it is an indescribably miserable feeling.

I will briefly describe a morning. I sit at my desk and work. I have a great deal to do, much that I have been looking forward to. But a tormenting restlessness keeps me from finding quiet. I jump up, walk to and fro, stop again and again in front of the cupboard where my bread is. I eat some of it; ten minutes later I jump up again and eat some more. I firmly resolve not to eat anymore now. Of course, I can summon up such willpower that I actually eat nothing. But I cannot suppress the desire for it. All day long I cannot get the thought of bread out of my mind! It so fills up my brain that I have no more room for other thoughts; I can concentrate neither on working nor on reading. Usually the end is that I run out into the street. I run away from the bread in my cupboard and wander aimlessly about. Or I take a laxative. How can that be analyzed? From where does this unconquerable unrest come? Why do I think I can dull it only with food? Why then does eating make me so unhappy? One might say, "Eat up the bread, then you will have peace." But no, when I have eaten it, I am unhappier than ever. Then I sit and constantly see before me the bread I have eaten. I feel my stomach and have to keep thinking, "Now you will get that much fatter!" When I try to analyze all this, nothing comes of it except theory. Something thought up. All I can feel is the disquiet and the dread. But all this is only fantastic pictures; I must exert my brain to think them up. It would be easy to analyze someone else like this. I myself, however, continue to wander about in my deathly dread and must go through thousands of frightful hours. Every day seems to me to have a thousand hours, and often I am so tired from this spasmodic thinking that I no longer wish for anything but death. After dinner my mood is always at its worst. I would rather not eat at all so as not to have the horrible feeling after dinner. All day I am afraid of that feeling. How shall I describe it? It is a dull, empty feeling at the heart, a feeling of dread and helplessness. Sometimes then my heart pounds so strongly that it makes me quite dizzy. We've explained it in the analysis this way: I attempt to satisfy two things while eating—hunger and love. Hunger gets satisfied—love does not! There remains the great, unfilled hole.

Perhaps I would find liberation if I could solve this puzzle: the connection between eating and longing. The anal-erotic connection is purely theoretical. It is completely incomprehensible to me. I don't understand myself at all. It is terrible not to understand yourself. *I confront myself as a strange person,* I am afraid of myself, I am afraid of the feelings to which I am defenselessly delivered every minute.

This is the horrible part of my life: It is filled with dread. Dread of eating, dread of hunger, dread of the dread. Only death can save me from this dread. Every day is like walking on a dizzying ridge, an external balancing on cliffs. It is useless to have analysis tell me that I want precisely this dread, this tension. I see nothing anymore, everything is blurred, all the threads are tangled.

The only work I do is mental. In my innermost being nothing changes, the torment remains the same. It is easy to say everything is transparent. I long to be violated—*and indeed I do violence to myself every hour.* Thus I have reached my goal.

But where, where indeed is the miscalculation? For I am boundlessly wretched; it sounds silly to me to say: "That is just what I want: to be wretched." Those are words, words, words, . . . and in the meantime I suffer as one would not let an animal suffer.

On November 7 Ellen makes her second suicide attempt by taking twenty tablets of a barbiturate compound. The following day she is in a condition that the analyst describes as a "hysterical twilight state." She cries and whimpers the entire day, refuses all food, and declares that in some unguarded moment she will take her life after all.

On November 9 she again takes food greedily. On the tenth she attempts several times on the street to throw herself in front of a car. On the eleventh she tries to throw herself out of a window in her analyst's office. On the twelfth she moves with her husband into her internist's clinic.

In the clinic a spiritual relaxation sets in, along with a complete revolution in her nourishment. From the first day on she eats everything set before her, including things she has not touched for years, such as soup, potatoes, meat, sweet dishes, chocolate. Her weight, which was 102 pounds on admission, nevertheless does not increase to more than 114 pounds in two months.

From the clinic Ellen attends lectures at the university in the morning and afternoon, taking notes with great concentration; in between, from three to four o'clock, she undergoes analysis. In the evening she often goes for a walk or to the theater. It seems to her husband as if real improvement is now beginning. Her notes and poems show new hope and new courage. She wants once again "to be human among humans." "Softly on sun-billows comes a new time"; "and thus I was reborn and the world has me again"; "deep gratitude quivers through my heart that I have lived through this night."

But, still, she does not quite trust this peace:

I see the golden stars and how they dance;
It's night as yet, and chaos utterly.
Will with the early morn's clear countenance
Peace come to me at last, and harmony?

All of the poems reproduced here (merely in small extracts) were written during the night of November 18–19. Of them she writes:

As soon as I close my eyes, there come poems, poems, poems. If I wanted to write them all down I should have to fill pages and pages—hospital poems . . . weak and full of inner restraint. They only beat their wings softly; but at least something is stirring. God grant that it may grow!

From the same night we have the following diary entry:

I have been awake for two hours. But it is beautiful to be awake. Once before it happened, in the summer. But then everything fell apart again. This time, I believe, it will not fall apart. I feel something sweet in my breast, something which wants to grow and become. My heart throbs. Is love coming back into my life? More serious, more quiet than previously, but also more holy and more purified. Dear life, I will ripen toward you; I spread out my arms and breathe deeply, timid and glad.

   I am reading Faust again. Now for the first time I am beginning to understand it. I am beginning; much will have to come, and many more heavy things in my life, before I may say, "I understand it. Yes, now I understand it." But I am not afraid of what is coming. It is sweet to fear and to suffer, to grow and to become.

But on the very next day (November 19), "The beautiful mood of the night is as if blown away. I am tired and sad."

Ellen continues to go to lectures, to write, to read, but the thought of eating never leaves her. For the attraction of this thought she finds a very characteristic comparison:

The murderer must feel somewhat as I do who constantly sees in his mind's eye the picture of the victim. He can work, even slave, from early until late, can go out, can talk, can attempt to divert himself: all in vain. Always and always again he will see the picture of the victim before him. He feels an overpowering pull toward the place of the murder. He knows that this makes him suspect. Even worse—he has a horror of that place, but still he must go there. Something that is stronger than his reason and his will controls him and makes of his life a frightful scene of devastation. He goes to the police and accuses himself. In the punishment he atones for his crime. I can find no redemption—except in death.

Ellen is painfully aware that

by this fearful illness I am withdrawing more and more from people. I feel myself excluded from all real life. I am quite isolated. I sit in a glass ball. I see people through a glass wall; their voices come to me muffled. I have an unutterable longing to get to them. I scream, but they do not hear me. I stretch out my arms towards them; but my hands merely beat against the walls of my glass ball.

At this time she begins to write the "History of a Neurosis." We quote from it:

Since I acted only from the point of view of whether things made me thin or fat, all things soon lost their intrinsic meaning. My work too. I sought it for the purpose of diverting myself: away from my hunger or my fondness for sweets. (During the time that I was working from nine to one and from two to six, I was not tempted to eat things that would make me fat.) For a time work served its purpose. It also gave me joy. When everything collapsed in me, that too broke to bits: Work neither diverted me nor gave me joy. However, that did not come till later.

In the fall of 19—— (at the beginning of my thirty-second year) I felt dread for the first time. Only a very indefinite and faint dread, really rather an inkling of the fact that I had become enslaved to an uncanny power which threatened to destroy my life. I felt that all inner development was ceasing, that all becoming and growing were being choked, because a single idea was filling my entire soul, and this idea something unspeakably ridiculous. My reason rebelled against it, and I attempted by willpower to drive this idea out. In vain. Too late—I could no longer free myself and longed now for liberation, for redemption which was to come to me through some method of healing. Thus I came to know psychoanalysis. I wanted to get to know the unknown urges which were stronger than my reason and which forced me to shape my entire life in accordance with a guiding point of view. And the goal of this guiding point of view was to be thin. The analysis was a disappointment. I analyzed with my mind, and everything remained theory. The wish to be thin remained unchanged in the center of my thinking.

The months which followed were the most terrible I have ever experienced, and I have not yet gotten over them. Now it was no longer the fixed idea alone which embittered my life, but something far worse was added: the compulsion of always having to think about eating. This compulsion has become the curse of my life; it pursues me waking and sleeping, it stands beside everything I do like an evil spirit, and never and nowhere can I escape it. It pursues me as the Furies pursue a murderer; it makes the world a caricature and my life a hell. It seems to me that I could stand any other pain more easily. If my existence were darkened by a really heavy sorrow, I would have the strength to bear it. But the torture of having each day to tilt anew against the windmill with a mass of absurd, base, contemptible thoughts, this torment spoils my life.

When I open my eyes in the morning, my great misery stands before me. Even before I am entirely awake I think of— eating. Every meal is associated with dread and agitation, every hour between meals filled with the thought "When shall I get hungry again? Would I perhaps even like to eat something now, and what?" . . . and so on; a thousand different forms, but always the same content. No wonder I can no longer be glad. I know only dread and sorrow, lack of pleasure and lack of courage.

Because the clinical course again takes a serious drop, at the beginning of December, Kraepelin is consulted. He makes the diagnosis of melancholia. The analyst considers this diagnosis incorrect and continues the analysis.

In the first half of December Ellen's course is again uphill. She again attends lectures, reads *Faust,* Part II, but is torn by the differing views of the doctors regarding her illness and treatment. The internist, who judges the illness most correctly, considers continued hospital treatment necessary; the analyst advises leaving the clinic and "returning to life." This advice completely shakes her faith in the analyst. In her diary entry of December 19, she notes, among other things, the following:

I continue living only because of a sense of duty to my relatives. Life has no further lure for me. There is nothing, no matter where I look, which holds me. Everything is gray and without joy. Since I have buried myself in myself and can no longer love, existence is only torture. Every hour is torture. What formerly gave me joy is now a task and intrinsically senseless, something contrived to help me pass the hours. What formerly seemed to be a goal in life, all the learning, all the striving, all the accomplishment, is now a dark, heavy nightmare of which I am afraid.

For her condition she again finds pertinent analogies. Her husband, Karl, she tells us, says that she does have joy in some things; but he should ask a prisoner of war sometime whether he would rather stay in prison camp or return to his homeland. In the prison camp he studies foreign languages and concerns himself with this or that, of course, only to help himself get over the long, hard days. Does he really enjoy the work? Would he for its sake remain in the prison camp even a minute longer than necessary? Certainly not, and nobody will even dream up such a grotesque idea. But of me it is required. Life has become a prison camp for me, and I long as ardently for death as the poor soldier in Siberia longs for his homeland.

The comparison with imprisonment is no play on words. I am in prison, caught in a net from which I cannot free myself. I am a prisoner within myself; I get more and more entangled, and every day is a new, useless struggle; the meshes tighten more and more. I am in Siberia; my heart is icebound; all around me is solitude and cold. My best days are a sadly comic attempt to deceive myself as to my true condition. It is undignified to live on like this. Karl, if you love me, grant me death.

Another analogy:

I am surrounded by enemies. Wherever I turn, a man stands there with a drawn sword. As on the stage: The unhappy one rushes toward the exit; stop! an armed man confronts him. He rushes to a second, and to a third exit. All in vain. He is surrounded; he can no longer get out. He collapses in despair.

So it is with me: I am in prison and cannot get out. It does no good for the analyst to tell me that I myself place the armed men there, that they are theatrical figments and not real. To me they are very real.

Ellen complains that for months she has "had not one hour of complete freedom." At the same time, she says the daily picture keeps changing. In one week the morning hours are the worst, in another the evening hours, in a third midday or the late afternoon hours, but in no week is she "completely free." What is constantly denied her is unconcern. She "knows" about herself unceasingly, does everything "with awareness," can never be simply here and live. If once in a while she "grasps at the faith" that her life does still make sense, that she can still be useful to others and help them, then fear comes clearer to her that she cannot live on if she does not succeed in "breaking the ban" and getting out of the preoccupation with self. Her "spiritual confusion" during and after meals is terrible. She swallows every bite with awareness and an inexplicable feeling of sadness.

> *The entire worldpicture is disarranged.* As if I were bewitched. An evil spirit accompanies me and embitters my joy in everything. He distorts everything beautiful, everything natural, everything simple, and makes a caricature out of it. He makes a caricature out of all life. . . . Something in me rebels against becoming fat. Rebels against becoming healthy, getting plump red cheeks, becoming a simple, robust woman, as corresponds to my true nature. . . . It drives me to despair that with all my big words I cannot get myself further. I am fighting against uncanny powers which are stronger than I. I cannot seize and grasp them.

At the beginning of the new year, on January 3, the internist intervenes decisively, prohibits the continuation of the analysis, to which the patient agrees, and advises her transfer to the Kreuzlingen Sanatorium in Kreuzlingen. On January 7 Ellen writes her younger brother to pardon her for writing him so frankly, but she will no longer lie to him; she wants to tell him that she is full of dread, even though she does not know of what. "Life burdens me like a cloud."

During the preparations for her trip to Kreuzlingen, increased depression and agitation set in. The trip, which takes place on January 13–14, is undergone amid states of fear, feelings of hunger, and depression.

The Stay at Kreuzlingen Sanatorium, January 14 to March 30, 19——— . The referral note of the internist states that menstruation has been absent for years and the salivary glands are slightly enlarged. Certainly, therefore, there are endocrine disturbances too. The neurosis has expressed itself for many years in obsessive ideas, especially in the fear of becoming too heavy and then again in a compulsive urge to eat copiously and indiscriminately. Between these opposing feelings the exceptionally intelligent patient, many-sided in her interests, vacillates back and forth. To this was added in July of the previous year a very severe cyclothymic depression with exacerbations approximately once a month, strong feelings of dread, and periodic suicidal ideas. During the periods of increased depression the obsessive thoughts have been more in the background. In the clinic her condition improves decidedly during the constant presence of her husband, who has a very favorable effect upon her. Her body weight increases markedly on an initial diet of seventy calories per 2.2 pounds (kilo) and at the present time is steady at about 114 pounds on a diet of fifty calories per 2.2 pounds. Because of her last depression she is to undergo the prolonged rest urgently recommended by Kraepelin in our institution. Admission to the locked ward seems necessary.

The second analyst states in his detailed report that the patient is suffering from a severe obsessive neurosis combined with manic-depressive oscillations. He is convinced that the patient is on the way to a cure! Evidence of this is also a far-reaching physiognomic alteration; for whereas during the summer she was repulsively ugly, since then she has grown more and more feminine and almost pretty. The report confirms in general the above anamnesis but also contains some important additions and opinions of the psychoanalyst. He considers the depression as "strongly and purposefully aggravated." The patient stated at one time, he says, that her father did not understand her obsessive ideas but that he did have full understanding of the depression. She had feared that by becoming fat she would displease her previous fiancé (the student), and anyway, for her, being thin was equated with a higher intellectual type, and being fat with a bourgeois Jewish type. After the termination of her engagement her first action was, with a sigh of relief, to raid her own larder! "But when she learned from a statement of the gynecologist that she would have no success along the womanly—motherly—line, despite her renunciation of higher intellectuality (in her marriage she concerned herself ostentatiously with the household and the copying of recipes, especially when in the presence of her younger brother's wife, who is a slim blond, artistically oriented, has children, and so on), she now resolved 'to live for her idea' without any inhibitions, and began to take large daily doses of laxatives."

Because she saw the blond, higher type in the person of her analyst, he succeeded in quieting her during the first consultation (a fact that her husband also confirms). She has also shown pronounced hysterical traits, visibly calculated to impress her husband. Anal-eroticism was the focus of treatment for a long time. She recognized the relationship between chocolate and anal-eroticism, as well as this equation: "Eating = being fertilized = pregnant = getting fat." The transference then became so clear that on one occasion she sat down quite suddenly on the analyst's lap and gave him a kiss, which in spite of their previous friendly relations, was very unusual. On another occasion she came to him with the wish that she might lay her head on his shoulder and he should call her "Ellen-child." Since the beginning of December the analysis had flagged more and more, and this is as a sequel to their discussion on the father complex, which however could only be treated peripherally. She has made it clear to herself that "her obsessional idea" meant turning away from the paternal (Jewish) type. For the incest wish, no material could be obtained, not even from her dreams. The infantile amnesia, unfortunately, was not illuminated by either analysis.

During the intake interview at the sanatorium on January 14, after a few words the patient bursts out into loud wailing and cannot be calmed down for a long time, but reports abruptly and intermittently disconnected fragments of her case history. She readily follows her husband to her room and is glad that she has an opportunity to report details of her illness. She then tells circumstantially the main features in the development of her suffering, from its inception thirteen years ago to the latest events in the university town. Kraepelin has rejected the analyst's assumption of an obsessive neurosis, has assumed a genuine melancholia, and has declared to her that the obsessional thoughts will surely disappear with the melancholia; what will happen to her fixed idea after that will then be seen. She differentiates between the obsessional idea of always having to think about eating and the "fixed idea," the "one goal" of not becoming fat.

She reports that during the last weeks she has felt a slight improvement, but has never really been happy and glad. She came here with a thousand good resolutions, but even on the way now she has become terribly hopeless. Every trifle now seems to her like an insurmountable obstacle. She has the feeling that if one of her symptoms is better, another is so much the worse. "I need the carefree feeling again while eating; to me every meal is an inner conflict. Constantly, I have the feeling that if somebody really loved me he would not let me live on."

In the clinic, she says, she finally became afraid of everyone because she must always expect they will tell her she looks well. "Everything agitates me, and I experience every agitation as a sensation of hunger, even if I have just eaten." She has the feeling that all her inner life has ceased, that everything is unreal, everything senseless. She also reports readily on her suicidal attempts. She wishes for nothing so much as to be allowed to go to sleep and not wake up again, for she does not dream that she can ever become healthy again. After the second attempt she constantly thought about only this: If only her husband would come back soon; otherwise she would throw herself under some car. She constantly longs for him when he is away.

Ellen turns against psychoanalysis with particular vigor. In contrast to this, her husband states that she let herself be analyzed quite willingly and that she was by no means detached from the second analyst.

Some extracts from the case record:

January 16 After a discussion of the daily schedule as to rest, walks, etc., and the question of eating, the first night went well, with the help of a mild sedative. The patient is allowed to eat in her room, but comes readily with her husband to the afternoon coffee, whereas previously she had stoutly resisted this on the basis that she did not really eat but devoured like a wild animal—which she demonstrated with utmost realism.

Her physical examination showed nothing striking. She is a woman of medium height, adequately nourished, tending toward pyknic habitus, whose body build is characterized in the case record as boyish. However, signs of pronounced male stigmatization are missing. The skull is described in the case record as relatively large and massive, but otherwise no signs of acromegaly are present. Facial form oval and evenly modeled. Salivary glands are markedly enlarged on both sides. Thyroid gland not palpable. An earlier gynecological examination is said to have revealed "infantile genitalia." On the clavicle, callus formation from a horseback riding accident. Internal organs, no comment. Pulse full and soft, but the rate is unstable. Periods absent for several years. The neurological examination showed, except for a very weak (Jendrassik enforced) patellar reflex (with a moderately active Achilles' reflex), absolutely nothing remarkable, nor any tremor of hands.

January 21 The facial expression is very changeable, corresponding to frequent fluctuations from one active state to another; on the whole, however, somewhat stiff and empty, her look now empty, now strongly "saturated with feeling." Also, her posture is somewhat stiff.[3] Her gait is erect and very quick. Her behavior is very amiable; she seeks contacts but without noticeable eroticism. Basic mood hopelessly despairing. Even at this time I noted: "One has less the impression that she suffers under a genuine depressive affect than that she feels herself physically empty and dead, completely hollow, and suffers precisely from the fact that she cannot achieve any affect. Strong feeling of illness in the sense of a flagging of her mental energy. Seriously longs for death. In the foreground, vexation and torment because of the obsession of always having to think of eating. Feels herself degraded by this. Striking is the objectivity with which she reports things from which properly the release of a strong affect must be expected. Train of thought shows neither flight of ideas nor dispersion;

[3]*Translator's note:* This posture, which is frequently seen in schizophrenia, was not due to neuroleptic medications because none were used or available. When this stiffness is seen today, it is usually attributed to side effects of medication. The work of Erwin Straus (1952) has demonstrated that the stiffness and lack of associated movement is a symptom of schizophrenia.

but she has difficulty concentrating since her thoughts keep revolving about her "complex." Hence will not yet let her husband read to her. Power of apprehension, attention, and memory intact, however. The Rorschach test was unfortunately not available at that time; the result would have been of the greatest interest in presenting experimentally a picture of the patient's entire world-view.

January 22 Nights tolerable with mild sedatives. Only during her second night so agitated that her husband had to call the head nurse. Mood fluctuates from day to day and often several times during the same day. On the whole, quieter; slight attacks of dread beginning with a "fluttering" in the cardiac region, "as if there were bats there."

Eats nearly everything that is set before her; only makes occasional difficulties about desserts. Has lost one pound in the last week, since then has eaten better. During walks lets herself be diverted from her despair with relative ease. Though as a child she was wholly independent of the opinion of others, she is now completely dependent on what others think about her appearance and her being fat.

Because everything now depends on our arriving at a definitive diagnosis, I ask the patient and her husband to work out an exact anamnesis, a labor that visibly calms the patient.

February 8 She suffers greatly from obsessional impulses to throw herself upon food and gulp it down like an animal (confirmed by observation). One night devoured seven oranges in succession. By contrast, during the meals there appear ascetic impulses, forcing her to deny herself this and that, especially the dessert. She is least restrained during walks but is also quite orderly with the other patients; however, she can never get away from herself and constantly has the feeling "of being like a corpse among people."

February 15 The findings already noted in the report of the internist are again shown clearly: feelings of hunger, ravenous desire, and "compulsive thoughts" about eating superseded by a severely depressive dejection, indeed, despair. Suicidal impulses, self-reproaches for beginning to lie once more—it has come to that today. Has recently taken six tablets of laxative daily but in response to a direct question lies to the physician, saying she is taking nothing.

February 26 Agitation, quickly subsides again. Has attached herself to an elegant, very thin female patient. "Homo-erotic component strikingly evident." Dreams very vividly and always about food or death; sees the finest things before her, feels terrible hunger, but at the same time the compulsion not to be allowed to eat. Her death dreams:

Dream 1: "I dreamt something wonderful. War had broken out; I was to go into the field. I say goodby to everyone with the joyous expectation that I shall soon die. I am glad that before the end I can eat everything; have eaten a large piece of mocha cake."

Dream 2: In a semisomnolent state she dreams she is "the wife of a painter who cannot sell his paintings." She herself has to work at sewing or the like, cannot do it because she feels sick, both have to go hungry. She asks him to get a revolver and shoot them both. "You're just too cowardly to shoot us; the other two painters shot themselves too."

Dream 3: Dreams that on her trip overseas she jumps into the water through a porthole. Her first lover (the student) and her husband both attempt artificial respiration. She eats many chocolate creams and packs her trunks.

Dream 4: She orders goulash. She says she is very hungry but only wants a small portion. Complains to her old nursemaid that people are tormenting her very much. Wants to set herself on fire in the forest.

For psychotherapeutic reasons, an analysis of her dreams was not made.

During a morning agitation in a semisomnolent state Ellen speaks of the deceased, who have eternal rest whereas she is still tormented; she speaks of her burial. She will eat no oranges because her husband will tell the doctor, and offers a farmer fifty francs if he will shoot her quickly. She speaks of her younger brother, who has left the New World because he has been tormented day and night by the buzzing of a fly; she herself, though in the same tormented state, is not allowed "to leave from overseas" but must continue to live. If she knows no other way of dying, she will set fire to herself or ram her head through a pane of glass. She says the medical personnel at the sanatorium are all sadists and take pleasure in tormenting her, the doctor included.

It is very easy for her husband to achieve rapport with her, not only when she is half asleep but when she is fully asleep.

March 9 After fourteen relatively good days, there are five days of agitation, which reached their climax yesterday. In the foreground a "colossal gluttony," to which, however, she did not yield. She says she cannot wait until her "melancholia" is cured. It is terrible that her husband has such a "bad" influence on her, since his presence makes it impossible to take her life. Wants to look at the locked wards, possibly to transfer there. "I feel myself, quite passively, the stage on which two hostile forces are mangling each other."

She has the feeling that she can do nothing at all about her condition and must look on in complete helplessness.

March 11 Her visit to the locked wards has had a rather unfavorable effect. "I would want to smash in the solid panes immediately." She feels gluttony again, "as when a wild animal throws itself on its food."

Full of self-reproaches for having eaten too much. Wants permission from the doctor to take her life. Attempts obstinately to convince her husband and doctor of the correctness of this trend of thought, rejects every counter-argument.

Even as a young girl she could not sit quietly at home,

but always had to be on the go. At the age of eighteen she wrote to a girlfriend, "Melancholy lies over my life like a black bird, which hovers somewhere in the background until the time has come to pounce upon me and kill me."

Now, too, she has the feeling that in everything she does a ghost stalks her in order to kill her, or she is only waiting until "insanity comes and, shaking its black locks, seizes me and hurls me into the yawning abyss."

Periods absent for four and one-half years, sexual intercourse discontinued for three years; previously normal.

March 21 Suicidal threats become more serious. Wants only to wait for the consultation scheduled for March 24.

> If there were a substance which contained nourishment in the most concentrated form and on which I would remain thin, then I would still be so glad to continue living. . . . I want to get thinner and thinner, but I do not want to have to watch myself constantly, and I do not want to forego anything; it is this friction between wanting to be thin and yet not wanting to miss any food which is destroying me. . . . On all points I am clear and sensible, but on this one point I am insane; I am perishing in the struggle against my nature. Fate wanted to have me fat and strong, but I want to be thin and delicate.

The capacity to enjoy spring increases more and more, but also the torment while eating.

Second postscript to the anamnesis: She says she has already had depressive dejections, even before the appearance of the fixed idea in her twenty-first year. In her diary, some months before the appearance of this idea, she expressed wonderment that a damper suddenly tones down her cheerful mood, so that she feels like crying. She wonders whether she is too sensitive for the great battle of life.

> How often I begin a morning cheerily, my heart full of sunshine and hope, and before I am able to understand why

I am so happy, something comes and strikes my mood down. Something quite insignificant, perhaps a cold tone in the voice of a person whom I love, or some other usually insignificant thing to disappoint me in someone.

In response to my request her husband gathers together the following material on the theme of suicide: The wish to die runs through her entire life. Even as a child she thinks it "interesting" to have a fatal accident—for example, to break through the ice while skating. During her riding period (at ages nineteen, twenty, and twenty-one) she performs foolhardy tricks, has a fall and breaks her clavicle, and thinks it too bad that she does not have a fatal accident; on the next day she mounts her horse again and continues to carry on in the same manner. When sick as a young girl, she is disappointed each time the fever subsides and the sickness leaves her. When she studies for the college entrance examination (at twenty-two), she wants her tutor to repeat this sentence over and over again: "Those whom the gods love die young." The teacher is annoyed by this and finally refuses to do this again and again. When she hears of the death of girlfriends, she envies them and her eyes shine at the death announcement. While working in the foundling home, despite the warnings of the supervisor, she visits children who have scarlet fever and kisses them in the hope that she, too, will catch it. Attempts also to get sick by standing naked on the balcony after a hot bath, putting her feet into ice cold water, or standing in the front of a streetcar when there is an east wind and she has a fever of 102 degrees. The first analyst at the first consultation in late December 19—— calls her behavior a "slow attempt at suicide."

March 22 Was very cheerful yesterday during her walk; sat down to her meal at noon quite calmly, but then, as always, was suddenly as if inwardly transformed. Wonders whether she can make herself leave something on her plate. Becomes more agitated, the more the meal progresses.

Everything in me trembles, the desire to eat up everything fights within me a furious battle against the resolve not to eat everything, until finally I jump up and have all that I have left taken away, in order not to get into the danger of eating it up after all.

Then feels as if beaten up, completely exhausted, her whole body covered with perspiration; all her limbs ache as if she had been whipped; would like to shoot herself at once. Only after some time (one or two hours) does this condition fade away.

March 24 Consultation with Professor E. Bleuler and another psychiatrist. The preliminaries of this consultation are as follows. In view of the increasing risk of suicide, continued residence of the patient on the open ward cannot be justified. I have to put before her husband the alternative of giving permission to transfer his wife to the closed ward or leaving the institution with her. The very sensible husband sees this clearly but says he can give his permission only if a cure or at least a far-reaching improvement of his wife can be promised him. Because on the basis of the anamnesis and my own observations I have to diagnose a progressive schizophrenic psychosis (schizophrenia simplex), I can offer the husband very little hope. [If shock therapy had existed then, it would have offered a temporary way out of the dilemma and a certain postponement, but it would certainly have changed nothing in the final result.] Because it is clear that a release from the institution means certain suicide, I have to advise the husband in the light of his responsibility not to rely upon my opinion alone—certain as I am of my case—but to arrange for a consultation with Professor Bleuler on the one hand, and on the other hand with a foreign psychiatrist whose views are not too close to the Kraepelin-Bleuler theory of schizophrenia. The complete anamnesis as well as our case record is handed to the consultants in advance.

Result of the consultation: Both gentlemen agree completely with my prognosis and doubt any therapeutic usefulness of commitment even more emphatically than I. For Bleuler the presence of schizophrenia is indubitable. The second psychiatrist declares that schizophrenia can be diagnosed only if an intellectual defect exists. In our case he would label it a psychopathic constitution progressively unfolding. The "idea" of wanting to get thin he correctly designates not as a delusional idea (because logical motivation is absent), but with less justification as an overvalued idea. All three of us agree this is not a case of obsessional neurosis and not one of manic-depressive psychosis, and that no definitely reliable therapy is possible. We therefore resolve to give in to the patient's demand for discharge.

March 30 The patient is visibly relieved by the result of the consultation, declares that she will now take her life in her own hands, but is much shaken when she sees that despite her best intentions she cannot master her dilemma with regard to eating. Externally, she controls herself powerfully and is quiet and orderly, but inwardly she is very tense and agitated. She ponders this way and that what she is to do now, and finally resolves to go home with her husband this very day. She continues precisely her whole way of life until the last because every change "confuses" her and throws her "completely off the track." She is tormented in the extreme by her "idea" up to the last moment. Weight upon leaving approximately same as upon arriving, namely, 104 pounds.

Death

On her trip home Ellen is very courageous. The reason for taking it gives her strength. The glimpse into life that the trip gives her hurts her. Even more than in the institution she feels incapable of dealing with her life. The following days are more harrowing than all the previous weeks. She feels no release of tension; on the contrary, all her symptoms appear more strongly. The irregularity of her way of life upsets her completely; the reunion with her relatives only brings her illness more clearly into view.

On the third day of being home she is as if transformed. At breakfast she eats butter and sugar, at noon she eats so much that—for the first time in thirteen years!—she is satisfied by her food and is really full. At afternoon coffee she eats chocolate creams and

Easter eggs. She takes a walk with her husband, reads poems by Rilke, Storm, Goethe, and Tennyson, is amused by the first chapter of Mark Twain's "Christian Science," and is in a positively festive mood. All heaviness seems to have fallen away from her. She writes letters, the last one to a fellow patient to whom she has become attached. In the evening she takes a lethal dose of poison, and on the following morning she is dead. "She looks as she had never looked in life—calm and happy and peaceful."

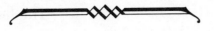

11

Providing Supportive Care

All of the interventions used in the treatment of mental and emotional illness and behavior problems can be classified under two major rubrics. The first of these is variously described as insight-oriented, definitive, expressive, and curative psychotherapy. The purpose of such therapy is to cure the disease, fix the problem, terminate the condition, and bring about a general cessation of illness.

However, there are conditions that we do not know how to cure and cannot terminate. These fall under the second rubric and require other kinds of therapy, variously called supportive care, ameliorative care, repressive psychotherapy, palliative treatment, or rehabilitation model therapy. The purpose of supportive care is to improve the patient's life with his or her disease and to minimize dysfunction, pain, and suffering while maximizing function, comfort, and pleasure. Supportive care is the treatment of choice for schizophrenia because we do not know how to cure it. Supportive care does not alter the length of the schizophrenic illness or the presence of the illness. It does alter the life of the individual who lives with schizophrenia.

The Rehabilitation Model

The rehabilitation model requires that we stabilize the disabilities caused by the illness and then develop a social, psychological, and physical system that allows the patient to function in the best possible way in spite of his or her disabilities. Treatment of schizophrenia according to the rehabilitation model is very similar to the treatment of a physical disability. If, for example, someone has a paralyzed right arm that cannot be fixed, we then provide her with a brace to help with function. We may modify her car so that she can drive and work the controls with only one hand. We may retrain her to use her left hand for all the things she used to do with her paralyzed right hand. We may also give her psychological support for accepting herself with the defect and help her focus on what she can do rather than what she cannot do.

In the rehabilitation model for the treatment of schizophrenia, we are not going to be able to fix the three nuclear defects, namely, the high level of free-floating anxiety, the clumsiness in interpersonal relationships, or the failure of historicity. We can however help schizophrenic patients compensate for these defects, learn to live with them, and have a satisfying life in spite of them. They may have to learn special skills, they may need a very supporting, nourishing relationship for all of life (Knight, 1946), and they may have to have some chemical help to manage anxiety. They may also need a special structure in their lives to compensate for the failure of historicity. All of this becomes part of supportive care.

The Therapeutic Alliance

Supportive care, like all treatment transactions, is carried within the framework of one of the oldest and most highly systematized human interactions (Gillespie, 1982). The participants in this transaction, the patient and the therapist, engage with each other for the purpose of relieving or changing some form of feeling, behavior, or thinking in the patient. The changes occurring in the therapist are not the primary concern of the treatment transaction, although they too must be understood and recognized for the proper management of treatment. But the changes in the patient are the primary focus of the transaction. Both parties come to the treatment situation with a history of many relationships that bear considerable similarity to it. A child-parent relationship is the prototype of all human relationships and closely parallels the patient-physician transactions as it includes dependence and independence, helplessness and improvement, growth and regression, development and arrest, being in the care of others and caring for others. There are other relationships in our human society that also prepare the patient for the therapeutic transaction. These interactions include those between the devout and the priest, the apprentice and the magician, the student and the teacher (Mendel, 1975b).

What all of these relationships have in common is that one individual goes to the other for the purpose of getting help, explanation, care, and concern (Mendel, 1970). Every person who enters the state of patienthood is prepared in part for such transaction by his lived history of other relationships that involve a situation in which he is dependent and moves toward being able to help himself, in which he does not understand and moves toward understanding, in which he cannot control and goes toward obtaining tools of control (Mendel, 1968c). Similarly, the therapist comes to the treatment transaction with a history of having been a child, a student, and patient and having mastered these states. As a therapist, she takes the adult caring role, handling her own need for care by caring for others.

Erikson (1950) describes the final state of maturity as ego-integrity, which he characterizes as the capacity to adapt oneself to the triumphs and disappointments of existence and the capacity to care for others in the human encounter. The psychotherapeutic relationship is one of the most intimate relationships possible (Frank, 1961). The formalities and the rules of the patient-therapist transaction allow for extremely rapid movement toward the intimacies necessary for treatment. It is a constant wonder how thoroughly the tradition of intimacy is incorporated into the patient-therapist relationship. One need only remind oneself that a physician, after only a few minutes of introduction, is given license by the patient and by society to explore every orifice, to probe the intimate secret recesses of the unconscious, or physically to lay open the patient's abdomen in order to alter anatomy by surgical intervention. In the medical transaction, the patient brings so much trust to the physician that he will literally place his life in the physician's hands without knowing any more about her than the fact that she wears a medical badge.

Each one of us as therapists inherits all of the feelings and attitudes that society holds toward the medical practitioner. Outside of this tradition, most relationships move much more slowly and it may take years to build up enough trust and confidence for one participant to trust the other with his or her life or to allow the type of physical and psychological intimacies that are inherent in the medical transaction. Certain of our social taboos are never transgressed in relationships other than the patient-doctor transaction. This transaction is the model for the therapeutic engagement regardless of whether it is conducted by a physician or any other mental health professional (Greenberg, 1986).

Treatment always includes the unspoken contract in which the therapist takes responsibility for treating the patient and the patient agrees to be treated and to compensate the therapist for his or her services. Built into this contract is the patient's hope, or at least his suspicion, that he can live differently, that better functioning is possible for him, and that he can exist with less anguish and pain (Frank, 1968). For the therapist, accepting a patient for treatment implies that he or she can intervene in some way helpful to the patient. Built into the contract is the concept of an open future. The open future implies to the patient that the therapist anticipates change in the direction of the therapeutic goal (Kernberg, 1981). It implies that the therapist can intervene in some way to offer care, to be helpful, and to keep the future open (Mendel, 1968b).

Because all treatment transactions are conducted within this powerful relationship, everything the therapist says or does tends to be overvalued and overinterpreted. Even novice clinicians quickly recognize how careful they must be in what they say and do during the therapeutic transaction with the patient. Because the patient often recognizes the therapeutic relationship as his only lifeline he cannot tolerate arbitrariness. He tends to believe that everything the therapist does, thinks, or feels is entirely related to the patient. If the therapist is grouchy because he or she has had an unpleasant start in the morning, the first patient of the day will certainly believe that the grouchiness is meant for him. Most patients have great difficulty appreciating that the therapist has a life outside of the therapeutic function with a particular patient. Therefore, everything the therapist does in therapy vis-à-vis the patient must be carefully considered and always run through a "therapeutic filter." The therapeutic filter consists of the question "Will what I am going to say or do be helpful in reaching the goal for the therapeutic transaction now, or is it going to interfere?" If the therapist keeps such a filter active, he or she will tend to make fewer mistakes, which will cause fewer disturbances in therapeutic process.

The therapeutic relationship is the matrix in which all treatment goes on, the backbone of all helping transactions. But by itself this relationship is not enough. Supportive care requires a careful assessment of the patient's problems, disabilities, and strengths. A detailed treatment program must be planned. Such a program needs to stabilize the defects and disabilities and then develop rehabilitation techniques to deal with the specific problems that interfere with the patient's ability to function and ability to feel good. Fundamental to the therapeutic relationship is the development of trust. It is this aspect of the treatment transaction that is so difficult for the schizophrenic patient. With appropriate support and proper management, trust can be generalized to other situations. The interpersonal transaction between the patient and the therapist is what makes treatment go (Mazzanti and Bessell, 1956).

Technique for Supportive Care. The content of therapy is also an important aspect of supportive care and must be managed. As patients talk about their feelings, thoughts, activities, and fantasies in the accepting atmosphere of the therapeutic transaction, they experience lessening of anxiety and some mastery over their distress. Moreover, the therapist uses discussion of the content of therapeutic transaction to help patients improve their reality testing. As patients describe their individual reality and compare it with the reality of the therapist, they begin to have the suspicion at least, that interpretations of reality other than their own are possible.

The content of the therapeutic session can help to demonstrate the therapist's acceptance of the patient regardless of thoughts or feelings that seem bizarre. The therapist can use content to

demonstrate a nonjudgmental attitude. The therapist is nonjudgmental in terms of deciding whether patients are morally good or
bad. However, the therapist must make judgments about patients'
functioning and behavior. It is possible to help patients try out new
modes of behavior in the safety of the therapeutic engagement. In
an atmosphere of acceptance and trust patients can use the
therapeutic transaction as a private laboratory in which to
experiment with attitudes and behavior prior to launching them in
life. The content of therapy sessions can be used to teach patients
the predictable attitudes of others toward them. In the therapeutic
transaction patients can learn to cope with certain minimal
rejections and failures. Here, in the safety of a trusting relationship
with the therapist, patients can prepare themselves for the real
world.

Therapists can help patients learn patterns of behavior to
develop the "as if" role (Deutsch, 1942). As the patients successfully
master the task of increasing their effectiveness in living and taking
on the as if normal role, new technical problems arise for therapists.
Unless they remember constantly how disorganized and disabled
their patients are, unless they can remind themselves of the
shallowness of the patients' adaptive capacities, therapists may fall
into the trap of forgetting how ill their patients really are. Certainly
a successfully treated patient who is receiving competent supportive
care can appear to the world as healthy. However, a skilled therapist
in a few moments of probing can confirm the extent of the patient's
disorganization underlying the facade of adaptation maintained by
supportive care. This facade, which may assume permanence in the
patient's life, can be likened to the snowcap on a dormant volcano.
The subterranean fires are not extinguished and may erupt at any
moment as the balance of internal and external forces is altered.

The relationship between therapist and patient needs to be
viewed as a two-person transactional system (Buckley, 1986). As is
true in all complex and dynamic human relationships, each
participant in this transaction has his or her own set of needs and
fears and expectancies. The degree to which the therapist successfully identifies these needs, fears, and expectancies in himself or
herself and the patient will determine the degree to which the
transaction can be successfully therapeutic. Obviously, there is no

such thing as a neutral relationship between a therapist and a patient. Each behavior or event is significant in the outcome of the transaction, and every action on the therapist's part will either contribute to or impede the therapeutic process.

In all therapeutic encounters the first requirement is that therapists be less anxious than patients. Although this requirement is usually met, the therapists' degree of comfort as well as their effectiveness in the situation will be increased if they are aware of their tendency to adopt what Balint (1957) has called the "apostolic role" of the doctor; meaning the physician's need to have the patient respond to him or her in the role that the physician privately cherishes—be it as healer, magician, scientific investigator, experimenter, friendly adviser, advocate, god, judge, or any of a broad variety of such other unspoken images. The treatment of schizophrenia will be impaired if patients must respond to such private needs on the part of therapists. Such a requirement imposes a demand on patients that they are quite unable to fill. Not only must therapists be aware of any tendency on their part to bring some hidden agenda to the therapy, they must also make themselves aware of those unspoken needs that patients bring to the transaction. Does a particular patient have a wish to be a helpless infant, a loyal child, an inexpert apprentice in the art of living, or a love object or to play some other role that his chronic illness has made him prone to adopt?

Patients are very much influenced by therapists' expectancies. Many studies in the literature demonstrate how expectancy influences outcome (Karon and Vandenbos, 1970). If therapists believe that their patients are hopeless, the therapeutic transaction will be ineffective. If therapists expect their patients to get better, the therapists will consciously and unconsciously transmit that expectation to the patients and give them hope. The effect of expectancy on patients' response to pharmacological agents is very much in evidence (see Chapter Thirteen). In the old diagnostic scheme, schizophrenia was associated with a decline of function. The Kraepelinian view of dementia praecox expected longitudinal deterioration as part of the disease (Kraepelin, 1904). Patients entered hospitals that had over their doors "Hospital for the Incurably Insane." Obviously, patients entering such portals and seeing that inscription would not expect to get well and therefore could not get better. When physicians were hopeless about schizophrenia, when they believed with Kraepelin in the relentless progressive deterioration of the minds of these patients, when they reinforced this pathology by "putting them away" in asylums, then patients responded by deteriorating. When the role expectancy changed to conform to modern concepts of brief crisis care combined with supportive treatment, the mental deterioration was usually not seen.

In supportive care, therapists attempt to maintain an attitude that demonstrates that they value the human worth of patients and will do whatever is necessary to prevent the alienation that schizophrenia frequently imposes on the patients' relationships with others. Yet therapists exercise their judgment as to the appropriateness or inappropriateness, the health or illness of patients' behavior. The future of the therapeutic relationship is both inclusive and exclusive and does not depend on a patient's achieving any particular goals stated by a therapist.

Often patients fear that the supportive relationship may be threatened by their inability to meet the needs and expectancies, real or imagined, of the therapist. But patients with schizophrenia are also threatened by the opposite turn of events, when they become aware of marked improvement. In the usual doctor-patient relationship, a patient presents himself with symptoms that are "removed" by the physician and the result is the termination of the relationship. If patients bring such expectancies to the therapeutic transaction, then they will feel threatened by becoming asymptomatic (Zilboorg, 1941). This requires special techniques to reassure them that the therapeutic alliance continues and is not dependent on their symptomotology alone. A supporting relationship is offered throughout the life of the individual patient.

As patients learn to be confident about the predictability and reliability of a therapeutic relationship, some of their anxieties become manageable and they can devote more of their energies to the task of learning from their therapist the techniques of attending to what they do and less to what they think and feel. As patients grow in their skill of attending to their behavior and its consequences, there will be more adequate adaptive functions and less need to borrow the therapist's personality (Zilboorg, 1941). This transition represents one of the most critical periods of the therapist-patient relationship. Because of the therapist's natural reluctance to continue the charismatic role and because of patients' understandable urge to function autonomously, it is easy for the therapist to conspire in arranging plans for patients that they are unable to carry out. Patients with schizophrenia are much more vulnerable to failure than are normal people. Failure devastates patients and can remove important gains that were made in the supportive relationship. It is easy for patients to misinterpret the therapist's encouragement as a demand to achieve. It is vital to a patient's continued good functioning that the therapist in no way imply an end to the relationship if the patient cannot succeed with plans. Each suggestion on the part of the patient that he undertake a new and higher level of adjustment must be interpreted by the therapist as a question with the latent meaning "Is it necessary for me to function better to warrant my continuing to see you?" The therapist must be sure that his or her communication, both overt and covert, carries the meaning "I accept you as a person worthy of my concern no matter what your level of achievement." The opposite condition can produce another potential pitfall for supportive care. If the therapist responds to increasingly healthy behavior of the patient by implying a diminution or even termination of therapy, he or she may be setting up failure. Many patients respond to the suggestion of termination of therapy because they are "better" or "well" by becoming sick again in order to regain the concern and care of the therapist.

The therapist-patient relationship can serve as a learning laboratory where therapeutic experiences for individual patients are arranged. These experiences are subsequently generalized into their lives. Eventually, the patients can find sources of support in real life. At that point the need for formal supportive care may indeed be diminished, though it is never finished (see Chapter Fifteen). All supportive care must deal with the issue of dependency. Every therapeutic relationship involves the management of dependency. Patients who are suffering from schizophrenia and are severely ill, simply by reason of their dysfunction and disability, are dependent.

In the therapist-patient relationship there is also a naturally occurring dependency. The literature abounds with many warnings about the dangers of prolonged overdependence of the patient on the therapist. Yet it is generally agreed that the development of dependency is a necessary part of all psychotherapeutic transactions. It is also true that as the patient grows and develops in the psychotherapeutic transaction, it is advisable to give up some of that dependency. In the treatment of a schizophrenic patient the problem of dependency becomes especially complicated.

The development of a consistent trust in anyone is an extremely difficult task for people with schizophrenia. Yet they cannot live unless they can at least learn to act as though they trust something or someone. Like all human beings, these people must be willing to accept on faith that tomorrow will come. Although they realize that perhaps it will not come, they must plan and act as though it will. Similarly, they must develop some trust in other human beings. To live in a world in which they can trust no one is impossible.

Each day requires acts based on faith. We cross a street on the basis of a green light, having faith that others understand red and green in the same way we do. We pay fare to a bus that claims to go to San Francisco, and we have faith that the bus will indeed go to the right place. Each person is necessarily a member of society; social relationships are built on feelings of trust. The interpersonal situations that produce a major rupture of trust, such as concentration camps or other human disasters, cause people to be so betrayed by their fellow humans that they are irreparably changed thereafter. Similarly, patients with schizophrenia are frequently unable to develop trust in anyone because they, too, feel totally betrayed by themselves, their bodies, and other human beings. Whether this lack is the result of a betrayal by a mother or due to organic defects in a patient's ability to develop trust has been argued for many years. It is probably the result of a biochemical defect in the brain. Whatever the cause, the fact that schizophrenic patients have great difficulty developing a trusting relationship is a major problem for therapy and for life. Patients are caught in a very difficult position. They cannot develop trust in anyone. Yet in order to be helped they must develop trust in the therapist or at least be willing to take the chance of developing such trust. They must take the risk of developing a dependency on another human being.

This therapeutic task assumes major importance in the effort with schizophrenic patients. Techniques for helping with this are based on offering a consistent and totally reliable relationship that does not demand closeness beyond patients' means. At the beginning of developing dependency, schizophrenic patients cannot tolerate even the slightest unreliability. Appointments must be kept on time, never cancelled. The therapist must be available and must withstand constant testing of his or her availability, consistency, and reliability. The therapist must manage the distance between self and patients throughout all tests patients will put the therapist through, including hostility, seduction, exacerbation of symptoms, and remission. A therapist may need to withstand such maneuvers for years without feeling secure that a patient finally trusts him or her and has developed a useful therapeutic dependency. Even when the therapeutic relationship is going well, the therapist may suddenly be surprised to face a new test of his or her reliability and dependability. The long history of a therapist's reliability and dependability does little to reassure patients. They may have been well-managed for years, the therapist may have made no errors and demonstrated no unreliability and then on one occasion is not available to them. Often patients react with the feeling that they have once again confirmed what they knew all along, namely, that no human being can be relied upon.

If dependency is well-managed, if patients are able to develop some consistent trust and therefore dependence on the therapist, and if they can use this trust and this dependency in altering their behavior outside of the therapeutic transaction, eventually they can allow themselves to develop dependency on others.

In a well-managed therapy program the following process unfolds: The patient develops a dependency on the therapist. She relies on and trusts in the reality of the psychotherapeutic transaction after many tests of it. Finally, she makes an attempt to depend on reality outside of the therapeutic transaction and invest other human beings with trust by allowing herself to become dependent on them. She is always on guard. She is always ready to withdraw into a shell, always ready to say, "People have turned out to be as unreliable and undependable as I knew they would be." Such a patient behaves much like a testing, exploring snail. She sticks out her head very tentatively; if she touches the slightest bit of rejection or unreliability, she withdraws into her shell. Each time this happens she stays in the shell a little longer and eventually refuses to come out at all. The patient is going to find many rejections in real life outside of the therapeutic transaction and she is going to find out that the others are not entirely dependable.

Throughout treatment the therapist must help patients extend trust to others. He or she must help patients to live as if they could depend on tomorrow to come, as if they could depend on others to do what needs to be done, as if they could predict other people's behavior. The therapist can help by preparing patients for what may happen to them. For example, before attempting a relationship outside of psychotherapy, patients might discuss all possible outcomes of a relationship with the therapist and work them through by considering all alternatives. Having thus prepared themselves, they will be less surprised by anything that happens and in effect will develop a trust in their own ability to cope. Once patients can depend on their own predictions, the next stage is the development of trust in themselves.

Supportive care is a slow process. Perhaps the most important generalization we can make to the therapist caring for the schizophrenic patient is to say, "Don't be in a hurry." Even long after the patient has maintained an excellent remission, the therapeutic transaction remains important in the maintenance of a comfortable and adaptive homeostasis. Even when the patient uses the therapist only once every three or six months, a therapeutic transaction may be the insurance that makes the difference between adequate function and consistently recurring crises. The schizophrenic patient who is in good remission and who is older and functioning well may not require much active intervention but still needs the lifelong maintenance of a therapeutic relationhip. Supportive care must never end. Although this is a somewhat disquieting requirement, it does not mean that there cannot be certain shifts throughout the patient's life in the sources of support.

Changing the Therapeutic Relationship. The need that therapists not be in a hurry must be emphasized. Supportive care is a long-term process. However, even though supportive care involves a nonending process, it is appropriate to consider the factors involved in changing the social support in the patient's life so as to allow the formal psychotherapeutic process to almost terminate. When the patient has developed security in the relationship with the therapist and has developed some trust in other human beings and when that trust has expanded into a trust of the patient in himself or herself and the world, then it is possible to make some major shifts in the relationship. Even though the therapist must constantly be on guard that therapeutic zeal does not interfere with the patient's therapeutic needs, he or she must also be alert to changes in the patient. As the patient improves, the therapist can refer more and more of the supporting activities to normal life. (See Chapter Fifteen.) As the therapist refers the patient to life and becomes active and assisting in a friendly and fraternal supportive role, he or she must still maintain the role of a therapist. In many subtle and rather complicated ways there is no ending. There is a shift in roles. The patient is referred to life. He or she is encouraged to use the trust developed in the psychotherapeutic relationship by investing trust in others. He or she is instructed to use the relationship with the therapist as a prototype for other relationships. There is a decrease in the number of actual therapy contacts. But support still needs to be maintained, even if only by an annual meeting or a telephone call or greeting card. Supportive care is never ended by planning not to meet again, never to see each other again, not to keep track of each other.

At this point the reader may feel that I am proposing a dangerous policy of fostering chronic dependency. Nothing could be further from the truth. I simply recognize the patient's continuing need for a source of support that comes from having had a corrective emotional experience in the psychotherapeutic relationship. My experience with schizophrenic patients has brought me to an awareness that even with patients whom I began treating many years ago, the relationship has never ended. It has merely changed. Positive transference continues, and indeed should continue, as a source of further growth and development throughout the patient's life.

Special Challenges with Schizophrenic Patients

It is not surprising that a large untreated population of schizophrenic patients exists and that they suffer from neglect. It is difficult to find therapists who are willing to devote the time, energy, personal investment, and "ongoingness" that are required. It is easy to understand why many young clinicians shy away from the treatment of these patients. It is difficult to face the limitations of our science and art, which these patients represent. They constantly show us our failures. There is much therapeutic frustration in caring for this patient population because of the slowness of treatment and many patients' lack of progress. Some therapists find themselves responding with boredom or anger. Neither one of these feelings is therapeutic for the patient. Caring for the schizophrenic patient involves therapeutic problems for the therapist in the area of expectation. The patient's hope, wish, and expectancy for the future are important aspects of treatment. Very early in the therapeutic engagement, the therapist reinforces this expectancy and helps the patient to see that life can be different, that the future does not have to be like the past, and that choices are available. As the years roll by, the therapist may find it more difficult to keep the future open. The patient is usually not nearly so concerned about the passage of time as is the therapist. The therapist may respond to his or her own uneasiness about the future with concerns about having promised more than he or she can deliver. Such feeling on the therapist's part occurs only when the therapist misunderstands the real function of hope in the therapeutic transaction. The function of hope is to pull the patient into the future. This pull allows the patient to continue to exist and to be exposed to new experiences that do bring about changes. It is important for the therapist to focus on the fact the patient, in spite of being ill, has many areas of strength and health.

Clinicians who understand the problem of treating the schizophrenic patient and who are willing to engage in such treatment interactions will never have a shortage of patients. Such clinicians will be busy and well paid, with many grateful patients who have feelings of loyalty and respect for them and who function better because of their skill and understanding.

12

Hospital Care
for Acute Intervention

A great deal has changed in the treatment of the severely and chronically mentally ill schizophrenic patient over the past forty years. One of the major areas of change is the amount of time patients spend in the hospital (Mendel, 1968a). The 497 patients described in our study are different from those in other long-term studies of chronic psychiatric patients with a diagnosis of schizophrenia in that the former spend very little time in the hospital. For them, the hospital was used only for acute intervention when they required more than could be provided with supportive care in the community. As already noted, over their lifetime these patients have spent an average of 8.5 days per year in the hospital. Most of this time was spent early in their illness.

Assessing the Benefits and Risks of Hospitalization

The reason for the practice of brief hospitalization becomes clear with an understanding of what hospitalization can do that is helpful and what its side effects are. As in all other treatment, when we make the decision to hospitalize, we must consider the risk-benefit ratio (Mendel and Rapport, 1969). Just as when we are prescribing medication, we must see whether the potential beneficial effects outweigh the potential negative side effects of treatment.

This must not only be done when hospitalization is first considered but each day that hospitalization is continued. As clinicians, we must have a clear idea as to what is to be accomplished, what the specific goals are for the hospitalization, and what the potential negative side effects are. At this point in the history of our knowledge we are fortunate in having accurate instruments with which to assess the patient's status in regard to symptom relief and cognitive level function. Such measures are available on a daily basis to allow us to make informed clinical decisions about the continuation or cessation of hospitalization for acute care (Table 10).

Benefits of Hospitalization. The benefits of hospitalization are many (Dozier, Harris, and Bergman, 1987). Hospitalization provides rescue from impossible situations that patients cannot manage. It provides the setting that may keep patients from doing permanent harm to themselves by such acts as suicide, destruction of a social support system, or destruction of their resources. Hospitalization also takes patients off the hot seat in whatever situation they are in and helps them to focus their lives in an appropriate way. Moreover, hospitalization may be used to teach new behavior, to adjust medication, to do extensive observation and testing that cannot be done on the outside. Often hospitalization is necessary to develop a detailed rehabilitation program or to develop or re-cement a therapeutic alliance. Hospitalization also offers the opportunity to decrease pain and suffering, to give relief to the supporting network, or to reorganize the support system.

Negative Effects of Hospitalization. Against all of the benefits we must consider the negative effects of hospitalization. Hospitalization certainly increases dependency. It reifies failure and tends to teach one how to get attention by being sick and having symptoms. Many patients learn new ways of being crazy in the hospital. One of the important negative side effects is that the patient is taken out of the circumstances, and a near-exhausted support system often reorganizes and closes up, leaving no room for the patient to return to.

The important question for hospital treatment is when it should be prescribed. In the natural history of schizophrenic illness

Table 10. Active Patients by Attending Doctor as of 5/28/88.

Name Last First Middle			Birth Date	Adm. Date	P. A	A. B	T. C	S. D	Diagnosis Description	T.P.S Prob. Area/Score		Cognitive Level Score
Jones, Rebecca		A	10/8/46	6/30/87	10	05	11	04	Paranoid schizo-chronic	12/1	18/2	4.2
Black, Wayne		C	9/4/58	5/15/58	01	02	02	01	Schizo-affective disorder	10/5	14/5	5.8
Crawford, Mary		J	12/12/63	12/23/88	10	04	11	05	Paranoid schizo-chronic	12/1	21/1	4.8
Black Owl, Roger		C	11/21/54	1/5/88	01	11	13	05	Schizo, undiff. chronic	15/1	27/3	4.9
Eisenhau, Mollie		A	8/31/12	3/7/88	01	05	04	01	Schizo, undiff. chronic/exac	15/5	16/3 27/3	3.2
George, Willis		D	11/08/16	11/10/87	02	02	01	04	Mild mental retardation	13/2	23/3	3.0
Gonzales, Juan		P	7/16/48	1/5/88	10	04	11	05	Paranoid schizo-chronic	17/1	23/2	3.7
Fitzgerald, Sue		E	5/24/46	4/27/88	07	06	04	11	Adjustment dis. dep. mood	03/3	03/1	6.3
Hall, Kris		A	12/24/66	3/24/88	03	02	05	07	Schizo, undiff. chronic	11/1	21/1	4.6
Pedro, Juan		G	10/8/63	2/13/88	01	02	02	01	Schizo-affective disorder	10/5	11/5	5.3

it has been observed that the undulating course is related to the age of the patient. The purpose of supportive care is to prevent the inevitable exacerbation from being a life crisis for the patient. If that prevention fails, then hospitalization must be considered.

Hospital Treatment

Once the decision to hospitalize has been made, it is important to clearly differentiate between what the geographic change of coming into the hospital does to help the patient and all the other things we do in the hospital, such as provide medication. A simple technique for clarifying this is not to medicate the patient for the first twenty-four hours in the hospital. We have made that procedure standard practice at our facility and have found that the patient improves markedly simply by coming into the hospital and being taken out of the environment in which he or she disorganized. When we reinstitute or begin medication after twenty-four hours, we can use much lower dosages because the patient has already improved markedly just from the geographic change. This allows us to assess the part that medication in itself plays in the treatment.

The treatment approach during hospitalization and the goals for such treatment are determined by the reason for the decision to hospitalize. There are three basic principles of hospital treatment: (1) it must have a consistent focus on reality, (2) it must have a consistent focus on activity, and (3) it must provide a structured life experience. The hospitalization must also be the beginning of a newly focused rehabilitation program.

At the beginning of hospitalization goals must be set and scales must be set up for the observation of symptoms so that the clinician can decide on a daily basis when the goals have been met and the patient should be discharged (Mosher, Kresky-Wolff, Matthews, and Menn, 1986).

Monitoring Symptom Relief. We have developed a system of monitoring the patient's progress for symptom relief. This is based on the Treatment Progress Scale (TPS). (See Exhibits 1 through 4.) This scale is an adaptation of Kiresuk's Goal Attainment Scaling (Lewis, Spencer, Haas, and DiVittis, 1987), which was developed in

Exhibit 1. Treatment Progress Scale Overview.

The Hastings Regional Center's Treatment Progress Scale (TPS) is the product of the efforts of numerous center personnel to provide a standardized method to document patient progress and treatment outcomes. The TPS is built around a "dictionary" that lists behavioral indicators associated with each of the following twenty-eight problem areas.

1. Activity level
2. Aggression
3. Assertiveness, lack of
4. Attention, lack of
5. Bizarre habits or rituals
6. Chemical dependency, alcohol
7. Chemical dependency, other drugs
8. Coherent speech, lack of

9. Compliance, lack of
10. Delusions
11. Denial
12. Dependency
13. Disruptiveness
14. Hallucinations
15. Hostility
16. Judgment, impaired
17. Memory, lack of
18. Motivation
19. Obsessive-compulsive

20. Psychosomatic complaints
21. Sadness/depression
22. Self-esteem, lack of
23. Self-help skills
24. Self-injury
25. Socialization, lack of
26. Stealing
27. Suicide
28. Suspicion
29. Other

Users can enter the dictionary through either the alphabetized *problem area* or any one of the alphabetized *behavioral indicators* that are cross-referenced to the problem area. The problem area becomes the title of each scale developed, and the behavioral indicator selected is rated according to the following levels:

5 = best anticipated success with treatment
4 = more than expected success with treatment
3 = expected level of treatment success
2 = less than expected success with treatment
1 = most unfavorable treatment outcome thought likely

Minnesota some thirty years ago. At the time the patient comes to the hospital, his or her problems are listed and appropriate treatment needs and goals are specified. For each problem, an individual scale is developed by the admitting psychiatrist during the admission interview and becomes part of the evaluation leading to the decision for hospitalization. These scales, although they follow the general format in a TPS manual, are individualized and quantifiable. Scores range from 1 to 5; 1 is the worst possible treatment outcome, 3 is the expected treatment outcome, and 5 is the best possible treatment outcome. For each problem to be treated, scores are assigned at the time of admission, twenty-four hours after admission, and thereafter on a regular basis.

The TPS scores for each patient are available to the clinician

Exhibit 2. Sample of TPS Scale Development Work Sheet.

Patient's Name _____ Ward _____
Number of Previous Admissions to HRC _____ Attending Physician _____

Scale Attainment Levels	Scale Headings (Problem Areas)		
	Scale 1: _____ (Problem Area No. =)	Scale 2: _____ (Problem Area No. =)	Scale 3: _____ (Problem Area No. =)
5 Best anticipated success with treatment			
4 More than expected success with treatment			
3 Expected level of treatment success			
2 Less than expected success with treatment			
1 Most unfavorable treatment outcome thought likely			

MD _____ _____
                Signature   Date

Nursing _____ _____
                Signature   Date

Psychologist

_____ _____
                Signature   Date

Primary diagnosis (Check):
1. ____ Alcohol dependency
2. ____ Substance use disorder
3. ____ Bipolar disorder
4. ____ Major depression
5. ____ Anxiety disorder
6. ____ Organic mental disorder
7. ____ Schizophrenic disorders
8. ____ Adjustment disorder
9. ____ Mental retardation
10. ____ Personality disorder

Source: Nebraska Department of Public Institutions Hastings Regional Center.

Exhibit 3. Examples of Developed Scales.

Problem Area	Scale Levels
11. Denial	5 Approaches staff on own initiative to discuss problems 4 Requests counseling sessions 3 Willing to discuss problems once a day 2 Admits to having problems but won't discuss them with staff 1 Denies having any problems
15. Hostility	5 Exhibits alternative methods for expressing anger 4 Discusses alternative ways to exhibit anger 3 States reason for feeling angry 2 Expresses anger by using passive aggressive technique 1 Expresses anger by using verbal obscenities
16. Judgment, impaired	5 Verbalizes why behaves differently drunk than sober 4 Pursues reasons why behaves differently drunk than sober 3 Admits behaves differently drunk than sober 2 Will discuss possibility behaves differently drunk than sober 1 Denies behaving differently drunk than sober
18. Motivation	5 Seeks additional counseling to work on goals, values, priorities 3 Follow treatment plan and does not use alibis and excuses 1 Refuses to follow treatment plan and uses alibis and excuses
21. Sadness/depression	5 Reports feeling happy and motivated 4 Reports looking forward to getting up in the morning 3 Does not mention being depressed or sad 2 States is sad or depressed once or twice a day 1 States is sad or depressed two to five times per shift

on a daily computer printout. With this information the clinician can decide on discharge, change of program, or continued hospitalization. (See Table 10.) The computer also graphs the patient's progress. A typical graph shows rapid improvement during the first

Exhibit 4. Sample TPS Score Recording Sheet.

Scale Area	TPS Dictionary Problem Area (Number)	(On Adm.) DR	(24 hr) RN	(CTP) T_1	T_2	T_3	Evaluation Data T_4	T_5	T_6	T_7	T_8	Discharge
1												
2												
3												
4												
5												
6												

Recorded by:

Signature   Date

T_1 _____ _____

T_2 _____ _____

T_3 _____ _____

T_4 _____ _____

Recorded by:

Signature   Date

T_5 _____ _____

T_6 _____ _____

T_7 _____ _____

T_8 _____ _____

Discharge _____

Note: Scores are entered into a computer and the numbers are manipulated to present data in tabular and graph forms on a daily basis.

twenty-four hours (without medication), a plateau for the next several days, then further rapid improvement, and then another plateau. If hospitalization is prolonged—more than thirty-five days—there is usually a drop in the curve, indicating that the anti-therapeutic effect of hospitalization has outweighed the therapeutic effect (see Figure 1). If this drop occurs, obviously the patient has stayed in the hospital too long (Fromm-Reichman, 1947). Such a drop is not noticed in our follow-up study on patients who are returned to the community at precisely the correct time.

Testing Cognitive Function. Hospital treatment must be arranged so that the patient has a good therapeutic experience that reinforces the therapeutic alliance with the representative of the helping situation and provides some measure of help with all of the major problems for which the patient has entered the hospital. Obviously, this requires that the patient see the hospital experience as successful. It is absolutely essential that we know what the patient can do and what is beyond his or her means. To assign a patient to a program of either psychotherapy or activity in which that patient is going to fail because of limited cognitive function is a therapeutic disaster. Unfortunately, this occurs in many hospitals simply because the patient is not matched to an individualized treatment program based on his or her daily changing needs and capacities.

A simple, reliable, and valid test for cognitive function is available and can be administered by any trained mental health professional. In our hospital this test is administered by the occupational therapy department and consists of a five-minute evaluation that uses leather lacing as the instrument for cognitive level assessment. This particular test was developed by Claudia Allen (1987) at USC. An alternate that at times can be used as a check or substitute is the Scratch-Pad Assembly, which was developed by Herzig in 1978, also at USC. With these simple tests we can get regular (sometimes daily) cognitive level assessment on each patient. From the test score (a range of 1.0 to 6.6, with 6.6 being the highest), we make assignments to activities and to psychotherapy. For example, to do insight-oriented psychotherapy on anyone with a cognitive level of less than 6.0 is useless and frustrating to

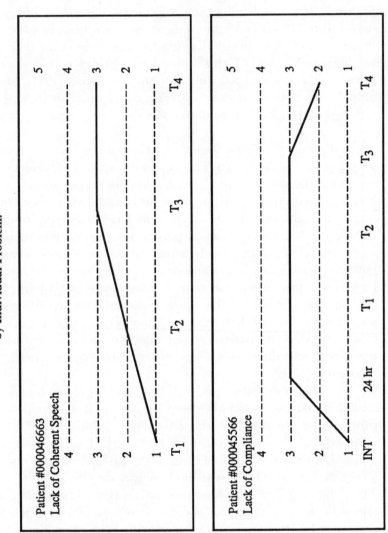

Figure 1. Computer-Generated TPS Graphs for Individual Patients and Institution by Individual Problem.

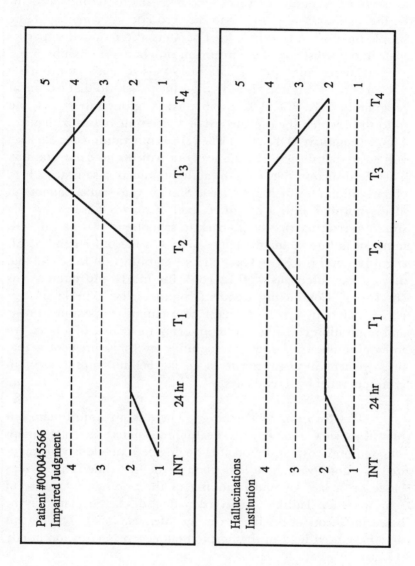

the patient. For anyone to drive a car safely, a cognitive level of 5.0 is necessary. A cognitive level of 4.0 is necessary to live independently, but it takes a level of 5.0 to buy groceries and manage basic simple finances. A cognitive level of 5.0 is also required to participate in our substance abuse treatment program. (See Exhibit 5.)

Having this kind of data allows us to make appropriate discharge decisions and also to assign the patient to that treatment program in O.T., R.T., I.T.; psychotherapy; group interaction, and so forth in which she can succeed. To place one of our patients in a level 4 cognitive O.T. group when she is functioning at a 3.5 level will mean that she will fail. None of our patients need more failure. They need success; they need the ability to function satisfactorily to obtain support for their self-esteem. Similarly, to send a patient out of the hospital with a cognitive level of only 4.0, when his life situation requires that he go back to school and drive a car, will result in failure of the discharge plan. On the other hand, if his cognitive level is 5.8, we know that he can function in school and drive a car safely, as well as cook his meals and balance his checkbook. Conducting frequent cognitive level checks on our patients gives us a measure that is as useful as temperature, pulse, and respiration checks are in monitoring the course of a fever. An interesting observation of our cognitive level measurement is that improvement in cognition tends to lag behind improvement in symptom relief by several days.

The Decision to Discharge. There is an unfortunate but prevailing view among mental health professionals that any patient who requires hospitalization after having been previously hospitalized was not hospitalized long enough the first time. This view is based on a lack of understanding of the undulating nature of schizophrenia. Failure to succeed with a discharge plan may be based on incorrect discharge timing (Mendel, 1966). The patient may have been held in the hospital either too long or too briefly (Cohen, 1958).

The decision of when to discharge (Ellsworth and others, 1971), that is, when maximum hospital benefit has been reached, should be based on completion of the treatment goals that were set when the decision for hospitalization was made. The decision

Exhibit 5. Expected Behavior by Cognitive Level.

Level	Supervisory Needs	Grooming	Dressing	Housekeeping	Cooking
6	None	No disability	No disability	Able to organize and plan schedule and long-term maintenance	Able to plan menus and anticipate problems
5	May require standby assistance	No disability	No disability	May neglect long-term maintenance; things may not be organized efficiently	May not make sense of new recipe, may not anticipate burning or timing, may forget to preheat oven
4	A supportive person should live in or check in frequently; may refuse assistance	Is independent, but makeup may not match; neglects back of body and head; misses whiskers when shaving	Is independent, though colors and patterns may not match, garments may not be the right size or may be old-fashioned	Will usually complete familiar tasks acceptably, but may forget trash removal	May not handle hot food or boiling water safely, may not turn off electric appliances, may not follow a diet but can prepare simple familiar dishes if materials are supplied
3	24-hour supervised living arrangement	May be independent, but may need reminding; quality is diminished	May be independent, but may need help selecting clothes and getting them on right side out	May dust furniture, sweep the floor, or fold linens	May set the table or peel potatoes
2	24-hour nursing care	May be able to assist care giver a little or may resist	May be able to assist care giver a little or may resist	Cannot function	Cannot function
1	24-hour nursing care, most likely in a hospital	Cannot function	Cannot function	Cannot function	Cannot function

Exhibit 5. Expected Behavior by Cognitive Level, Cont'd.

Level	Shopping	Money Management	Telephone	Laundry	Work
6	Anticipates and plans for shopping needs	Anticipates expenses and plans for future financial security	Uses classification system for finding numbers in Yellow Pages	Anticipates clothing needs and different cleaning procedures	Able to plan, organize, direct others, use deductive reasoning
5	Can do routine shopping, but may not follow budget or plan for long-range needs	May have difficulty planning ahead or be immobilized or incorrect when comparative shopping or planning a budget	May use white pages accurately, but may get confused by having to transfer a call	Will sort clothing, but may not notice that some items will shrink	May hold a job but not one requiring planning and organizing
4	May shop for small familiar items, but may not have enough to pay or may not be able to do comparison shopping	May have periods of being short on funds due to mismanagement, theft, or loss, a limited daily allowance might help	May call information for numbers, not look up new numbers	May do familiar hand laundry or use washer; may not sort or consider care instructions or recognize items for cleaners	May get a job, but usually will not hold it more than a month; cannot last in sheltered workshop more than one or two months
3	Needs assistance; may run out of money, give it away, or lose it	Can go to the store but may not recognize change or remember what to buy	May answer phone, but may not take messages or may leave phone off the hook	Cannot do laundry; may not even realize clothing needs washing	Cannot work
2	Cannot function	Cannot manage money	Does not use phone	Cannot do laundry	Cannot work
1	Cannot function	Cannot manage money	Does not use phone	Cannot do laundry	Cannot work

Level	Driving	Medication	Safety	Social Relationships	Psychotherapy
6	Plans ahead and anticipates problems	Complies with directions and anticipates effects correctly	Anticipates hazards and takes steps to avoid danger	Relationships are not strained by a cognitive disability	Uses deductive reasoning to choose alternative forms of behavior (insight, cognitive training)
5	May drive, but may not plan ahead for cost or buying gas or note where car is parked	May comply with directions, but may not understand side effects going away or probable complication	Unable to anticipate problems; should practice steps to avoid hazards	Strains relationships by self-oriented behavior, may violate laws	Uses techniques of inductive reasoning for new behavior; patterns (role playing) may help
4	May not drive safely; may disregard fines, insurance, license; may get lost, stay on familiar routes at slow times	May take simple dose at routine time, may not understand reason for medication, may refuse it, may need reminding	May cause fires and get burns; access to cars, power tools, poison, should be restricted; neglects safe storage of possessions	Activities must be organized by others; does not understand the need to share, take turns, wait in line	Verbal discussions have little value; no new learning occurs
3	May travel independently in vehicles driven by others if route is familiar (bus)	May forget the time, may be unable to tell one pill from another, needs assistance	Usually need escort outside the home; mobility may need to be restricted	Will respond to familiar activities; conversation often not understood by strangers	No new learning occurs
2	Cannot drive	Must be administered by others	Must be taken care of by others, often need one-to-one supervision	Has only marginal awareness of others	No new learning occurs
1	Cannot drive	Must be administered by others	May be bedridden or in tray chair to prevent injury	Loses relationships	Is unaware of others

Source: Compiled from material researched by Claudia Kay Allen, LAC/USC Medical Center.

should also be based on appraisal of cognitive function (Allen, 1988) to make sure that individual patients are able to succeed in their discharge plans, that they are able to handle the setting in which they will be placed and to carry out the rehabilitation program designed for them (Allen and Allen, 1987).

Often adjustment and fine-tuning (Schlesinger and Hoizman, 1970) in the support network are necessary during the hospitalization. The experience of how the patient disorganizes during his last exacerbation leading to the crisis that required hospitalization can be used to plan the new rehabilitation program. There is considerable urgency in getting these things done before the patient leaves the hospital. Yet the patient must be discharged before the negative side effects of hospitalization accumulate and cause damage.

Summary

Acute hospitalization is an excellent, but not the only, tool for dealing with crisis resulting from exacerbation of schizophrenia (Odenheimer, 1965). It is a tool that must be used correctly and carefully monitored. Like any other effective treatment, it has beneficial effects for which it is instituted, and it has negative side effects that must be considered in the risk-benefit assessment. The proper length of hospitalization requires a clinician to set specific goals for the treatment intervention and to terminate hospitalization at the appropriate point. Clinical judgment necessary to make that decision can be enhanced considerably by monitoring the patient's treatment progress and cognitive level with the excellent instruments currently available. In making the decision for discharge it is absolutely essential that one consider both the TPS score and the cognitive level so as to place the patient back in the community at the optimal point in his or her recovery from crisis.

13

Psychology of
Prescribing Medication

Since antiquity, medications have been administered to patients by physicians and other representatives of the helping professions. Drugs have been used to alleviate discomfort, to alter the state of pathology, to bring about changes in consciousness, to revive or to poison, to alter development, and to change behavior. In the treatment of patients with psychological disturbances, a number of psychopharmacological agents are used to influence behavior and thinking and feeling in a systematic way (Kety, 1959). The primary purpose of these drugs is to alter specific target symptoms of disease. The effect of the medication on the patient is determined only in part by chemistry. It is also determined by the relationship between the therapist who gives the medication and the patient who receives it and the particular dynamics of the symptom that is to be altered. Response to medication is highly idiosyncratic. Although medications are classified according to their effect, such as antipsychotics, antidepressants, anxiolytics, and sedatives, it is difficult to predict patient response on the basis of pharmacology, physiology, and pharmacokinetics alone. How a particular pharmacological intervention will work with a given patient at a given time is determined by many variables (Mendel, 1967) other than chemistry and physiology.

157

Medication and the Patient's Own Past

The patient's own past in relation to a medication will necessarily be an important factor in his response. The individual who has adopted the chemical intervention as part of a life-style, the patient who easily reaches for the aspirin bottle to relieve a headache or the laxative bottle to relieve constipation will also be ready to seek a pill to alter his feelings, behavior, and thinking. In many ways this kind of intervention is a passive, magical, and distant one. The patient takes something into his mouth that produces changes inside of him, changes that he cannot control and cannot see and does not understand. Through a complex biological change his behavior is altered in a way that he and the world may judge as more adaptive. The patient takes very little part in changing his behavior and has very little control over the change. The use of medication reinforces his passivity, allowing him to let the therapist take over in the administration of his destiny. For some patients who feel helpless and overwhelmed by the inner world or by external reality as well as the demands of interaction with others, this passive approach to problem solving is seen as control from outside. For patients such as this, medication can be therapeutic for purely psychological reasons. For patients who are in crisis because they feel as if they were sitting on a volcano about to erupt, the introduction of medication into the treatment is seen as a chemical restraint. As a result of this psychological factor, anxiety is often lessened.

On the other hand, the patient who comes to treatment with a tendency to feel loss of control over her own life—for example, the paranoid patient—will react very differently to a chemical intervention. She sees the world as influencing her and allowing her no freedom. She lives in a situation in which mysterious influences from outside alter her behavior. She may see chemical intervention as a further attempt to subject her to external control and may feel an even greater loss of her autonomy when asked to take medication. Many patients who see the chemical intervention in this way and discover that the drug further impairs their ability to function, refuse to take medication.

For still other patients medication becomes a representative of the psychological components of the interaction and symbolizes "being given to." For the patient who is deprived, isolated, and unable to make human contact, the administration of a pill may represent the only impingement of the outside world on the prison of a psychotic existence. When the patient takes medication three times a day, it is at these three times each day that he has contact with reality. This contact may be the only means through which he can perceive, however dimly, that others are concerned or interested or that they care. Being given the pill and swallowing it may be the most significant contact with reality each day.

The giving and taking of medication is a highly structured contact. The purpose of the contact is known to both the people who give the medication and the patients who take it. The expectations are simple. Doctors or their representative give the pills and expect patients to take them. Patients take the pills from the givers and expect that the pills will work in some mysterious way to alter their feelings, thoughts, and behavior to a more comfortable state.

We should remember that, for some patients, being given the pill may have undesirable effects. For example, the paranoid who is certain that he is about to be poisoned will naturally refuse the pill. If he is forced to take the pill, it will confirm the suspicion that others are trying to poison him. Similarly, the psychotically disturbed patient who is depressed may see a pill as something that she does not deserve, or she, too, may see it as a poison but welcome the poison because in her thinking she deserves to be killed. The pharmacological reaction of a particular drug in a specific patient at a specific time can be predicted only when one knows the dynamics of the patient. The great variability in such dynamics makes drug research so difficult that at times it appears that all responses to medications are idiosyncratic.

For many patients, the medication serves as a talisman of health or a symbolic representation of the physician and the helping situation. For some patients, it is apparently not even necessary that they take the medication; they merely carry it. The fact that the medication is available seems to give security to these patients, who continually feel the threat of an impending loss of control. I have seen patients who carry several neuroleptics in a medication vial wherever they go. They never ingest the medication, because they feel they do not need it. However, they feel secure in the thought that if they need help at some time when the physician is not readily available, taking a pill will help them until they get back to the medical transaction.

What individual patients believe about the medication to a very large extent determines how they will respond to it. One of the factors of this belief is the physician's opinion and how that is conveyed. If the physician really feels that the medication is helpful in managing the patient's behavior or feelings or thinking and if the physician conveys this idea to the patient, the psychological effectiveness of the medication can be greatly enhanced.

Medication in Concert with Other Treatment Interventions

It is difficult to assess the patient's response to medication when many other treatment interventions are being used at the same time. If the physician administers medication to the patient on the first visit, one cannot attribute a subsequent change in behavior to the medication alone. The change may be due entirely or partly to the beginning of the interaction, which is part of the treatment. As already noted, in our hospital we generally do not medicate for the first twenty-four hours to see the effect of hospitalization by itself. When the experienced therapist makes it a practice *not* to administer medication during the first visit or the first day of hospitalization, the number of patients requiring medication is reduced as is the subsequent dosage necessary. Many patients respond to beginning treatment with a marked reduction in anxiety, an improvement in their ability to think and function, and a considerable reintegration of their adaptive capacity and personality, even before any medication is administered or has a chance to work.

Other patients are so disorganized in their perception of their world (Anscombe, 1987) and in their behavior that a chemical intervention is necessary immediately, being the only way to reach them for a therapeutic interaction. This chemical intervention may work either by lessening the awareness of anxiety or by allowing the interaction to proceed at a more chemical and therefore less personal level.

When the therapist delays the administration of drugs until the second outpatient visit or the second day of hospitalization, the amount of medication may be decreased by as much as 70 percent. To administer as little medication as possible is not only of value from an economic point of view and from a physiologic point of view in terms of avoiding unnecessary side effects. One must also remember that psychological factors of giving and taking medications can be antitherapeutic for some patients. The administration of medication in a particular patient may be psychologically contraindicated. It may reinforce further feelings of helplessness and passivity. Taking medication may again convince the patient that she has no stake in controlling her own destiny. It may reinforce her tendency to look for magical answers to her problems and thus support a stereotyped, distant approach to the external world in her interpersonal relationships.

The major purpose of administering medication is to reduce symptoms that interfere with patients' comfort or their ability to adapt to their surroundings (Van Praag and Korff, 1974). However, the symptoms may be the last adaptive maneuver available to particular patients, and the removal may result in further or even total disorganization of personality. For example, if patients are frightened to death of being overwhelmed by their angry, aggressive impulses and literally feel that if they let go of this control they may murder someone or destroy the world, they may then develop a catatonic stupor as a symptom. Such patients spend virtually all of their energy in holding in the body as tightly as possible to prevent any of this potentially fatal anger from leaking out. If such patients are given a chemical agent to loosen their control, the effect may be the opposite of what is expected. The medication may have been given with the intent of lessening the anger, and thus lessening the need for control. However, it may in fact lessen patients' ability to control themselves. Giving a neuroleptic to such patients may result in the appearance of overt, wildly psychotic, and very destructive behavior that is frightening to the patients and to the environment and may require physical restraint.

Such an effect of medication has been called paradoxical. However, it is not paradoxical at all if one remembers that the effect of medication is the sum of its chemical and psychological impact on the patient and his or her environment. The response to medication is markedly altered by the function of a particular symptom in a specific patient and by the total economics of the patient's psychological makeup. The therapist must consider that symptoms are formed in response to stresses, either external or internal, and that they thus serve a function. If a symptom is removed chemically, there must necessarily be a shift in the homeostasis of the patient. The purpose of the chemical intervention is to shift this homeostasis in the direction of better adaptive capacity and better function. Because symptoms are restitutive in nature, this shift to a more adaptive state occurs only if the medication is administered in the context of a total treatment program that allows the patient a better level of function.

We can understand symptoms on the basis of the thought, mood, and behavior disorders that occur in patients. However, the content of the particular delusions or feelings is based entirely on the patient's dynamics and is generally restitutive in nature. That is, the symptom serves the purpose of helping the individual's psyche to adapt to the basic conflict. An example is the patient who has developed grandiose delusions. The basic conflict is the impaired feelings of self-esteem. Because the patient has a thought process disorder, he is able to engage in magical, nonrealistic thinking. Because he has impaired self-esteem, which is painful to him, he develops the delusion that he is somebody very powerful and very important. He may believe that he is the president of the United States, Jesus Christ, or Napoleon. If we give him medication to reduce his psychosis and the thought process disorder that makes it necessary for him to give up his thoughts that he is somebody very important, he again experiences more severe impairment of his self-esteem and may in response to medication get worse.

It is absolutely essential, even for the totally biologically trained and oriented psychiatrist, to thoroughly know the patient and to understand the patient's dynamics as well as the dynamics of interaction in order to be a successful psychopharmacologist. If the psychiatrist simply prescribes medications without understanding and managing the rest of treatment, he or she will be therapeutically much less effective than it is possible to be. A thorough knowledge and understanding of modern pharmacology is necessary for the best possible treatment of schizophrenia (see Chapter Fourteen) but it is not enough. There must also be a thorough knowledge and understanding of supportive psychotherapy and the patient's dynamics (see Chapter Eleven).

14

Guidelines for the Use of Psychoactive Medications
*by Patricia J. Lobeda, Pharm.D.**

The use of medications to treat psychiatric illnesses continues to change as our experience and knowledge grow. Since the 1950s we have seen the use of antipsychotics change from the practice of giving megadoses of three to four grams of Thorazine to the practice of using microscopic homeopathic doses to the current practice of using guidelines for treatment as established by the Committee on Peer Review, American Psychiatric Association (1985). More changes in drug therapy will occur as research into the causes and treatment of mental illness continues.

    This chapter discusses general guidelines for the use of antipsychotics, antidepressants, lithium, and anxiolytics. These medications are not specific for certain illnesses but are used to treat specific target symptoms. Polypharmacy should be avoided, but the use of drugs from more than one therapeutic class is occasionally indicated. As with the use of any drug, the risks and benefits of the medication must be weighed. Antipsychotics can have very serious side effects; yet they may provide enough relief from psychotic symptoms that an otherwise nonfunctioning individual can live a productive life outside the hospital. In the same way, the benefits

*Dr. Lobeda is Director of Pharmacy at the Hastings Regional Center, Hastings, Nebraska.

of an anxiolytic should be weighed against the risk of addiction and withdrawal problems. It is advisable to use the lowest possible effective dose in an effort to avoid adverse effects.

Antipsychotics

Antipsychotics are effective in treating the signs and symptoms of psychosis in illnesses such as schizophrenia, schizo-affective disorder, organic mental disorder, and major depression with psychosis. Antipsychotics are also used for acute treatment of the manic phase of bipolar illness. Target symptoms include hostility, combativeness, paranoia, hallucinations, altered sleep patterns, delusions, and anxiety. Target symptoms are useful as monitoring parameters of drug effectiveness. The anxious, distraught, agitated patient can be calmed within twenty-four to seventy-two hours after initiation of antipsychotic therapy. The hostile combative patient can be effectively controlled with aggressive dosing of a sedative antipsychotic. It is important to bring hallucinations, altered sleep patterns, and anxiety under control. Gradual improvement in delusions, social skills, and affect will occur over time. Symptoms of poor judgment, lack of insight, and impaired social skills are less responsive to drug therapy.

Approximately twelve different antipsychotics are currently available, and several others are under investigation for marketing. Antipsychotics, sometimes referred to as neuroleptics or major tranquilizers, can be classified according to their chemical structures (Table 11). Phenothiazines are grouped according to their side chain: the aliphatic type, chlorpromazine (Thorazine); the piperidine types, mesoridazine (Serentil), thioridazine (Mellaril); and the piperazine types, perphenazine (Trilafon), trifluoperazine (Stelazine), and fluphenazine (Prolixin). The four nonphenothiazine antipsychotics have varying structures and are generally not classified as a group. They are thiothixene (Navane), haloperidol (Haldol), loxapine (Loxitane), and molindone (Moban). All antipsychotics appear to act by blocking the dopamine receptors in the limbic system. Recent literature suggests that the decreased neuronal firing rate of dopaminergic neurons also plays a role. Receptor studies show differing affinities of antipsychotics for dopamine receptors (Black, Richelson, and Richardson, 1985). The more potent antipsychotics such as haloperidol (Haldol) and thiothixene (Navane) have a greater affinity for dopamine receptors and are effective in a lower dose than chlorpromazine (Thorazine). All of the antipsychotics have the same effects, but to a varying degree, on the basis of their chemical structures. The aliphatic and piperidine phenothiazines (chlorpromazine [Thorazine], thioridazine [Mellaril], and mesoridazine [Serentil]) have a high incidence of sedation, orthostatic hypotension, and anticholinergic side effects. They cause extrapyramidal side effects less often than the more potent antipsychotics such as fluphenazine (Prolixin), thiothixene (Navane), and haloperidol (Haldol). Knowing the side effect profile of a specific antipsychotic helps us choose drug therapy for a particular patient. For example, in an elderly patient with prostatic hypertrophy, we want to avoid the use of a drug that is strongly anticholinergic. We would avoid the use of chlorpromazine (Thorazine) in favor of something like haloperidol (Haldol). The strong sedative side effect of chlorpromazine is also a disadvantage in an elderly patient, who may be more susceptible to adverse effects.

When anticholinergic effects become a problem, the dose of antipsychotic should be decreased. If this is not possible, treatment of anticholinergic side effects may be necessary. Treatments include the use of ice, lozenges, or artificial saliva for dry mouth; a bulk laxative for constipation; or a cholinergic agent such as bethanechol for blurred vision, urinary retention, or more serious anticholinergic side effects.

Extrapyramidal side effects include akathisia, akinesia, pseudo-parkinsonism, and acute dysthymic reactions. Anticholinergic medications such as benztropine (Cogentin), trihexyphenidyl (Artane), and amantadine (Symmetrel) are useful in treating extrapyramidal side effects. We avoid the prophylactic use of these agents because many patients do not develop extrapyramidal side effects. Thus the extra expense, side effects, and trouble of taking an anticholinergic are unnecessary. When it is necessary to use an anticholinergic, do so for one to three months, then begin to taper the dose to examine the need for continued treatment. The sedative side effect of antipsychotics may be beneficial initially to calm the

Table 11. Antipsychotics and Their Relative Potency.

Phenothiazines	(CPZ Equivalent)	Usual Daily Dose (mg)
Aliphatic		
Chlorpromazine (Thorazine)	100	400–1600
Piperidine		
Thioridazine (Mellaril)	100	400–800
Mesoridazine (Serentil)	50	100–500
Piperazine		
Perphenazine (Trilafon)	10	8–64
Trifluoperazine (Stelazine)	5	10–80
Fluphenazine (Prolixin)	2	5–40
Nonphenothiazines		
Thiothixene (Navane)	4	10–60
Chlorprothixene (Taractan)	100	400–1600
Haloperidol (Haldol)	2	5–100
Loxapine (Loxitane)	10	5–250
Molindone (Moban)	10	20–225

agitated or combative patient. In an effort to diminish the sedation, the dosage can be decreased or given in a single bedtime dose. Tolerance to initial sedative effects usually occurs.

Tardive dyskinesia, a potentially irreversible side effect of antipsychotics, involves involuntary movements of the mouth, lips, tongue, and sometimes the limbs or trunk. It has been associated with all classes of antipsychotics. Clinical experience suggests that the earlier tardive dyskinesia is recognized, the better the potential for recovery. Close observation of the patient's tongue, mouth, and face musculature is recommended. Antipsychotics should be discontinued, at least temporarily, when tardive dyskinesia is recognized to allow for a complete evaluation of the symptoms. An assessment of the risks versus benefits should be made to determine the need for resuming antipsychotic therapy. If necessary, the antipsychotic should be started again at a lower dose. Clozapine, a new drug used in the treatment of schizophrenia, is claimed by many to cause no extrapyramidal side effects or tardive dyskinesia. However, blood dyscrasias are a serious side effect of clozapine. At the time of this writing, clozapine has not yet been released on the market.

All antipsychotics lower the seizure threshold. This appears to be significant only in patients with a preexisting seizure disorder. In these patients, we monitor seizure frequency and serum levels of anticonvulsant medications, then increase the dose of anticonvulsant if necessary. Photosensitivity reactions may occur in patients taking antipsychotics. Limited exposure to the sun and the use of a sunscreen containing PABA will help control these reactions. Skin pigmentary changes to a tan, blue, or purple color seem to be related to exposure to the sun and to high doses of antipsychotics, especially phenothiazines. Skin discoloration is reversible upon discontinuation of the phenothiazine. Phenothiazines are also associated with pigmentary deposits in the lens and cornea of the eye. If routine slit lamp examination of the eye shows pigmentary lens deposits, phenothiazines can be discontinued in favor of an antipsychotic that does not cause eye deposits. Doses of thioridazine (Mellaril) greater than 1,000 mg per day are associated with pigmentary retinopathy. Metabolic and endocrine side effects include weight gain, irregularities in temperature regulation, galactorrhea, amenorrhea, and gynecomastia.

The use of antipsychotics has been associated with a potentially lethal reaction known as neuroleptic malignant syndrome (NMS). The estimated incidence of this syndrome is 0.5 to 1.5 percent of all patients taking neuroleptics. The mortality rate may be as high as 20 percent. The onset of NMS may occur at any time during neuroleptic therapy but is most often seen after the start of therapy or after an increase in dose. It is associated with both oral and injectible neuroleptics. An episode usually lasts from eight hours to thirty days, but with depot medication the syndrome lasts much longer (Lavie, Olmsted, Ventura, and Lepler, 1986). By sex, the incidence is 2:1, male to female, and it is more common in patients under the age of forty. The incidence of NMS increases in hot climates. Moreover, evidence suggests that the tendency to develop NMS is inherited, just as has been found to be the case with malignant hyperthermia secondary to inhalation anesthesia. Taking a good family history for heat stroke, NMS, or malignant hyperthermia may alert the clinician to high-risk patients.

The clinical presentation of NMS includes the four cardinal symptoms of muscular rigidity, hyperthermia, autonomic dysfunctions, and altered consciousness. The muscular rigidity is a lead pipe rigidity rather than a cogwheel presentation. The fever ranges from 38° C to 42° C. Diaphoresis, tachypnea, rapid pulse, and labile blood pressure with either hypertension or hypotension are the usual autonomic dysfunctions. Altered consciousness ranges from lethargy to coma. Laboratory studies are not diagnostic but may help to rule out other disorders. Laboratory abnormalities may include an elevated creatinine phosphokinase, leukocytosis, and elevated levels on liver function tests. The differential diagnosis of a patient with fever, muscular rigidity, and altered autonomic function may be complicated. It is necessary to rule out allergic, infectious, metabolic, and toxic etiologies. Other syndromes in the differential diagnosis of NMS include malignant hyperthermia, acute lethal catatonia, and heat stroke.

The initial treatment of NMS is prompt discontinuation of the offending neuroleptic. Supportive measures include antipyretics, cooling blankets, ice packs, and so on to treat the hyperthermia. Treat dehydration with IV fluids and electrolytes. Anticholinergics may help muscular rigidity. Bromocriptine and amantadine are thought to restore the balance between dopamine and acetylcholine, and have been used successfully to treat NMS. Dantrolene helps lower temperature and relax skeletal muscle stiffness. Diazepam is also useful as a muscle relaxant. Significant consideration must be given to the question of whether to restart neuroleptic therapy. Again, risks versus benefits must be evaluated. When it is deemed necessary to restart neuroleptic therapy, it is best to avoid the agents that caused the NMS. Choose a neuroleptic from a different class or a low-potency agent such as thioridazine (Mellaril) (Janicak, Bresnahan, and Comaty, 1987). Start with a low dose and avoid parenteral agents. Monitor the patient on a regular basis and discontinue the neuroleptic at the first sign of fever or any other symptom of NMS.

Given in equipotent doses, all of the antipsychotics appear to be equally effective. That is not to say that a particular patient will respond positively to all of these medications. In fact, it is not unusual for a patient to respond favorably to chlorpromazine

(Thorazine) and not at all to thiothixene (Navane), or vice versa. How, then, do we make a choice of antipsychotics? We choose antipsychotics on the basis of the patient's past history of response and the side effect profile of the drug. Cost may also be a significant factor. The patient who has responded favorably to a particular antipsychotic in the past is likely to have a favorable response again. The importance of an accurate history from the patient or the patient's family is clear. We can determine what medication has worked in the past, as well as the effective dosage. Of added importance is the patient's experience with the side effects of neuroleptics. A medication the patient stopped taking because of side effects would not be a good choice to try again. The patient would probably exhibit the same side effects and possibly be noncompliant. On the other hand, it may be worth trying to treat the side effects in order to give the neuroleptic an adequate therapeutic trial. The drug should not be discounted solely on the basis of side effects if it is thought to be therapeutic.

On initiation of antipsychotic therapy, multiple daily dosing is suggested to increase the patient's tolerance of side effects. This also helps to provide a sedative effect throughout the day in an effort to calm the agitated, hyperactive, or aggressive patient. Once acute symptoms are under control, a single daily dose may be given at bedtime. Occasionally, neuroleptics are dosed on an "as needed" or "prn" basis in an effort to bring target symptoms of hostility, aggression, or hyperactivity under control. Initially, prn use may be effective in sedating the patient, but tolerance to the sedative effect will develop. The antipsychotic effects of the drug have a slower onset than the sedative effect. If the patient continues to require prn drug therapy intervention, the daily dose of the neuroleptic should be increased or the neuroleptic changed. The prn use of a benzodiazepine anxiolytic along with the regularly scheduled neuroleptic is also useful. One of the many fashions in the use of neuroleptics has been called rapid neuroleptization. This consists of giving frequent intramuscular doses of neuroleptics (particularly haloperidol) to manage the behavior of acutely psychotic patients. There is no evidence that this is a useful technique. It must be remembered that the onset of the antipsychotic effect of neuroleptics is very slow. The sedative effect occurs within a few minutes, but the antipsychotic effect may take several days to weeks. Rapid neuroleptization has been associated with an increase in extrapyramidal side effects and an increased incidence of the potentially fatal neuroleptic malignant syndrome (Aubree and Lader, 1980; Kane, 1985). Therefore, the frequent (every hour or so) injection of a neuroleptic cannot be justified as a treatment of acute psychosis.

Antipsychotics can be given orally to most patients. Several of the antipsychotics are available in concentrate or liquid form. These are useful in a patient who cannot swallow a tablet or who may be "cheeking" and disposing of medication. For those who refuse oral medication, many of the antipsychotics are available parenterally. The injectable form is more bioavailable than the oral form, so dosage adjustments must be made. For example, the I.M. form of chlorpromazine (Thorazine) is four times more bioavailable than an equivalent oral dose. Therefore, 25 mg I.M. should have the same effect as 100 mg of chlorpromazine given orally. Two long-acting parenteral antipsychotics are also available: haloperidol decanoate (Haldol) and fluphenazine decanoate (Prolixin). These agents provide therapeutic blood levels for two to four weeks (Comaty and Janicak, 1987; Kane, 1986). Once patients are controlled on the oral medication, they may be switched to the decanoate. It may be necessary to continue the oral medication initially because of the slow pharmacologic onset of the decanoate.

Although therapeutic serum levels of antipsychotics are not yet well defined, studies show evidence of their potential usefulness. Many of the neuroleptic drugs have suggested therapeutic plasma concentrations that seem to correlate with antipsychotic effect (Baldessarini, Cohen, and Teicher, 1988). There is also evidence of a biphasic relationship of efficacy to plasma concentration, or a "therapeutic window," where higher plasma levels correlate to decreased therapeutic efficacy and increased side effects (Dahl, 1986). Further studies are essential to more clearly define the clinical usefulness of antipsychotic blood levels.

A patient should be given four to six weeks to respond to the antipsychotic. Acute symptoms such as hostility, hyperactivity, aggression, irritability, and suspicion may respond within a few days. Symptoms of hallucinations, delusions, and bizarre behavior may take up to a month or more. Rapid changes from one antipsychotic to another are not recommended. There is evidence that a rapid switch from one antipsychotic to another, after only a few days of therapy and before the medication has had a chance to be effective, may increase the risk of the neuroleptic malignant syndrome.

Polypharmacy, or the use of more than one antipsychotic, should be avoided. There is no convincing evidence that the use of more than one antipsychotic is any more effective than an adequate dose of one antipsychotic for an adequate length of time. The increase in cost and side effects is also a disadvantage. Any patient who does not respond to the therapeutic dosages of neuroleptics may be tried on the addition of one of the following drugs: lithium, in dosages of 900 mg to 1800 mg daily, a benzodiazepine such as lorazepam or clonazepam in dosages of 0.5 mg to 4 mg daily (Black, Richelson, and Richardson, 1985; Lewis, Spencer, Haas, and DiVittis, 1987), or carbamazepine in dosages of 400 mg to 1400 mg daily. Carbamazepine is particularly useful in the treatment of violent, assaultive, or impulsive behavior that has not responded adequately to antipsychotics. Other medications with reported success as adjunctive therapy in the treatment of schizophrenia include reserpine, clonidine, and calcium channel antagonists such as verapamil and diltizem.

Antidepressants

Affective illness is the most common psychiatric disorder in the United States. It has been estimated that 15 to 20 percent of the population will suffer from some form of depression in their lifetime. The decision to treat depression pharmacologically depends on the severity, duration, and type of symptoms seen. Symptoms that interfere with day-to-day functioning, impair interpersonal relationships, or reveal a high risk of suicide indicate the need for treatment. Target symptoms include weight loss, anorexia, altered sleep patterns, psychomotor retardation or agitation, loss of pleasure in usual activities, diminished ability to think or concentrate, feelings of worthlessness, and suicidal ideation.

Antidepressants can be classified into three broad groups.

The tricyclic antidepressants, the monoamine oxidase inhibitors, and the newer, nontricyclic antidepressants, which are similar in effect to tricyclics but differ structurally (Table 12). Both tricyclic and nontricyclic antidepressants are thought to act by blocking the re-uptake of neurotransmitters into the presynaptic neuron. This increases the availability of serotonin and/or norepinephrine in the synaptic cleft. Studies suggest that long-term antidepressant use may alter the number and sensitivity of postsynaptic receptors (Sulser, 1983). Monoamine oxidase inhibitors are thought to act by inhibiting the enzyme responsible for the breakdown of norepinephrine and serotonin, thereby increasing the number of neurotransmitters in the presynaptic neuron.

Because of the number of antidepressants available today, it may be difficult to choose an appropriate drug for a particular patient. A logical way to make a choice is to evaluate each drug's side effects and determine the patient's tolerance to those side effects. The tricyclic antidepressants (TCAs) can be divided into subgroups on the basis of their chemical structures. The incidence of side

Table 12. Classification of Antidepressants.

Tricyclic	Usual Daily Dose (mg)
Dimethylated	
Amitriptyline (Elavil)	100–300
Imipramine (Tofranil)	100–300
Doxepin (Sinequan, Adapin)	100–300
Trimipramine (Surmontil)	100–300
Monomethylated	
Protriptyline (Vivactil)	20–60
Desipramine (Norpramin)	100–300
Nortriptyline (Pamelor)	50–150
Nontricyclic	
Amoxapine (Asendin)	100–300
Trazodone (Desyrel)	100–400
Maprotiline (Ludiomil)	100–300
Fluoxetine (Prozac)	20–80
Monoamine Oxidase Inhibitor	
Isocarboxazid (Marplan)	30–80
Phenelzine (Nardil)	30–90
Tranylcypromine (Parnate)	30–80

effects correlates to these structures. There are the dimethylated TCAs and the monomethylated TCAs (Table 12). While all TCAs can cause drowsiness and sedation, the dimethylated TCAs cause the side effects to a greater degree than the monomethylated. The dimethylated TCAs also cause a higher incidence of weight gain and orthostatic hypotension. Trazodone (Desyrel) is highly sedative, similar to a dimethylated TCA. Maprotiline (Ludiomil) and amoxapine (Asendin) are less sedative. Fluoxetine (Prozac) is not associated with sedation and may cause nervousness and insomnia.

Antidepressant drugs are potent blockers of the muscarinic receptors in the brain. Blockade of these receptors leads to the anticholinergic side effects of blurred vision, dry mouth, constipation, urinary retention, tachycardia, and memory dysfunction. The dimethylated TCAs are the more potent blockers of muscarinic receptors and thus cause a higher incidence of anticholinergic side effects. Based on this evaluation of side effects, a dimethylated TCA would be a good choice for a young, agitated, depressed patient in whom the sedative effect would be of advantage; it would be a poor choice for an elderly patient with a history of heart disease. A definite advantage of the nontricyclic antidepressants trazodone, maprotiline, amoxapine, and fluoxetine is their low incidence of anticholinergic side effects.

Antidepressants may cause a variety of cardiovascular side effects. Palpitations, orthostatic hypotension, tachycardia, and arrhythmias may occur. In patients with preexisting heart disease, exacerbation of congestive heart failure has been noted. Dermatological side effects include skin rashes and vasculitis. Transient hematologic changes are associated with the use of antidepressants. Tricyclic antidepressants can cause an anticholinergic psychosis or delirium. This is more common with high TCA plasma levels and in the elderly. Because of this neurologic side effect, the Committee on Peer Review, American Psychiatric Association (1985), recommends half the standard adult dose for patients over sixty-five years of age. TCAs and amoxapine can lower the seizure threshold but only at high doses, and these drugs are not generally contraindicated in patients with a history of seizures. Because of amoxapine's ability to block dopamine receptors, it has caused extrapyramidal side effects and tardive dyskinesia. Trazodone causes a higher incidence of erectile dysfunction than the other antidepressants.

Antidepressants should be started at a low dose and increased every two to four days to allow the patient to adjust to side effects. Because of their long half-lives these drugs can be dosed once a day, usually at bedtime because of the sedation. Some clinicians prefer to divide the daily dose in an effort to decrease the intensity of the side effects. When a dosage of 150 mg per day of amitriptyline is reached, signs of improvement in at least one symptom (for example, improved sleep or appetite) should be seen in about one week. If no improvement is seen, the dose should be increased to the maximum dose of 300 mg per day or the maximum that the patient can tolerate and then held there for three weeks. While the side effects occur within the first twenty-four hours, the antidepressant effect will not be seen for two to three weeks. Patients should be counseled about this delay in therapeutic effect, the side effects to expect, and treatment of those side effects. Maximum tolerable doses should be maintained for at least three weeks to determine therapeutic benefit.

Because of the wide variation in the metabolism of antidepressants, serum level determinations are often of value. Tricyclic antidepressants are completely absorbed, but a large amount is metabolized on the first pass through the liver. Serum level studies show substantial variations among patients, variations that can probably be attributed to intrapatient variations in hepatic metabolism, protein binding, and concurrent physiologic processes. Tobacco smoking, concurrent drug therapy, and renal, hepatic, and inflammatory diseases are all known to affect plasma levels of antidepressants. Optimum therapeutic serum levels have been defined for most of the antidepressants. Reliable therapeutic plasma levels have been defined for nortriptyline (Pamelor), desipramine (Norpramin), and imipramine (Tofranil). Other antidepressants have suggested therapeutic plasma levels that may become more reliable with further studies (American Psychiatric Task Force, 1985). Serum levels are drawn after the drug has reached steady state, approximately five half-lives or about one week for most antidepressants. These are of particular value in the patient with medical problems, who may not tolerate the adverse effects, in the elderly patient who is more prone to adverse effects, in the suicidal patient, and in the patient who is unresponsive at the usual therapeutic dose.

Serum levels give valuable information on the dosing of the antidepressant and, when combined with clinical evaluation of the patient, help to determine the patient's response to drug therapy. Once adequate clinical response is seen, the patient should be maintained on the antidepressant for six to twelve months to prevent a relapse. An adequate maintenance dose may be as little as half the initial therapeutic dose. Once the decision is made to discontinue therapy, it is necessary to taper the dosage over four to eight weeks. Abrupt discontinuation causes an anticholinergic withdrawal syndrome characterized by nausea, vomiting, headache, chills, malaise, dizziness, abdominal cramps, diarrhea, insomnia, anxiety, restlessness, and irritability. Thus patients should be cautioned against abruptly discontinuing drug therapy.

The Dexamethasone Suppression Test (DST) can be used in several ways to evaluate the depressed patient. Abnormal plasma cortisol levels occur within seventeen to twenty-four hours after dexamethasone is administered to depressed patients. This test can be a diagnostic aid, as well as an aid to evaluate when to discontinue drug therapy. The DST is not to be used as a definitive diagnostic tool but as an adjunct to support or confirm a clinical diagnosis. As the patient improves, the response to the dexamethasone challenge may become normal. A good prognosis is associated with a normalized DST. A persistent, abnormal DST identifies a group at risk for relapse. Before discontinuing antidepressant therapy, it may therefore be of value to perform the DST.

When an adequate dose of antidepressant has been given for an adequate length of time and is not effective, several alternatives are available. Another antidepressant, of a different chemical structure, can be tried. For example, after a dimethylated TCA such as amitriptyline has failed, a monomethylated TCA such as desipramine (Norpramin) or a nontricyclic antidepressant such as trazodone (Desyrel) is a reasonable alternative. Another choice is to try a monoamine oxidase inhibitor. Other treatments for resistant depression include the addition of lithium carbonate, synthetic thyroid hormone, a psychostimulant, or L-tryptophan or the use of electroconvulsive therapy (Paykel and Van Woerkom, 1987; White and Simpson, 1987).

Monoamine oxidase inhibitors (MAOIs) are the third major pharmacologic class of antidepressants. These agents are used less often than the tricyclics and nontricyclics because of their potential for serious adverse effects and the necessary dietary restrictions that go with their use. Three monoamine oxidase inhibitors are on the market in the United States: isocarboxazide (Marplan), phenelzine (Nardil), and tranylcypromine (Parnate).

MAOIs are thought to be as effective as tricyclic antidepressants when used at adequate doses (Pare, 1987). Some studies suggest that MAOIs are more effective in atypical depressions involving symptoms such as phobia, panic, anxiety, somatic preoccupations, and mood variations. MAOIs may also be effective in treating depression refractory to other antidepressant medications. Monoamine oxidase inhibitors have been shown to be more effective when combined with L-tryptophan. The measurement of monoamine oxidase activity in blood platelets is under investigation in an effort to correlate MAO activity with illness and treatment outcomes in schizophrenia and affective illness. Further investigation is needed to define any clinical usefulness of MAO platelet activity measurements.

The common side effects of MAOIs include dry mouth, blurred vision, bad taste, constipation, drowsiness, insomnia, tremor, dizziness, palpitations, and agitation. The various MAOIs cause these side effects to varying degrees. Therefore, a patient who cannot tolerate one MAOI may not have the same adverse reaction to another one.

MAOIs may affect cardiovascular function by decreasing heart rate and blood pressure and causing ECG changes. Orthostatic hypotension may be seen. The concurrent use of MAOIs and certain amines has been associated with a hypertensive crisis characterized by elevated blood pressure, headache, and sometimes fever. Tyramine is the amine most often implicated in these reactions. Tyramine-containing foods include aged cheeses, beer, wine, pickled herring, liver, and ripe bananas. Drugs containing indirect-acting sympathomimetics, such as phenylephrine, phenylpropanolamine, or ephedrine, may also cause a hypertensive crisis.

These drugs are found in several over-the-counter cold products and diet control products. Patients therefore need to be educated about diet and drug interactions. Although the incidence of hypertensive crisis is rare, the risk of more serious effects such as stroke or death is cause for concern.

It is now recognized that to be effective MAOIs must be used at higher doses than were previously used in clinical practice (Davis and Janicak, 1987). Recommended dosage ranges are shown in Table 12. Orthostatic hypotension is usually the dose-limiting factor. Onset of action is slow, with two to four weeks being required before maximum monoamine oxidase inhibition occurs. Four to six weeks of drug treatment is considered an adequate therapeutic trial period. MAOIs may cause either drowsiness or excitation. Because they can be given on a twice-daily schedule, the larger part of a divided dose may be given in the morning or in the evening, according to which effect is seen.

Monoamine oxidase inhibitors should be given prophylactically for six to twelve months to prevent relapse. Abrupt discontinuation has been reported to cause muscle weakness, headaches, parasthesia, and nightmares. Slowly decreasing the dose over a two-week period should prevent such withdrawal symptoms.

Lithium

Lithium is effective in 60 to 70 percent of manic patients in the acute phase of mania and in prophylaxis of both bipolar and unipolar affective disorders. Some benefit from lithium may also be seen in treating schizo-affective illness. Moreover, recent reports show benefit from the adjunctive use of lithium in treating schizophrenia and major depression. Lithium has been studied in a variety of other psychiatric and behavioral disorders with inconsistent reports of effectiveness (Jann, Garrelts, Ereshefsky, and Saklad, 1984).

Lithium's mechanism of action is not completely understood. It is thought that lithium may stabilize catecholamine receptors, preventing the changes in catecholamine receptor activity that are hypothesized to occur in manic-depressive illness. Upon initiation of lithium therapy, there is a lag time of five to ten days before therapeutic efficacy is seen. During this time, it may be necessary to use an antipsychotic to control the increased motor activity, hostility, grandiosity, or suspiciousness that may be present in acute mania. As the patient improves, the antipsychotic can be titrated down and discontinued.

A serum level of between 0.8 and 1.5 mEq/L is usually required to control an acute manic attack. Serum lithium levels are most reliable when drawn twelve hours after the last dose of the drug. Initially, serum levels should be drawn twice a week because the clearance of lithium may change as the patient becomes less active. Once the patient is stable, lithium levels may be monitored weekly for one month, then monthly for a few months, and every three to six months thereafter. A therapeutic trial of lithium is considered to be three weeks at therapeutic serum levels. The minimum serum level for prophylaxis is 0.4 mEq/L. The usual daily dose of lithium carbonate is 300 to 3600 mg per day. Lithium has a long half-life and can be dosed once a day but is more often given in a divided dose to help control the nausea and vomiting associated with high serum levels. The use of lithium is associated with a high incidence of side effects upon initiation, but tolerance develops within a few weeks. The initial side effects include gastrointestinal irritation, tremor, muscle weakness, thirst, and polyuria. Other side effects of lithium use are more serious and require careful monitoring. A pre-lithium workup is necessary to obtain baseline data so that side effects can be monitored (Salem, 1983). In patients over forty years old or with heart disease, a baseline ECG should be obtained. Lithium can cause ECG changes or cardiac arrhythmia, and leukocytosis occurs during lithium therapy. A complete blood count will monitor these changes.

Lithium often induces a transient hypothyroidism and on long-term use can cause hyperparathyroidism. Baseline and follow-up thyroid function studies, as well as serum calcium levels, are therefore necessary. Lithium may cause a variety of adverse renal effects including polyuria, polydypsia, decreased ability of the kidney to concentrate urine, and tubular-renal necrosis. This lithium-induced diabetes insipidus can be alleviated by reducing the dose of lithium or discontinuing its use. Periodic renal function tests should include urine osmolalities, serum creatinine, and BUN. Lithium also causes a high incidence of weight gain, which correlates to the length of treatment. Patients on long-term prophylactic therapy report more of a weight gain. Edema is another side effect of lithium. Sodium-restricted diets and sodium-depleting diuretics should be avoided or used only with careful supervision. Decreased serum sodium can cause increased lithium reabsorption and toxicity.

Lithium intoxication usually occurs at a serum level greater than 2 mEq/L. A flu-like syndrome is the earliest sign of toxicity, which is characterized by nausea, vomiting, drowsiness, lethargy, tremors of the hands, and diarrhea. More serious intoxication involves impaired consciousness, generalized tremors, hypertonic muscles, dysarthria, seizures, cardiac arrhythmias, coma, and death. Treatment of lithium toxicity depends on its severity. For toxicity caused by an acute overdose of lithium, emesis or gastric lavage is necessary. For mild toxicity, discontinuation of lithium may be sufficient, whereas for more serious intoxication, osmotic diuresis will increase lithium excretion. Hemodialysis is also effective in removing lithium from the body. In all cases fluid and electrolyte balance must be maintained.

Anxiolytics

The ideal anxiolytic should be safe and effective in treating all types of anxiety disorders, cause minimal side effects, and not cause sedation or impair cognitive performance. In addition, the ideal anxiolytic should have a low addiction and suicide potential and minimal interaction with other drugs (Gershon and Eison, 1987). Unfortunately, the ideal anxiolytic has not been discovered, although advances are being made in the treatment of anxiety.

The use of propanediols (for example, meprobamate) and barbiturates has been abandoned because of the potential for serious adverse effects, including addiction, overdose, and suicide. Today we have benzodiazepine and nonbenzodiazepine anxiolytics that provide safe and effective treatment of anxiety. Benzodiazepines have been the drug of choice since the early 1960s. In addition to treating various anxiety disorders, they have been used as muscle relaxants, hypnotics, anticonvulsants, and premedication in anesthesia; they have also been used in the treatment of drug and alcohol withdrawal.

Benzodiazepines are as effective as, and in some studies more effective than, propanediols and barbiturates in treating anxiety. Benzodiazepines have a higher therapeutic index, which makes suicide unlikely. They also have a lower addiction potential and do not cause enzyme induction. Although their mechanism of action is not completely understood, benzodiazepines are thought to act in the limbic system and affect the inhibitory neurotransmitter gamma-aminobutyric acid (GABA). Specific receptors for benzodiazepines have been identified in the brain.

Most of the significant side effects of benzodiazepines involve the central nervous system. Common adverse effects include drowsiness, dizziness, headache, and muscle weakness. These CNS depressant effects tend to decrease with continued use of the drug. Although the elderly are significantly more susceptible to the CNS depressant effects than younger people, all patients should be cautioned about driving and operating hazardous machinery during initial treatment with benzodiazepines. Other neurologic side effects that occur less frequently are hostility, behavioral disinhibition, mental depression, and paradoxical excitement.

Known to be both physically and psychologically addicting, benzodiazepines are a class IV controlled substance because of their potential for abuse. Dependence is a product of drug dose and duration of use. Upon abrupt discontinuation, potentially severe withdrawal syndrome may be seen. Withdrawal symptoms include nausea, vomiting, diarrhea, insomnia, nervousness, confusion, psychosis, hallucinations, tremors, and seizures. The onset and severity of withdrawal symptoms are a function of the half-life of the benzodiazepine. Upon discontinuation of long-acting diazepines such as diazepam (Valium) or chlordiazepoxide (Librium), the withdrawal symptoms may not be seen for several days to a week. With shorter-acting benzodiazepines such as alprazolam (Xanax) and lorazepam (Ativan), abrupt discontinuation may lead to severe withdrawal symptoms within twenty-four hours. Patients should be cautioned not to stop taking their medications except under medical supervision.

All benzodiazepines are equivalent in their clinical effectiveness. The choice of a particular benzodiazepine for a specific patient is based on the pharmacokinetic properties of the drug (Greenblatt and others, 1983). Knowledge of the half-life of each benzodiazepine is useful. With the exception of lorazepam (Ativan), oxazepam (Serax), and alprazolam (Xanax), the benzodiazepines have long half-lives. This is an advantage in providing once daily dosing and an anxiolytic effect throughout the day. A shorter half-life is useful in preventing accumulation of the benzodiazepine on repeated dosing. Accumulation with long-acting benzodiazepine is particularly a problem in the elderly because of their decreased ability to metabolize and their increased volume of distribution, which allows the drug to be stored in the body. This accumulation, storage, and decreased metabolism puts the elderly patient at an increased risk of side effects.

The benzodiazepines are given orally in multiple or single daily doses, depending on the half-life of the particular drug. Oxazepam (Serax), lorazepam (Ativan), and alprazolam (Xanax) are short-acting and must be given more than once a day for continuous anxiolytic effect. The larger portion of the dose can be given at night to avoid the need for a hypnotic in those patients with a sleep disturbance. Unlike other benzodiazepines, oxazepam (Serax) and lorazepam (Ativan) are metabolized by glucuronidation only and are probably safer to use in the presence of liver dysfunction. Diazepam (Valium), chlordiazepoxide (Librium), and lorazepam (Ativan) are available as parenterals. However, lorazepam (Ativan) is the only benzodiazepine that is well absorbed intramuscularly and provides satisfactory clinical effects.

Many nonbenzodiazepine substances are under investigation for their anxiolytic activity, including pyrazolopyradines, imidazole derivatives, quinolone derivatives, and azospirodecanediones. Of these, buspirone (Buspar), an azospirodecanedione, is the only one now marketed in the United States. Buspirone has antianxiety activity similar to that of the benzodiazepines; however, it lacks their anticonvulsive, muscle relaxant, and sedative/hypnotic properties.

The exact mechanism of action for buspirone is not completely understood. Buspirone has a high affinity for serotonin receptors and a moderate affinity for dopamine receptors. It does not affect GABA and has no affinity for benzodiazepine receptors. Its anxiolytic effect is probably the result of its influence on serotoninergic activity.

Buspirone has several advantages over existing anxiolytics. It is not a CNS depressant. It does not cause sedation, drowsiness, cognitive disturbances, or impairment of motor skills and does not potentiate the effects of alcohol or other CNS depressants. Buspirone's lack of potential for abuse or addiction is another advantage (Goa and Ward, 1986). Additionally, patients taking buspirone experience no withdrawal syndrome, even with abrupt discontinuation.

The side effects of buspirone are generally mild and include dizziness, nausea, headache, nervousness, light-headedness, and excitement. At higher doses it may cause dysphoria. Euphoria, or the feeling of well-being associated with a benzodiazepine, is not present with buspirone. A patient familiar with this feeling of well-being from benzodiazepines may conclude that buspirone is not effective. Upon investigating the patient's complaint, however, we may find that the symptoms of anxiety are gone; buspirone is effective, but the euphoric feeling is missing.

Buspirone is available in oral tablet form. The initial dose is 5 mg three times a day, increasing to 30 mg a day over one week. The maximum daily dose is 60 mg per day. Buspirone has a very gradual onset, with a lag time of seven to ten days, and maximum therapeutic effect may not be seen for three to four weeks. Patients should be cautioned about the lag time and cautioned against prn use of buspirone. Because buspirone has no effect on benzodiazepine receptors, a patient taking benzodiazepines cannot be switched directly to buspirone. As already noted, benzodiazepines need to be tapered off slowly to avoid withdrawal symptoms. Buspirone presents a reasonable alternative for treating anxiety, especially in patients with potential for abuse or in those who cannot tolerate the sedation or impaired cognitive functioning of benzodiazepines.

Summary

The four classes of psychoactive drugs discussed in this chapter—antipsychotics, antidepressants, anxiolytics, and lithium—are not illness-specific but are used to treat specific symptoms in a variety of illnesses. Polypharmacy, the use of more than one drug in a particular therapeutic class, should be avoided. There is rarely any advantage to giving two antipsychotics, or any other two drugs of the same class. On the other hand, there are indications for the use of more than one class of psychoactive drug. For example, the use of an antipsychotic and an antidepressant may be necessary in the chronic schizophrenic patient who presents with a depressive episode. The addition of an anxiolytic to the treatment of schizophrenia is sometimes necessary to treat the symptoms of anxiety. In the chronic, excited schizophrenic, or the schizo-affective patient, the use of lithium in conjunction with an antipsychotic may be indicated (Jann, Garrelts, Ereshefsky, and Saklad, 1984).

Although lithium is the mainstay of drug therapy in the treatment of affective illness, combination drug therapy is sometimes indicated. Antipsychotics may be used to control the symptoms of insomnia, hostility, hyperactivity, or aggression in the acute manic patient (Janicak and Boshes, 1987). In the bipolar patient on lithium, an antidepressant may be indicated to treat the depression. This combination of drug therapy may also be the result of treating a major depressive episode with an antidepressant, and the antidepressant precipitating a switch to mania. In treating a psychotic major depression, an antipsychotic in conjunction with an antidepressant may be indicated when the antidepressant alone does not control the psychotic symptoms.

As with the use of any medication, the risks must be weighed against the benefits of using a psychoactive drug. When use is called for, the lowest effective dose should be given in an effort to minimize adverse effects, and the need for continued drug therapy should be reevaluated periodically. The elderly patient may no longer require continuous drug therapy or may benefit from a reduced dose. Whereas some patients require long-term maintenance therapy, others may benefit from intermittent targeted drug treatment (Carpenter, 1986; Herz, 1982). Intermittent dosing involves the identification of target symptoms or prodromal signs of relapse in the schizophrenic outpatient. This limits drug therapy to psychotic episodes and may decrease the side effects of long-term neuroleptic therapy.

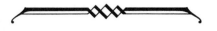

15

Supported Living
in the Community

The 497 patients who form the basis for this book spent, as already noted, an average of only 8.5 days in the hospital per year over a period of thirty-five years. This is probably fairly typical for most schizophrenic patients treated in the United States in the 1970s and 1980s. Treatment methods have changed in a major way (Shrala, 1972) so that patients no longer live in the hospital but rather reside in the community.

Many forms of community treatment are available. All of these must take into account the treatment needs of schizophrenic patients as well as their limitations of function. Chapters Eleven and Twelve describe in detail how these needs and limitations can be monitored and met and how they must result in a highly individualized treatment program for each patient. Such programs must be constantly reassessed and frequently changed to meet the changing needs and altered limitations of the patient.

The Supporting Family

Among the wide range of supporting resources in the community, first and foremost is the supporting family, when such a family is available. Even when there are problems within the family (Hatfield, 1987), it is better to keep the family together with

185

appropriate education and family support (Leff, 1976). A common error inexperienced clinicians make is to blame the family and suggest the patient move out of the family. In fact, with minimal effort at education and family support, patients usually function best in their natural supporting environment (Falloon and others, 1981). Using the natural family for support requires the least therapeutic effort and, if done correctly, will offer considerable satisfaction to the family (Freeman and Simmons, 1963) as well as to the patient. Unfortunately, many patients do not have families, or by the time the patients get to us, their families are so totally alienated and destroyed that they can no longer provide support and care. In such cases we must look for other supporting resources.

Patient Group Living

Resources for support vary in the amount of support and structure they offer and the amount of rehabilitation treatment possible (Roberts, 1984). Where patients should be placed among the various types of facilities must be a clinical decision based on needs, limits of function, and availability (Pasamanick, Scarpitti, and Dinitz, 1967). In "board and care" homes patients simply get room and board and nothing else (Schwartz and others, 1986). In halfway houses, patients get board and care but also supervision of medication and a minimal program. One variation of this is the quarterway house, which we have developed and which is for those patients who have such limitations at the time of leaving the hospital that they are not able to function in a halfway house. The quarterway house is on the hospital grounds but is independent of the hospital. Here patients get room and board and supervised medication in addition to which they are also seen as frequently as necessary in the outpatient department of the hospital. They participate in day-care programs. If they have an exacerbation resulting in crisis, they can be seen immediately by a psychiatrist and appropriate treatment can be instituted, including changes in medication, a change of program, or rehospitalization.

Partial hospitalization programs are now carried out by many modern hospital units in the United States. These programs allow the patient to function in the normal world outside the hospital during the day, as for example going to work at a regular job, and then returning to the hospital for treatment, sleep, and support during the night. Another version allows the patient to do just the opposite. The patient is in the hospital all day for treatment and then returns home to the family at night.

Many models are used for group living of schizophrenic patients. These include the Fairweather Lodge (Fairweather, 1980), which moves an entire ward of the hospital out into the community and has patients live, work, and function together with decreasing staff support. There is the Fountain House model (Beard, Propst, and Malamud, 1982), where patients use the organization's clubhouse and support system while living independently in various apartments. Another example of group living is the recent innovation of using HUD housing for schizophrenic patients. In this program patients live in groups of four per apartment, at low rent with some housekeeping supervision, and also participate in a community program or a day treatment center. Yet another example of group living, which is particularly successful, is called the transitional living center (TLC). Here patients live together, are treated together, and obtain jobs in the community. This system was developed in New York and exported to California. Now there are various TLCs in a number of states.

In my opinion the problem with all of these programs is that they group mentally ill schizophrenic patients together (Serban and Thomas, 1974). Such grouping causes each patient to have major interpersonal contact with other severely ill and severely disturbed psychiatric patients in a "sick"-oriented environment. Even when a patient gets intensive care to the extent of seeing a psychotherapist an hour a day or participating in groups or in a milieu program for two or three hours per day, this represents only a small portion of the 168 hours in each week. The major portion of the week is spent with other psychiatric patients.

Most psychiatric patients improve clinically not only as a result of interventions of medication or psychotherapy but also because they learn how to be normal people (Torrey, 1986). They do this by learning from others how to be normal and how to behave, and they model themselves after the people around them. One crucial function of psychiatric treatment is to offer severely ill, psychotic patients a role model. How do people respond to anxiety in ways other than going crazy? How do people respond to anger in a socially acceptable way? How do people respond to fear other than by cutting their wrists or overdosing on medication? How do people respond to loneliness and sexual frustration other than by being delusional, hallucinating, and acting inappropriately?

In considering the 168-hour week of the psychiatric patient, we must pay attention to the kinds of role model we provide. Those people from whom the psychiatric patient learns how to respond to feelings, behavior, and impulses should be healthy models. Because a schizophrenic patient has an impaired ability to respond to the crises of life (Zusman, 1967), he or she must learn to respond in a more adaptive way to the usual life problems. Social remission is achieved when a patient has learned to manage anxiety, to develop interpersonal skills, and to live as an "as if" person (Will, 1958). The basis of the "as if" personality of the schizophrenic patient is the role models available to the patient.

Mainstreaming

The mainstreaming program I have developed utilizes the normal support system available in the community. The support system is not a mental health system. It is clear that we can never provide all of the support that is necessary with mental health personnel. The resources are simply not available or feasible.

Community Support. We need to use the normal support system in the community, including the churches, fraternal organizations and societies, police, and neighborhood organizations as well as public services such as the library, the telephone, the adult education system, colleges and universities, political organizations, special-interest groups, and so forth. Then the mental health system needs only to provide assessment and frequent reassessment of the patient, rehabilitation planning, and a "catalyst" to help the patient use the normal resources. We can maximize mental health program effectiveness with minimal expenditure of mental health resources. We use the mental health system for diagnosis, treatment planning, crisis intervention, and catalytic activity, but the support is given by the normal society.

Here is an example of how community resources can be used as support for patients. Recently I discharged a patient to a western Nebraska town of 250 people. No mental health clinic was available within fifty miles. The only resources in town were two bars, a sheriff, four churches, and a Future Farmers of America club. For this particular patient, we worked up a discharge plan so that he could return to his parents' home in that town. Because there had been some problems with noncompliance with medication, the town sheriff, with whom the patient had had a good prior relationship, agreed to give the medication to the patient each day. Every morning the patient would go to the sheriff's office and take his medication while the sheriff looked on. A program was also worked out so the patient could visit the two bars in town, learning to drink Coke and nonalcoholic beer. This involved our contacting the owners of the bars, explaining the special problems of the patient, and persuading them to stock nonalcoholic beer. It allowed the patient to go to the bars and to play pool, which he enjoyed, without getting into difficulty by getting drunk, which he had done on several previous occasions. We also called the minister of his church, a charismatic group, and explained the problem to him. He agreed to see that the patient was picked up for the Saturday and Sunday services, for the Wednesday night meeting, and for the youth group. The minister also assured us that he would see to it that if the patient didn't come to service someone would visit him at home and express interest and concern. The patient was also encouraged to join the Future Farmers of America and to partici-pate in their program. During hospitalization he had received some training from the recreation therapy department, through their leisure assessment and education program, to prepare him for these activities in his hometown.

A visiting nurse saw the patient and his parents on their farm once every two weeks. The nurse inquired about how the program was going and reported back to the hospital clinician the patient's progress and problems. Each time the nurse reported in she received instructions for her next visit. Once a month the patient's parents brought him by car to the hospital outpatient department for supervision of medication and evaluation of his ability to function. An adjustment in the rehabilitation program was often made. The total expense of this program to the mental health system consisted of one hour per month with the therapist. All the rest of the supportive therapy was done by normal resources in the community.

Our mainstreaming program was developed to treat patients according to the rehabilitation model. Ordinary people, normal environment, and everyday life activity in the real world become the matrix and technique of the treatment program when severely impaired patients are placed in the community in their own living situation (usually living alone in an apartment). They can live a nearly normal life while using the community resources for support, with the special addition of the supporting services of a catalyst or rehabilitation therapist (Mendel, 1980).

Team Support. This special support is sometimes given by three, four, or five individuals who spend time with the patient, helping the patient to live his or her life. At the beginning, individual teams will spend an average of four to six hours per day with the patient for shopping, cooking, housekeeping, swimming at the Y, looking for a job, going to work or riding a bicycle, riding the bus, taking a driver's test, going to the doctor's office, going fishing, or whatever. In all of these activities, the patient associates only with normal people. There is no grouping of patients for the convenience of carrying out these activities. Similarly, patients are not encouraged to meet with each other but rather encouraged to meet and be with nonpatient populations. The patients learn to cope with loneliness, failure, disability, and fear of loss of impulse control in a normal setting, and they are given role-model support by the team members. In short, mainstreaming uses the normal environment of the community to provide support, role models, and guidance with the additional support of special team members (Mendel and Goren, 1981).

The team assigned to each patient consists of the catalysts and the clinician in charge of the team. The team's primary function is to provide immediate and helpful feedback and emotional support to the patient and to interact as role models with the patient. Team members are social preceptors who coach their patients. Schizophrenic patients have great difficulty with interpersonal relationships and frequently are very socially isolated. They often have spent much time in hospitals, board and care residences, and day-care programs. As a result of their illness and experiences, patients' social skills are clumsy and their social behavior is rather regressive and idiosyncratic. The team provides a customized social circle in which undesirable behaviors can be selectively ignored or pointed out as maladaptive and more mature behavior can be reinforced. The team gives realistic and immediate feedback whenever possible so patients can gain understanding of society's reaction to them. Patients who are unaware of the effect of their behavior on others often experience rejection without ever learning why. When a team can point out that such behavior (for example, seeming rudeness) causes an effect in others (injury, withdrawal, wish to retaliate) and the resulting response (rejection), the patient is informed and thus helped to change his or her behavior and to master the situation.

Patients can gain some measure of intellectual control over their environment so that they can then incorporate into the development of their personality functions that will enable them to be more effective (Bellet, Hussain, and Williams, 1983). Team members offer support, encouragement, and positive reinforcement for patients from the start of the mainstreaming program. After patients begin to expect and even trust that they will be supported, they may choose one or more members of the team as special friends. For example, as a patient develops dependency on the team, she might occasionally phone one of the team members when she is feeling uncertain, fearful, or lonely. The opportunity for a team member to provide extra support on such an occasion can be a rewarding experience for the team member and helpful to the patient.

Some patients offer team members special invitations for unscheduled activities, such as going to dinner or seeing a movie, and can be quite insistent that a team member accept. Team members must remain alert to patients' dependency needs and impaired self-esteem as well as their poorly developed interpersonal skills. At the same time team members must take care to maintain a good therapeutic relationship. A team member, in his or her involvement and enthusiasm, may believe that a personal friendship with a patient may be possible. An important reason for being cautious in this area is that the patient may not be ready to participate in this kind of relationship. He or she may feel threatened by the prospect of closeness or intimacy with another individual. Such a situation could result in the necessity of replacing the team member.

The team also provides role models for the development of a patient's coping skills and problem-solving abilities. As the patient engages in various activities, team members demonstrate appropriate dress and manner, proper entertainment of people in the community, and useful coping devices to manage the usual problems in living. Team members of the same sex as the patient provide an opportunity for the patient to strengthen his or her sexual identity by adopting the appropriate role.

On occasion I have assigned a team member to a patient for the purpose of developing and practicing dating behavior. This situation must be closely monitored so the patient does not feel pressure to go beyond his or her emotional means or participate in sexual behavior. The program continues toward the goals of independent living, participation in the social network, and competitive employment. Involvement with a team of socially competent and emotionally mature individuals allows the patient the opportunity to identify with these role models and to develop and practice the skills he needed to cope successfully in society.

Team members are chosen to represent the dominant culture to which the patient must adjust. Because they serve the purpose of providing a useful and constructive role model for the patient, they are expected to react to the patient's attitudes, values, and behavior much as the ordinary person in the community would. Bizarre and idiosyncratic behavior by the patient is experienced by team members as sharply different from the norm and can be pointed out to the patient as unacceptable. Team members give the patient feedback with sensitivity and kindness so that the patient's maladaptive behavior can be modified to a more acceptable conduct without the patient's feeling rejected.

I have found that the ideal team member is one who resembles the patient in terms of family background, level of vocational expectation, and social class values. This rehabilitation technician has achieved some degree of self-sufficiency and demonstrated the ability to support himself or herself emotionally, intellectually, and economically. In other words, the ideal team member is very similar to the person the patient was becoming when he became ill. Rather than limiting the search to people who exhibit these ideal characteristics, however, the team can be composed in such a way that these qualities are strongly represented among a number of the team members for each case. In most instances our team members have been chosen from student populations at local colleges or technical schools that offer programs for human services. Often a student who becomes a team member and catalyst for a patient is rewarded not only by the hourly pay but also by receiving school program credit and the experience of working with difficult and interesting patients under his or her supervision. We have occasionally used community volunteers as team members for this program. However, the limited time that community volunteers are interested in devoting to the program each week is often not enough for them to participate effectively in a team. Obviously, each team member, either student or volunteer, must be carefully evaluated for appropriateness for each case and for the program. This screening of team members is probably best done by the senior clinician who is developing the rehabilitation program for a particular patient within the context of mainstreaming.

The size of the team also depends on the needs of the individual patient. When the patient's program involves leaving the hospital and becoming established in the community, the patient may need massive support for some time. At first the support may have to come from four or five members so the patient is accompanied many hours per day for the first few days. In other cases much less support is needed, even at the beginning of the program. Usually, as the program continues and the patient adjusts well, decreasing support is necessary and fewer team members are needed, and they spend less time with the patient. The long-term goal of mainstreaming is that the patient can function almost by himself, with support from the normal community and only a very small amount of supporting therapy from the mental health profession.

Being a team member and providing catalytic services to

severely ill schizophrenic patients can be very taxing, particularly to an inexperienced person. Obviously, team members need a great deal of guidance, support, and supervision. Also because progress with patients is slow, sometimes discouragingly so, team members have a tendency to burn out. Patients express behavior that they have developed over many years of illness. This behavior has often been learned from other psychiatric patients in a hospital or in group living situations, or as a result of their families' accommodation to idiosyncratic and bizarre patterns. Maladaptive behavior that has not been modified by the usual social contacts requires patience, consistency, and firmness on the part of the team members. Therefore, the work of team members can be stressful, exhausting, discouraging, frustrating, and irritating. Frightened and severely impaired patients require sustained supporting relationships that are demanding and difficult to maintain. There is a tendency in the inexperienced therapist to slide from the desired posture of supportive care to one of parental scolding, correcting, and nagging, which is antitherapeutic. Team members must not react to frustrations and irritations in a spontaneous and thoughtless way but must always run their response through a "therapeutic filter." They must ask themselves if their response of confrontation is helpful in accomplishing a therapeutic goal with this patient at this particular time. On the other hand, team members must be allowed the opportunity to vent and share their negative feelings in some way in order to guard their own well-being and effectiveness as helpers. This support and burnout prevention can be provided if all team members meet on a regular basis with the team leader (clinician in charge of the case) for the purpose of discussing the difficulties in their work with a particular patient. By sharing and supporting each other, a team spirit develops; this in turn provides more support to the patient. An effective in-service training and continuing education program for team members is also helpful. The senior clinician should be available to team members at all times for telephone or in-person consultation in regard to the case.

Role of the Senior Clinician. The senior clinician who is the team leader begins mainstreaming by setting specific goals for the program and the patient, identifying specific needs and carefully documenting and identifying the patient's limitations. Goal setting is done on the basis of the Treatment Progress Scale described in Chapter Twelve. The limitations are carefully documented on the basis of cognitive levels, also described in Chapter Twelve. Then the team leader puts together a team of specifically appropriate members, identifying the level of support necessary and the intensity of social action desirable. The team leader develops a schedule and assigns the members (also called catalysts or rehabilitation technicians) for specific hours and specific activities. All members of the team meet every two weeks with the patient and the clinician leader. At these meetings goals are set and attainment of goals is assessed. Everyone reports on what has happened during the previous two weeks, and plans are made for the following two weeks. When a family is involved, family members also participate in the team meetings.

Summary

There are many approaches to providing supported living in the community for the schizophrenic patient. Each approach has advantages and disadvantages. The mainstreaming approach, which uses the rehabilitation model, offers a useful alternative to hospitalization and the usual outpatient services. This technique makes it possible for schizophrenic patients to use healthy people as role models and social perceptors. Even during periods of massive intervention mainstreaming is generally less expensive than hospitalization. Eventually, most patients are able to obtain much of their support from the usual resources in the community, which are generally free of charge.

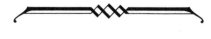

16

Crisis: Evaluation, Treatment, and Prevention

When the undulating course of schizophrenia moves to exacerbation and the exacerbation turns into crisis, the patient's life disorganizes and her behavior deteriorates. She may lose her job, be expelled from her family, get dismissed from school, be picked up by the police, or do serious damage to herself. At this point crisis intervention is necessary.

Chapter Two describes the index crisis, which is usually the second or third episode of exacerbation in the course of the illness in young patients. Later on in their lives other exacerbations lead to crises and require crisis intervention. Such interventions may or may not be carried out in the hospital. Crisis intervention in the hospital is described in Chapter Twelve, and crisis intervention within supportive-living programs in the community is described in Chapter Fifteen. Regardless where the crisis is treated, however, the intervention must begin with a crisis evaluation.

Crisis Evaluation

In any crisis evaluation a detailed history must be taken from the patient, from the family, from the police, and from all significant others who participated in and watched the crisis develop. This history needs to be taken immediately, when the

196

patient is first seen. The crisis evaluation must ask the clinician, not the patient, "Why now?" Why did the patient go into crisis today, July 12, rather than two days earlier or five days later? The answer to that question is never because the patient has schizophrenia. He has had schizophrenia for many years and will continue to have schizophrenia for the rest of his life. The answer is also never because the patient was experiencing an exacerbation. The patient will experience the undulating pattern of exacerbation and remission throughout much of his younger life and to some extent even to his older age. "Why now?" must be answered by the clinician when he or she finishes the crisis evaluation. The easiest way to accomplish this is to take a very detailed history, almost hour by hour for the previous forty-eight to seventy-two hours. From that information it will become clear to the clinician that something has changed in the world around the patient, something has dropped out of the supporting network, something has gone awry in the homeostasis of the rehabilitation program.

A sample crisis evaluation of a patient of mine will illustrate this point. John was thirty-six years old and had been hospitalized several times during the past decade. His last hospitalization was approximately two years prior to this crisis. He was brought by the police to the emergency room of our hospital. He appeared grossly psychotic and delusional and was apparently hallucinating. He had been seen for his regular aftercare appointment two weeks earlier and was doing well. He had been maintained on an appropriate dose of neuroleptics and had taken his medication regularly. What had happened in the previous seventy-two hours? The detailed history revealed that John had continued living in a small apartment complex typical of the 1930s construction in the Los Angeles area. Several bungalows were situated around a central court. Each bungalow consisted of a bedroom, small living room, kitchen, bathroom, and front porch. John lived in the last one in this U-shaped series of buildings. In order to leave the court, he had to walk past four bungalows plus the first bungalow at the street entrance to the property where the manager lived.

Each morning John would get up, have a cup of coffee, and walk out. Usually the manager's door would be open, and she would shout out through the screen door, "Good morning, Mr.

Seller, have a good day.'' He would then walk a block to catch the bus to go to work in a local factory, where he had been employed for the past two years. His work record had been satisfactory and he seemed to have gotten along quite well. Typically, when John finished work at four o'clock, he would catch the bus back to his neighborhood. He would get out one stop before his house and do his grocery shopping at the local Safeway store. Then he would walk home, carrying a brown paper bag with groceries and a newspaper. On his way into the bungalow complex the manager, who was an elderly, rotund, friendly lady, would greet him with appropriate remarks and he would go to his bungalow, where he would fix his dinner. Then later he would watch television and go to bed. Once a week he would go to a meeting of a local stamp collectors' club, where he participated peripherally. Once every two weeks John would come to the aftercare facility at the hospital for his medication and supportive care interview. Often on Sundays, he would see his brother or his mother for dinner and a short visit.

During the last few days before this crisis, John had continued with his routine but suddenly noticed that the manager's door was locked shut, and no one greeted him on the way in or out of the bungalow complex. When he recognized the absence of the social contact, he got up his courage in the afternoon and knocked at the door. Instead of a friendly, grandmotherly manager, a ''very large, very black man'' opened the door and, according to John, yelled at him, ''What do you want?'' After this episode, John returned to his room, became increasingly confused, and by the next morning was actively delusional. He left his home but didn't go to work. Next he was apprehended by the police for shouting and yelling at passing cars in downtown Los Angeles. When our social worker went to the complex where John lived and visited the manager, she discovered that he was of ordinary size and not black at all but rather an olive-skinned individual who was friendly and expressed concern about John. The manager told the social worker that he had taken over the job from the previous manager because she had retired and moved to Florida to be with her grandchildren.

It is obvious from this clinical vignette that John had obtained significant support from the daily recognition by the manager. Neither he nor we, his clinical team, were aware that this was a significant part of his support system prior to its failure. When it suddenly disappeared, he was unable to deal with his loss. This is typical of the kind of information we get in a carefully conducted crisis evaluation. This information becomes important in restructuring the patient's rehabilitation program. We often learn that besides the formal support system we set up, which consists of aftercare appointments, social work visits, membership in groups or contact with assigned catalysts, the patient also has an informal support system of which he or she is often not even aware. Patients develop informal systems such as John did quite on their own. I have known patients who have used telephone operators, time and temperature services, dial-a-prayer or joke-for-the-day services, or radio talk shows as such informal support systems.

Another very significant part of the crisis evaluation is a detailed history of the signs and symptoms that develop as the patient disorganizes into crisis. We have learned over the years that although the sequence of signs and symptoms is not consistent for the illness of schizophrenia, it tends to be entirely consistent for the individual patient. Throughout the lifetime of the individual, as the patient disorganizes, he or she tends to develop the same signs and symptoms in the same sequence. That information becomes a very important part of crisis prevention. The patient can learn to monitor his or her own behavior and take appropriate steps to prevent a crisis.

Crisis Treatment

Crisis treatment consists, first of all, of rescue. The patient is rescued from a situation either by hospitalization or by change of support or by acts of social intervention. The rescue is not only important in terms of relieving the patient's distress and pain but also as the start of the therapeutic alliance or the re-cementing of it. The effective rescue becomes the basis of future treatment planning and rehabilitation. Once the crisis evaluation has been completed and rescue has been accomplished, a long-term treatment program begins or begins anew. As with all other treatments, the least that does the job is the best. Prevention of the next crisis begins at the time the patient is rescued from the current crisis and the evaluation and treatment are conducted.

Crisis Prevention

An essential part of crisis prevention is to develop, document, and instruct the patient in his or her unique pattern of disorganization. The signs and symptoms usually fall into eight major categories.

1. *Change in eating pattern.* This may occur in either direction. The patient who has always eaten adequately suddenly stops eating or vice versa. A patient who has always had problems eating sudden eats voraciously. In some patients we see very specific food cravings. Suddenly they begin eating nothing but sweets when previously they didn't care for them. Sometimes patients go on extensive fasts in response to delusions or hallucinations.

2. *Change in sleep pattern.* This may occur in all directions. A patient who has always easily gone to sleep cannot get to sleep; another patient who always awakened with the alarm suddenly starts waking up in the middle of the night. A patient who has always gotten along well on eight to ten hours of sleep needs twelve or fourteen hours; another patient who has always needed six hours now only requires three hours of sleep.

3. *Change in attention span.* This may occur in either direction. The individual who has never been able to sit down to read a magazine suddenly is able to do so. Another individual who has always had patience and pleasure from sitting down and reading a book cannot even attend to the newspaper.

4. *Interpersonal change.* This may be noted by the patient and those around him or her. An individual who has always been friendly becomes unfriendly and irritable. An individual who has always been difficult interpersonally, somewhat paranoid and irritable, suddenly becomes very friendly and outgoing.

5. *Change in dream patterns.* This, too, may occur in either

direction. A patient who never remembers dreams suddenly starts remembering them, or vice versa. A patient who has always had pleasant dreams starts having nightmares, or vice versa.

6. *Repressed material returns.* Usually as the patient goes into remission from her crisis, the specific content of her delusional system will be forgotten. She is amnesic for the delusions. Often a sign of disorganization is the return of the amnesic material. Suddenly the patient remembers that the last time she "went crazy," she thought she was Cleopatra.

7. *Specific physiologic change.* This may affect any system. Some patients develop gastrointestinal symptoms, others respiratory or dermatological symptoms. Some female patients develop specific changes in their menstrual cycle, either stopping menses or suddenly flowing excessively and irregularly. I have had one patient who had very specific pain symptoms. Each time he experienced a crisis, he would have severe pain in his right leg, which was thoroughly studied neurologically and orthopedically, for which there was no basis other than his psychological condition.

8. *Change in medication, alcohol, or other drug intake.* This change may also occur in either direction.

In our facility information is carefully documented on a card before each patient is discharged from the hospital or other crisis treatment (see Exhibit 6). Patients take this "pink card" home with them; it spells out in detail what their particular pattern and sequence of disorganization is. The card also gives patients instructions on what to do when the signs and symptoms of crisis appear. In the hospital, as part of discharge planning, patients are trained not only in how and when to take their medication but also how frequently to check the pink card. Most of our patients are asked to check their card once a week at a specific time to see if any of the signs or symptoms are noticeable to them and if so, what to do about them. Patients who live with their families are also asked to have family members check the card on a regular basis to see if they have noticed any change. The purpose of the card is to get

**Exhibit 6. Sample Discharge Card Given Each Patient
After Crisis Evaluation Has Been Completed.**

Hastings Regional Center
Hastings, Nebraska
(Telephone: 402-463-2471)

Signs to Watch out for!

Below is a list of signs that mean you need help:

1. _____

2. _____

3. _____

4. _____

5. _____

If one or more of these things are happening to you, *CALL
YOUR THERAPIST*. Check at least one time each week.

(Phone: _____)

Your name: _____

Your therapist's name: _____

patients into crisis intervention early so that the situation does not
deteriorate to the point of requiring their removal from the social
rehabilitation program.

When patients are discharged from the hospital or from crisis
treatment, their rehabilitation program is readjusted so that the
program is appropriate for the level of function that the patients are
able to sustain at that time. This is not necessarily the same level
they had prior to their last crisis. The information for designing the
rehabilitation program is obtained from the clinical assessment,
which includes the TPS score, cognitive level score, and clinical
observation (see Chapter Twelve).

Summary

Crisis evaluation, treatment, and prevention are an important part of schizophrenia treatment throughout the life of the patient. The better this aspect of treatment is carried out, the less likely the patient is to have future crises and the better his or her life will be in the community.

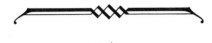

17

The Case of Amelia East

Amelia was born in 1941, the second child of an upper-middle-class family in Massachusetts. I first saw her in 1960 when she was nineteen years old. At that time she suffered from acute psychosis and was hospitalized with delusions, auditory hallucinations, and paranoid ideation. It was her first frank psychiatric illness. My diagnosis was schizophrenia.

Background

Amelia's father was the wealthy owner of a furniture store in Massachusetts. He was a jovial man somewhat distant from his family but very good as a salesman and marketer. He was a member of many organizations, but he participated in them primarily to market his products. Amelia's mother is a quiet, withdrawn, somewhat mousy woman who always stood in the background. Amelia has one older brother who is four years her senior and seems to be suffering from intermittent depression. He graduated from law school and is a practicing attorney, and he is not married. Amelia's family history revealed two maternal aunts who had been diagnosed as having schizophrenia, and her father had a brother who committed suicide.

Early History

Amelia was different from the other child in her family. Her mother remembered her early eating problems and difficulty with most foods. There were lots of visits to the pediatrician. Amelia was constantly on special diets for her eating problems. Even as a four-year-old she was described as "strange and different" in her preschool experience. She always had a very artistic tendency. She attended private schools and eventually a private boarding high school for girls. She was a *B* student, but in her junior year she developed mononucleosis and was out of school for approximately three months. After she returned she was more withdrawn and strange, according to the school authorities. However, she continued to do *B* work. She took on the role of being an artist, and much of her introverted and socially uncomfortable behavior was explained away on that basis. Although Amelia contributed cartoons, drawings, and paintings to various school activities, she made very little attempt to interact with others. She started writing poetry and sent one poem home to her parents.

Take what you want and let me go.
I only ask of you, be quick, be quick!
Do not explore this frozen continent.

The patient remained very slim throughout her high school career and had delayed menses. Eventually, she was given a series of injections that started an irregular pattern of menstrual periods when she was about seventeen years old.

At eighteen, Amelia graduated from the private high school and decided to go to the University of Wisconsin. At that time Wisconsin was popular with New York Jewish liberals. This was a rather unusual choice because her home state was on the East Coast and her family had attended private eastern universities. Her father was a very conservative Protestant, who thought that the Roosevelt presidency was the beginning of the end of the American republic. Quite obviously, her family background did not fit in with her university choice. Yet the family agreed that she could go to Wisconsin.

The Course of the Illness

In the fall of 1960, at age nineteen, Amelia entered the University of Wisconsin. She enrolled as an art major and intended to develop a career in fine arts. She spent much of the time by herself during her initial months at college and attended few classes, not even her much-cherished art classes. She had many appointments at the student health service for a variety of somatic complaints, most of which centered around her menstrual difficulty. Toward the end of her first semester she began writing strange letters home. Here are some examples.

I am like a zombie living behind a glass wall. I can see all that goes on in the world, but I can't touch it. I can't reach it. I can't be in contact with it. I am outside. They are inside and when I get inside they aren't there. There is nothing there, absolutely nothing. I am living in a make-believe world, and I fear I am being asked to pretend even more. It is a real fantasy. It has all the horrors of the fantastic. Should I find myself by giving myself up? Is it instead that myself must change, must become "lovely"?

It is an appearance that I can only maintain at times, that I am being asked not only to adopt but to replace myself with. I am different, can't fit into another's pattern. Most people seem to fit into a sort of group pattern, but mine is the absolute of such, it seems. I am not this or that, so easily classified as others wish me to be, and usually it is their classification they wish me to fit into. They call this "caring," "loving" me.

There is something wrong with me. I don't seem to feel about my family like others do. I notice when I talk about my parents, I talk about them like neighbors talk about their cars. They're really quite dispensable.

And at another time Amelia wrote:

To me the world is peopled rather than populated. What I mean by peopled is that it is filled with people. Much like others' houses are furnished with furniture. It is all the same to me.

When Amelia's worried parents came to see her, they found her sitting in her room, apparently not having eaten anything for several days and staring off into space. They took her to the student health service, which referred her to me for psychiatric evaluation. At this time I saw her for the first visit and, upon examining her mental status, made the following observations.

Amelia is a nineteen-year-old confused young lady who is very thin and gaunt looking. She cannot present a clear complaint. Her history shows no evidence of prior mental illness. There is a significant history of major changes in her life course since high school. She has no significant medical history other than her long history of allergies and her menstrual irregularity. She apparently has smoked marijuana on a couple of occasions but otherwise has no drug or alcohol history. The family history demonstrates genetic predisposition to schizophrenia and depression. Her general appearance is one of confusion, her behavior is cooperative, and her attitude shows mostly fright. Her thought processes demonstrate concreteness and loose association. Her mood is one of moderate depression and confusion. The thought content shows the presence of delusion, including the idea that others are following her and giving her signals on how to behave. It is not clear how the signals are transmitted, but it is not through the usual means of verbal and nonverbal communication. She is preoccupied with the question of who she is and what the meaning of life is. Her sensorium is clear; her estimated level of intellectual function is above normal. Memory is intact for recent, remote, and immediate events, and orientation is precise for time, place, person, and current news. There are illusions and possibly auditory hallucinations. She frequently hears her name called, but when she turns around no one is there. At times she thinks she heard an unknown voice asking her what she was all about. The patient shows minimal insight into her present predicament except that she knows something is wrong and her judgment is markedly impaired.

My diagnosis at that time was that Amelia was suffering from schizophrenia, with a history of at least four years' duration. This episode was the first frank psychotic episode.

Amelia seemed to be somewhat catatonic at the time of our first meeting, and I hospitalized her for a total of eighteen days. Neuroleptic medication (Thorazine) was initiated. Her signs and symptoms of disorganization were tabulated and found to be (1) loss of energy, (2) loss of appetite, (3) loss of ability to function in her scheduled activities, and (4) increasing confusion.

After her first psychiatric episode and the eighteen days of hospitalization Amelia was discharged back to the university to continue her schooling and to have outpatient supportive care. She was seen twice a week for therapy appointments and given low doses of neuroleptic (Thorazine, 100 mg b.i.d.). She did quite well for the next six months, continuing to live in the college dormitory and doing adequate work in school. In therapy she would talk a great deal about her misery and often communicated it in poetry.

I don't know what makes me tick
I don't know what makes me sick
This dying feeling is what I dread
And I keep wishing I were dead

She began developing some somatic symptoms focused primarily around her reproductive system, including cessation of menses, concern about whether she could ever become pregnant, and concern about whether she could finish college. During the summer vacation she went home to her parents in Massachusetts but found it difficult to relate to them. She also saw a local psychiatrist, who added anxiolytic medications to her neuroleptic regimen. In the fall she returned to the university and her supportive psychotherapy continued. At that time she wrote the following:

Who am I?
I shift with every change in wind to sometimes cool, some-
    times kind
Sometimes young, sometimes old
Sometimes warm, sometimes cold
Though I dig deep in every you
Trying to pull out what is true
For all of us, it is you I see
I can't find me.

Approximately one month after school started, Amelia
became increasingly confused, could no longer go to meals in the
cafeteria, and felt tearfully isolated. She was rehospitalized for a
period of seven days, during which her medications were slightly
increased and a new posthospitalization plan was drawn up. She
was not to continue living in the dorm but rather to transfer to
another school, a smaller college with only 600 students on campus,
and she was to live in her own apartment just off campus. At the
time of discharge her cognitive level was unimpaired and she was
maintained on neuroleptic medication alone. During the next few
months she seemed to get along quite well in school. She continued
taking her medication but had great difficulty living alone. Many
times she would call me in the middle of the night wanting to talk.
She was frightened of being alone and yet not able to be with
anyone. She seemed comfortable on the telephone, when there was
considerable distance between her and me. At that time she wrote
the following poem:

She sang softly and sobbed silently, so alone, so alone.
Who cares or wants her.
Shriveled and torn, so alone, wet, cold, like a smelly corpse.
So alone. Shouting for help. No one can hear.
No one can help.
People are fun but the upkeep is awful—you have to care
    about them.

And then:

Right and wrong
Blame and guilt
The flow of love
Is choked by silt

With considerable support, frequent night phone calls, and occasional outpatient supportive psychotherapy appointments, Amelia managed to get through that school year with satisfactory grades. At the end of the school year she decided to transfer to a large public univeristy on the West Coast because she would be near her aunt and uncle and her therapist. Again she spent the summer at home, but things did not go well. She felt that the family was putting considerable pressure on her to finish school, get married and have children, and get on with her life. During the summer she sent this poem to me:

Our cat has kittens
The trees are in leaf
But all I produce
Is more grief.

On the West Coast she changed much of her life-style. She seemed to be able to handle the large university and the large classes and began some normal dating. Although her poems in the last couple of years had much depressive content, she did not appear clinically depressed. She had a number of unfortunate experiences that seemed like sexual exploitation to me. She would meet someone, go out with him, sleep with him, and then discharge him. In many ways, however, this suited her because she could not really maintain long-term close relationships. Yet she had proven to herself that she could be sexually active, or "grown up" in that way. Still, something about the way she handled these relationships felt very uncomfortable to her. She continued to take her neuroleptic medication on a regular basis and continued twice-a-week outpatient supportive psychotherapy.

Then she accidently became pregnant. She could not tell her parents and did not want to involve the man because she really didn't like him. We had many hours of discussion about this. I expressed a consistent opposition to an abortion, not on the basis of my personal opinion but for therapeutic reasons. Her parents wanted a grandchild and I think could have accepted the situation. The patient was searching for self-esteem support and the meaning to life. She had many doubts about herself as an adult woman and a sexual person. I felt the baby could have helped in all of these areas. However, Amelia suddenly decided to go to Tijuana to have an illegal abortion. After the abortion she came back with a high fever and was in a toxic and delirious state. She continued to insist that her parents not be notified.

I hospitalized her at a general hospital, where she was treated for septicemia. She became extremely depressed and expressed many suicidal ideas. As an emergency measure to control the severe and immediate risk of suicide, I gave her three electroconvulsive treatments, which resulted in one week of confusion and immediate termination of the depression and suicidal risk.

She was discharged from the hospital after two weeks and returned to school. She spent much time in supportive psychotherapy, working through her guilt about the abortion. She became obsessed with the fear that she could never have children as a punishment by God. She wrote the following poem.

It is my counterpart
Yet the heart beats
Despite defeat
Sometimes races, sometimes slows
But it goes
This plodding victory is too much to bear.

Amelia graduated from college and enrolled in a graduate course at the local art institute. She became a very good artist and began associating with artist groups around town. Much of her unusual behavior, thinking, and feeling was, again, attributed to her status as an artist. She complained a great deal about her social isolation during the therapy hours. At that time a mainstreaming program (see Chapter Fifteen) was initiated for her. Because she was able to do her work at the art school and had certainly been able to manage her own apartment and finances, she needed no help in those areas. However, her social life was a constant pain to her. The mainstreaming program was designed to help her normalize her social life. Two "catalysts" were assigned to her, one male and one female. Each one spent an evening a week with her, taking her to various functions, accompanying her as a girlfriend or as a "date," depending on the catalyst's gender. Amelia went to concerts, the theater, folk dance clubs, discos, political meetings, and artist meetings with her two companions. They were at first very active in getting her into groups and keeping her there. Slowly they began to withdraw by standing in the background.

In one political group that was concerned with world overpopulation, Amelia met her future husband, a young physician. At first she would only see him at club meetings. Subsequently, he began asking her and her girlfriend (catalyst) for coffee, and then he began dating Amelia. She had originally introduced her catalyst as a cousin and even took her along a few times on the dates. Thereafter Amelia began dating regularly, and the catalyst was dropped from her program. Amelia spent much of her time in supportive therapy getting instructions on how to behave vis-à-vis her young physician friend and how to manage the relationship. She found him comfortable to be with and enjoyed the fact that he was rather domineering and provided highly structured time for her. She also enjoyed the fact that he did not make any sexual demands on her. After approximately two years of dating he asked her to marry him. He came from a totally different culture, being Jewish and a first-generation American, but this posed no particular problem to her. She even managed his difficult parents, who were shocked that she was not Jewish. Her future husband knew that she had some "neurotic" tendencies but did not believe that she was seriously mentally ill.

Amelia brought the man to see me so that I could explain her illness to him. I explained the natural history of schizophrenia and outlined her life-long requirement for supportive care. After that meeting the young physician continued to want to marry her. Amelia also wanted to marry him, and we spent much time in her subsequent therapy hours looking at the probable difficulties she would have in a close interpersonal relationship. She felt her future husband would not demand this, and she turned out to be right. The two were married in a traditional Jewish ceremony in which there were lots of tensions because of the differences in the cultures of the two families. I attended the wedding. Amelia and her husband went on a honeymoon and after approximately six weeks returned with Amelia in a state of near collapse. When I saw her, she appeared overtly psychotic, suffering from delusions and hallucinations. I hospitalized her for approximately one week and gave intensive support and increased neuroleptics. She returned home, and she and her husband took up housekeeping. Within three months it was obvious that she was pregnant. Both she and her husband were looking forward to the addition to the family. I now saw her approximately once a month for supportive psycho-therapy. I was concerned about the medications and discontinued them during the pregnancy.

The delivery of Amelia's first child, a daughter, was normal, and the child appeared to be normal. In the immediate postpartum period Amelia became severely depressed, although she did not develop psychotic symptoms. I again treated her with supportive care and reintroduced the medication that had been terminated during her pregnancy. This time I also placed her on appropriate doses of an antidepressant. After approximately three months the depression lifted and the patient was able to provide adequate care for her daughter. During the first three months she had some help at home; namely, one of the catalysts had spent time helping Amelia take care of the child, functioning much like a nursemaid. At the same time the catalyst was able to offer support to Amelia and teach her how to take care of her child. Amelia was particularly clumsy in the ordinary procedures of feeding and diapering but was able to learn with constant support, instruction, and reinforcement. Her husband was fairly unaware of her disabilities during this time because he was so busy, having joined a group practice.

When the baby was one year old, Amelia again became pregnant, much to the joy of her husband but much to her own horror. She felt totally overwhelmed by the idea of taking care of two children. During the second trimester of this pregnancy Amelia became acutely psychotic though not depressed. I had discontinued the neuroleptic medication during pregnancy. She was again hospitalized, this time for about a week, during which she got lots of rest and I reintroduced the medication. Amelia returned home, and in a conference between the husband, the patient, and me we again discussed Amelia's diagnosis. I pointed out to her husband that Amelia would need a great deal of attention during the next few years but that she could function as a mother and perhaps as an artist with much support from him. The second delivery was also normal, and the couple had another healthy girl. There was no depression following this delivery, and the patient seemed to be getting along quite well.

During the next few years Amelia had an improved relationship with her mother, who had come out to help with the second baby and spent considerable time on the West Coast; in part she wanted to help and in part she wanted to get away from Amelia's father, who was getting increasingly difficult with age. The mother was able to offer considerable support to Amelia, and Amelia seemed to feel comfortable enough to let her mother get close to her. The patient continued in outpatient supportive therapy, and her mother would join her in one of the weekly appointments about once every month. There were relatively few crises. Although a definite undulating pattern could be observed in her condition, she was able to get along without medication after 1975.

In 1980, when Amelia was thirty-nine and her children were thirteen and fifteen, she had her first solo art exhibition. The show met with considerable critical acclaim, including a very favorable article in the *Los Angeles Times,* and she sold several of her paintings. This thoroughly impressed her husband, who was very supportive of her artistic activity after that. The relationship between husband and wife was somewhat formal, never warm, but highly structured. This seemed to suit the patient particularly well. Her husband offered considerable leadership in the relationship and tended to treat Amelia like a junior partner in the family. He was concerned and paternal, giving directions and yet also giving support and love.

Amelia continued to be seen on a once-a-month basis in outpatient supportive psychotherapy. In 1981, shortly after her successful exhibition, she had another acute exacerbation of her illness leading to crisis. This time her psychotic symptoms were completely out of hand, to the point that she was picked up by the police and brought to the local county hospital. Here I saw her in the emergency room and admitted her to a local private psychiatric hospital for fourteen days of hospitalization. During that hospital-ization, neuroleptic medication was increased and proved effective in suppressing the delusions and hallucinations.

Amelia returned home and continued to function. She managed the adolescence of her two children particularly well, seeming to rise to the usual adolescent crises as they appeared. Her husband seemed happy in the relationship. Amelia continued to have outpatient supportive psychotherapy on a once-a-month basis and continued on a low dosage of neuroleptics.

Soon after this stable state began, I retired from active practice in order to sail around the world. The patient stayed in touch with me via radio/telephone contact to my boat. The conversations were necessarily brief, but they did continue. In 1986, when I returned to the United States and settled in Nebraska, Amelia came to visit me for several supporting interviews. After that our contact was again by telephone.

At the time of this writing, Amelia is forty-seven, and her children are twenty-one and twenty-three. Both attend a private eastern university. Her husband continues as a hardworking cardiologist, and their relationship seems to be stable. Amelia's father died and her mother has become very old. Amelia and her mother have a strained relationship now, in part because the elderly woman has chosen to live with her bachelor son in Boston. Amelia is active in two art galleries and continues to paint with much pleasure and considerable artistic success. She is very proud of the fact that one of her paintings has been bought by the Whitney Museum in New York for its permanent collection. Amelia continues to call me every two or three months for supportive therapy. She has not taken any medication for several years and seems to be getting along quite well without it. She has had no major psychotic symptoms for the past eight years, although she continues to have some fluctuations of her state. She reports that two or three days each month, she feels poorly, stating that she is not depressed but just out of sorts. Her husband believes that she is cured. Her children believe that their mother is different but loveable, and they appreciate the fact that she is a very fine artist. She herself says, "I still have the schizococcus, but it is dormant."

Postscript

It has been one hundred years since Emil Kraepelin grouped a number of disorders under the general heading of dementia praecox. It has been eighty years since Eugen Bleuler named that same disease schizophrenia. Three generations of physicians have toiled in the workplace of schizophrenia since then. Three generations of patients have been born with schizophrenia and lived and suffered with the illness. Today, at the beginning of the last decade of the twentieth century, *what do we know about schizophrenia?*

We know for sure that schizophrenia is an illness that has a describable course. We know that it has a genetically transmitted etiology (Ödegaard, 1972; Essen-Möller, 1977). We also know that it has predictable disabilities and that when all of the signs and symptoms of thousands of cases are subjected to cluster analysis, three nuclear defects appear: (1) inadequate anxiety management, (2) clumsy and failing interpersonal relationships, and (3) failure of historicity. We know, too, that the onset of the illness occurs in the teens and that the younger patient has a much stormier course than the older patient. As the patient ages, the illness becomes less of a problem; it is as though the illness ameliorates. We know that the course of illness is one of undulation between exacerbation and remission. We also know that the number of exacerbations per year is age-related. The younger patient has more exacerbations per year

217

than the older patient. We know that good treatment and rehabilitation programs do not prevent the undulation between remission and exacerbation, but they do prevent the exacerbation from becoming a crisis with social, personal, and physiological ramifications. And we know that if we treat the patient with a well-planned and well-managed rehabilitation program, the patient can live a life of considerable effectiveness, comfort, and satisfaction in spite of the illness. These are the things we know for sure.

We suspect that unknown factors are involved in precipitating the illness in individuals who are genetically at risk. A great deal of speculation and a small amount of research have attempted to identify these factors (Mednick, 1970) but have not yet yielded the answers.

We do not know how to cure or prevent schizophrenia. During the forty years I have been working in the field, there have been a variety of claims of cures by some serious clinicians and by many charlatans. These claims have proposed vitamin, medication (magic bullet), psychotherapy, social engineering, spontaneous remission, and physical therapy (hemodialysis—Wagemaker and Cade, 1977—pulling of teeth, psychosurgery, exercise) cures. When proposed by serious scientists, I have investigated each one of these by personally visiting the site, examining the patient supposedly cured, and interviewing therapists. Invariably the results of my investigation have been the same all over the world. Either the patient who was "cured" had been misdiagnosed, or the patient was experiencing a remission and the therapist had not picked up the persistence of the illness in his or her clinical examination. In other words, the therapist had simply mistaken clinical improvement for cure. We do not know how to cure schizophrenia. And we certainly do not know how to prevent it. Perhaps genetic engineering offers some hope for the near future.

In this volume I have presented three cases in some detail. Two of these cases were separated from the third by fifty years of time. The reader must judge what answers the comparison of these cases yields. Each case represents the most thoughtful and best treatment available at the time. The patients come from the same socioeconomic class and the same general culture even though they lived in different countries. This allows the reader to make a comparison that is difficult to find elsewhere. All too often bad treatment of one era or one theoretical framework is compared with good treatment in another. To make a fair comparison we must take the best of each era or each theoretical model and compare it with the best of another. There have always been good hospitals and bad hospitals, psychotherapeutic therapists and psychonoxious therapists.

This book delivers the clinical knowledge about schizophrenia to the next generation of clinicians and investigators. It is my fervent hope that my students and sons will take this knowledge and move on to find a cure for this disease. Perhaps forty years from now one of them will rewrite this book and be able to say that we know for sure how to cure the disease and even how to prevent it. I believe the answer lies in the synapse and at the cell membrane.

Good-bye, good fortune, love, and support to the many patients who have taught me so much and to my young colleagues who need to do so much.

References

Allen, C. K. "Activity: Occupational Therapy's Treatment Method." *The American Journal of Occupational Therapy*, 1987, 563–575.

Allen, C. K. "Occupational Therapy: Functional Assessment of the Severity of Mental Disorders." *Hospital and Community Psychiatry*, 1988, *39* (2), 140–142.

Allen, C. K., and Allen, R. E. "Cognitive Disabilities: Measuring the Social Consequences of Mental Disorders." *Journal of Clinical Psychiatry*, 1987, *48* (5), 185–190.

American Psychiatric Association Task Force on Laboratory Tests in Psychiatry. "Tricyclic Antidepressants—Blood Level Measurements and Clinical Outcome." *American Journal of Psychiatry*, 1985, *142*, 155–162.

Andrews, S., Vaughn, K., Harvey, R., and Andrews, G. "A Survey of Practising Psychiatrists' Views on the Treatment of Schizophrenia." *British Journal of Psychiatry*, 1986, *149*, 357–364.

Anscombe, R. "The Disorder of Consciousness in Schizophrenia." *Schizophrenia Bulletin*, 1987, *13* (2), 241–260.

Aubree, J. C., and Lader, M. H. "High and Very High Dosage Antipsychotics: A Critical Review." *Journal of Clinical Psychiatry*, 1980, *45*, 341–349.

Baldessarini, R. J., Cohen, B. M., and Teicher, M. H. "Significance of Neuroleptic Dose and Plasma Level in the Pharmacological Treatment of Psychosis." *Archives of General Psychiatry*, 1988, *45*, 79-91.

Balint, M. *The Doctor, His Patient, and the Illness.* New York: International Universities Press, 1957.

Beard, J. H., Propst, R., and Malamud, T. J. "The Fountain House Model of Psychiatric Rehabilitation." *Psychosocial Rehabilitation Journal*, 1982, *5* (1), 47-53.

Beck, J. C. "Social Influences on the Prognosis of Schizophrenia." *Schizophrenia Bulletin*, 1978, *4* (1), 86-101.

Bellet, W., Hussain, G., and Williams, M. A. "A Resocialization Group for the Socially Impaired Psychiatric Outpatient." *Vanderbilt Psychological and Counseling Center*, 1983, *7* (1), 41-46.

Bessell, H., and Mazzanti, V. "Diagnosis of Ambulatory Schizophrenia: A Case Study." *Psychiatric Quarterly*, 1959, *33*, 429-436.

Binswanger, L. "Symptoms und Zeit" [Symptoms and time]. *Schweizerische Medizinische Wochenschrift*, 1951, *81*, 510-512.

Binswanger, L. "Existential Analysis, Psychiatry, Schizophrenia." *Journal of Existential Psychiatry*, 1960, *1*, 157-165.

Black, J. L., Richelson, E., and Richardson, J. W. "Antipsychotic Agents: A Clinical Update." *Mayo Clinic Procedures*, 1985, *60*, 777-789.

Bleuler, E. *Dementia Praecox* or *The Group of Schizophrenias.* (J. Zinkin, trans.) New York: International Universities Press, 1950.

Bleuler, M. "A 23-Year Longitudinal Study of 208 Schizophrenics and Impressions in Regard to the Nature of Schizophrenia." In D. Rosenthal and S. S. Kety (eds.), *The Transmission of Schizophrenia.* Oxford: Pergamon Press, 1968.

Bleuler, M. "The Long-Term Course of the Schizophrenic Psychoses." *Psychological Medicine*, 1974, *4*, 244-254.

Bleuler, M. *Schizophrenic Disorders: Long-Term Patient and Family Studies.* (S. M. Clemens, trans.) New Haven, Conn.: Yale University Press, 1978.

Böök, J. A. "A Genetic and Neuropsychiatric Investigation of a North Swedish Population." *Acta Genetics*, 1953, *4*, 1-100.

Böök, J. A., Wetterberg, L., and Modrzewska, K. "Schizophrenia in a North Swedish Geographical Isolate, 1900-1977. Epidemiology, Genetics, and Biochemistry." *Clinical Genetics*, 1978, *14*, 373–394.

Bridge, T. P., Cannon, H. E., and Wyatt, R. J. "Burned-out Schizophrenia: Evidence for Age Effects on Schizophrenic Symptomology." *Journal of Gerontology*, 1978, *33* (6), 835–839.

Buckley, P. "Supportive Psychotherapy. A Neglected Treatment." *Psychiatric Annals*, 1986, *16* (9), 515–521.

Burton, A., Lopez-Ibor, J., and Mendel, W. "A Phenomenological Theory of Schizophrenia." In W. Mendel (ed.), *Schizophrenia as a Life Style*. New York: Springer, 1974, 106–155.

Cancro, R. "Increased Diagnostic Reliability in Schizophrenia: Some Values and Limitations." *International Journal of Psychiatry*, 1973, *11*, 53–57.

Caplan, G. *In Crisis Intervention*. (H. Parad, ed.) New York: Family Service, 1965.

Carpenter, W. "Early, Targeted Pharmacotherapeutic Intervention in Schizophrenia." *Journal of Clinical Psychiatry*, 1986, *47* (Suppl.), 23–29.

Carpenter, W., Strauss, J., and Muleh, S. "Are There Pathognomanic Symptoms in Schizophrenia?" *Archives of General Psychiatry*, 1973, *28*, 847–852.

Chapman, L., and Chapman, J. "Psychosis Proneness." In M. Alport (ed.), *Controversies in Schizophrenia*. New York: Guilford Press, 1985.

Chapman, L., and Chapman, J. "The Search for Symptoms Predictive of Schizophrenia." *Schizophrenia Bulletin*, 1987, *13* (3), 497–504.

Chase, L., and Silverman, S. "Prognostic Criteria in Schizophrenia." *American Journal of Psychiatry*, 1941, *98*, 360–368.

Ciompi, L. "The Natural History of Schizophrenia in the Long Term." *British Journal of Psychiatry*, 1980, *136*, 413–420.

Cohen, R. "The Hospital as a Therapeutic Instrument." *Psychiatry*, 1958, *21*, 29–35.

Comaty, J. E., and Janicak, P. G. "Depot Neuroleptics." *Psychiatric Annals*, 1987, *17*, 491–496.

Committee on Peer Review, American Psychiatric Association. *Manual of Psychiatric Peer Review*. (3rd ed.) Washington, D.C.: American Psychiatric Association, 1985.

Cooper, H. N. "Problems in Application of the Basic Criteria of Schizophrenia." *American Journal of Psychiatry*, 1960, *117*, 66–71.

Cutting, J. "Schizophrenic Deterioration." *British Journal of Psychiatry*, 1983, *143*, 77–84.

Dahl, S. G. "Plasma Level Monitoring of Antipsychotic Drugs, Clinical Utility." *Clinical Pharmacokinetics*, 1986, *11*, 36–61.

Davis, J. M. "A Two-Factor Theory of Schizophrenia." *Journal of Psychiatry*, 1974, *11*, 25–29.

Davis, J. M., and Janicak, P. G. "The Efficacy of MAO Inhibitors in Depression: A Meta-Analysis." *Psychiatric Annals*, 1987, *17*, 825–831.

Deutsch, H. "Some Forms of Emotional Disturbance and Their Relationship to Schizophrenia." *Psychoanalytic Quarterly*, 1942, *11*, 301–321.

Dozier, M., Harris, M., and Bergman, H. "Social Network Density and Rehospitalization Among Young Adult Patients." *Hospital and Community Psychiatry*, 1987, *38* (1), 61–65.

Edwards, G. "Diagnosis of Schizophrenia: An Anglo-American Comparison." *British Journal of Psychiatry*, 1972, *120*, 385–390.

Ellsworth, R., and others. "Milieu Characteristics of Successful Psychiatric Treatment Programs." *American Journal of Orthopsychiatry*. 1971, *41* (3), 427–441.

Erikson, E. *Childhood and Society*. New York: Norton, 1950.

Essen-Möller, E. "Evidence of Polygenic Inheritance in Schizophrenia?" *Acta Psychiatry Scandinavica*, 1977, *55*, 202–207.

Fairweather, G. (guest ed.). *The Fairweather Lodge: A Twenty-Five-Year Retrospective*. San Francisco: Jossey-Bass, 1980.

Falloon, I.R.H., and others. "Family Therapy of Schizophrenia with High Risk of Relapse." *Family Procedure*, 1981, *20*, 211–221.

Feighner, J. P., and others. "Diagnostic Criteria for Use in Psychiatric Research." *Archives of General Psychiatry*, 1972, *26*, 57–63.

Feurlein, W. "Kriseninterventionstechniken und Organisation der Krisenintervention, Eine Station fur Notfallpsychiatrie und Krisenintervention—Konzepte, Struktur, und Erste Erfahrungen" [Crisis intervention techniques and organization of crisis intervention. A unit for emergency psychiatry and crisis intervention concept, structure, and initial results]. *Wien Klin Wochenschr*, 1983, *145*, 13–27.

Foucault, M. *Madness and Civilization*. New York: Pantheon, 1965.

Fowler, R., and others. "The Validity of Good Prognosis in Schizophrenia." *Archives of General Psychiatry*, 1972, *26*, 182–185.

Frank, J. D. *Persuasion and Healing*. Baltimore, Md.: Johns Hopkins University Press, 1961.

Frank, J. D. "The Role of Hope in Psychotherapy." *International Journal of Psychiatry*, 1968, *5* (5), 383–400.

Freeman, H. E., and Simmons, O. G. *The Mental Patient Comes Home*. New York: Wiley, 1963.

Fromm-Reichman, F. "Transference Problems in Schizophrenia." *Psychoanalytic Quarterly*, 1939, *8*, 412–426.

Fromm-Reichman, F. "Problems of Therapeutic Management in a Psychoanalytic Hospital." *Psychoanalytic Quarterly*, 1947, *16*, 325–356.

Gershon, S., and Eison, A. S. "The Ideal Anxiolytic." *Psychiatric Annals*, 1987, *3*, 156–170.

Gillespie, J. "Supportive Care in the Community." *Nursing Focus*, 1982, *4* (3), 9.

Goa, K. L., and Ward, A. "Buspirone." *Drugs*, 1986, *32*, 114–129.

Greenberg, S. "The Supportive Approach to Therapy. Conference of the Department of Psychiatry, Mount Auburn Hospital (1977, Cambridge, MA)." *Clinical Social Work Journal*, 1986, *14* (1), 6–13.

Greenblatt, D. J., and others. "Clinical Pharmacokinetics of the Newer Benzodiazepines." *Clinical Pharmacokinetics*, 1983, *8*, 233–252.

Greinspoon, L., Ewalt, J., and Shader, R. "Psychotherapy and Pharmacotherapy in Chronic Schizophrenia." *American Journal of Psychiatry*, 1968, *124*, 1645–1652.

Hagstrom, W. O. *The Scientific Community*. New York: Basic Books, 1965.

Harding, C. H., Zubin, J., and Strauss, J. S. "Chronicity in Schizophrenia: Fact, Partial Fact, or Artifact?" *Hospital and Community Psychiatry*, 1987, *38* (5), 477–486.

Hatfield, A. B. (ed.). *Families of the Mentally Ill: Meeting the Challenges.* San Francisco: Jossey-Bass, 1987.

Herz, M. I. "Intermittent Medication for Stable Schizophrenic Outpatients: An Alternative to Maintenance Medication." *American Journal of Psychiatry*, 1982, *139*, 918–922.

Hoch, P., and Polantin, P. "Psychoneurotic Forms of Schizophrenia." *Psychiatric Quarterly*, 1949, *23*, 248–276.

Hollingshead, A. B., and Redlich, F. C. *Social Class and Mental Illness.* New York: Wiley, 1958.

Jacobs, L. I. "A Cognitive Approach to Persistent Delusions." *American Journal of Psychotherapy*, 1980, *34* (4), 556–563.

Janicak, P. G., and Boshes, R. A. "Advances in the Treatment of Manic and Other Acute Psychotic Disorders." *Psychiatric Annals*, 1987, *17*, 145–149.

Janicak, P. G., Bresnahan, D. B., and Comaty, J. E. "The Neuroleptic Malignant Syndrome: A Clinical Update." *Psychiatric Annals*, 1987, *17*, 551–555.

Jann, M. W., Garrelts, J. C., Ereshefsky, L., and Saklad, S. R. "Alternative Drug Therapies for Mania: A Literature Review." *Drug Intelligence Clinical Pharmacy*, 1984, *18*, 577–589.

Jaspers, K. *General Psychopathology.* (J. Hoenig and M. Hamilton, trans.) Chicago: University of Chicago Press, 1963.

Jens, L. *The Jewelled Flower.* Glen Ellyn, Ill.: National Writers Press, 1987.

Kane, J. M. "Antipsychotic Drug Side Effects: Their Relationship to Dose." *Journal of Clinical Psychiatry*, 1985, *46*, 16–21.

Kane, J. M. "Dosage Strategies with Long-Acting Injectable Neuroleptics, Including Haloperidol Decanoate." *Journal of Clinical Psychopharmacology*, 1986, *6*, 205–235.

Karon, B., and Vandenbos, G. "Experience, Medication, and the Effectiveness of Psychotherapy with Schizophrenics." *British Journal of Psychiatry*, 1970, *116*, 427–428.

Kernberg, O. F. "Supportive Psychotherapy with Borderline Conditions." *Grand Rounds Presentation.* New York: Department of Psychiatry, Albert Einstein College of Medicine, 1981.

Kety, S. "Biochemical Theories of Schizophrenia." I, II, *Science*, 1959, *129*, 1528–1532, 1590–1596.

Knight, R. P. "Psychotherapy of an Adolescent Catatonic Schizophrenia with Mutism." *Psychiatry*, 1946, *9*, 323–339.

Kraepelin, E. *Lehrbuch der Psychiatrie* [Clinical psychiatry: A textbook for students and physicians]. (6th ed.) (A. R. Defendorf, ed.) New York: Macmillan, 1904.

Kulhara, P., and Wig, N. N. "The Chronicity of Schizophrenia in North West India." *British Journal of Psychiatry*, 1978, *132*, 186–190.

Laing, R. *The Divided Self.* London: Pelican, 1965.

Lanzkron, J., and Wolfson, W. "Prognostic Value of Perceptual Distortion of Temporal Disorientation in Chronic Schizophrenia." *American Journal of Psychiatry*, 1958, *114*, 744–746.

Lassenius, B., Ottosson, J., and Rapp, W. "Prognosis in Schizophrenia. The Need for Institutionalized Care." *Acta Psychiatrica Scandinavica*, 1973, *49*, 295–305.

Lavie, C. J., Olmsted, T. R., Ventura, H. O., and Lepler, B. J. "Neuroleptic Malignant Syndrome." *Postgraduate Medicine*, 1986, *3*, 171–178.

Leff, J. P. "Schizophrenia and Sensitivity to the Family Environment." *Schizophrenic Bulletin*, 1976, *2*, 566–574.

Lewis, A. B., Spencer, J. H., Jr., Haas, G. L., and DiVittis, A. "Goal Attainment Scaling: Relevance and Replicability in Follow-up of Inpatients." *Journal of Nervous and Mental Disease*, 1987, *175* (7), 408–418.

Lewis, H. A., Bacher, N. M., and Field, P. B. "Addition of Lithium to Neuroleptic Treatment in Chronic Schizophrenia." *American Journal of Psychiatry*, 1986, *143*, 262.

McEvoy, J. P., Howe, A. C., and Hogarty, G. E. "Differences in the Nature of Relapse and Subsequent Inpatient Course Between Medication-Compliant and Noncompliant Schizophrenic Patients." *Journal of Nervous and Mental Disease*, 1984, *172* (7), 412–416.

May, P. *Treatment of Schizophrenia.* New York: Science House, 1968.

Mazzanti, V., and Bessell, H. "Communication Through Latent Language." *American Journal of Psychotherapy*, 1956, *10*, 250–260.

Mednick, S. "Breakdown in Individuals at High Risk for Schizophrenia: Possible Predispositional Perinatal Factors." *Mental Hygiene*, 1970, *54*, 50-63.

Mellor, C. "First Rank Symptoms of Schizophrenia." *British Journal of Psychiatry*, 1970, *117*, 15-23.

Mendel, W. "Outpatient Therapy of Chronic Schizophrenia." In J. Masserman (ed.), *Current Psychiatric Therapies*. Vol. 4. Orlando, Fla.: Grune & Stratton, 1964.

Mendel, W. "Effect of Length of Hospitalization on Rate and Quality of Remission from Acute Psychotic Episodes." *Journal of Nervous and Mental Disease*, 1966, *143*, 226-233.

Mendel, W. "Tranquilizing Prescribing as a Function of the Experience and Availability of the Therapist." *American Journal of Psychiatry*, 1967, *124*, 16-22.

Mendel, W. "On the Abolition of the Psychiatric Hospital." In L. Roberts and others (eds.), *Comprehensive Mental Health*. Madison: University of Wisconsin Press, 1968a, 237-247.

Mendel, W. "Responsibility in Health, Illness, and Treatment." *Archives of General Psychiatry*, 1968b, *18*, 697-705.

Mendel, W. "The Non-Specifics of Psychotherapy." *International Journal of Psychiatry*, 1968c, *5*, 400-402.

Mendel, W. "Authority: Its Nature and Use in the Therapeutic Relationship." *Hospital and Community Psychiatry*, 1970, *21*, 367-370.

Mendel, W. "Precision in the Diagnosis of Schizophrenia." *Psychiatria Fennica*, 1975a, 107-114.

Mendel, W. *Supportive Care: Theory and Technique*. Los Angeles: Mara Books, 1975b.

Mendel, W. *Schizophrenia: The Experience and Its Treatment*. San Francisco: Jossey-Bass, 1976.

Mendel, W. "Mainstreaming." *Hillside Journal of Clinical Psychiatry*, 1980, *2*, 95-128.

Mendel, W., and Goren, S. "Mainstreaming." In R. Lorsini (ed.), *Handbook of Innovative Psychotherapies*. New York: Wiley, 1981.

Mendel, W., and Rapport, S. "Outpatient Treatment for Chronic Schizophrenic Patients." *Archives of General Psychiatry*, 1963, *8*, 190-196.

Mendel, W., and Rapport, S. "Determinants of the Decision for

Psychiatric Hospitalization." *Archives of General Psychiatry,* 1969, *20,* 320-328.

Merskey, H. "Diagnosis of Schizophrenia." *Lancet,* 1972, *2,* 1246-1249.

Meyerson, A. T., and Herman, G. S. "What's New in Aftercare? A Review of Recent Literature." *Hospital and Community Psychiatry,* 1983, *34,* 333-342.

Minkowski, E. *Le Temps vécu* [Experienced time]. Paris: Collection de l'Evolution Psychiatrique, 1933.

Molchanova, E. K. "Results of Continuous Study of Population of Schizophrenic Patients Greater than 60 Years of Age." *Zhurnal Nevropatologii I Psikhiatrii Imeni S. S. Korsakova,* 1975, *75,* 898-905.

Mosher, L. R., and Keith, S. J. "Research on the Psychosocial Treatment of Schizophrenia: A Summary Report." *American Journal of Psychiatry,* 1979, *136* (5), 623-631.

Mosher, L., Kresky-Wolff, M., Matthews, S., and Menn, A. "Milieu Therapy in the 1980s: A Comparison of Two Residential Alternatives to Hospitalization." *Bulletin of the Menninger Clinic,* 1986, *50* (3), 257-268.

Ödegaard, Ö. "The Psychiatric Disease Entities in the Light of a Genetic Investigation." *Acta Psychiatry Scandinavica,* 1963, *169,* 94-104.

Ödegaard, Ö. "The Multifactorial Theory of Inheritance in Predisposition to Schizophrenia." In A. R. Kaplan (ed.), *Genetic Factors in "Schizophrenia."* Springfield, Ill.: Thomas, 1972, 256-275.

Odenheimer, J. "Day Hospital as an Alternative to the Psychiatric Ward." *Archives of General Psychiatry,* 1965, *13,* 13-46.

Pare, C. M. "Monoamine Oxidase Inhibitors in the Treatment of Affective Disorders." *Psychiatric Annals,* 1987, *17,* 309-316.

Parfitt, D. "The Neurology of Schizophrenia." *Journal of Mental Science,* 1956, *102,* 671-718.

Parsons, T. "Illness and the Role of the Physician." In C. K. Kluckhohn and H. A. Murray (eds.), *Personality in Nature, Society, and Culture.* New York: Knopf, 1953, 609-617.

Parsons, T. "Definitions of Health and Illness in the Light of

American Values and Social Structure." In E. G. Jaco (ed.), *Patients, Physicians, and Illness.* New York: Free Press, 1958.

Pasamanick, B., Scarpitti, F., and Dinitz, S. *Schizophrenics in the Community.* East Norwalk, Conn.: Appleton-Century-Crofts, 1967.

Patterson, T. "Electrophysiological Studies of Schizophrenia." *Bulletin of the Menninger Clinic,* 1986, *50* (3), 238–256.

Paykel, E. S., and Van Woerkom, A. E. "Pharmacologic Treatment of Resistant Depression." *Psychiatric Annals,* 1987, *17,* 327–331.

Polantin, R., and Hoch, P. "Diagnostic Evaluation of Early Schizophrenia." *Journal of Nervous and Mental Disease,* 1947, *105,* 221–230.

Roberts, R. "The Outpatient Treatment of Schizophrenia: An Integrated and Comprehensive Management-Oriented Approach." *Psychiatric Quarterly,* 1984, *56* (2), 91–112.

Rutter, M. "Meyerian Psychobiology, Personality Development, and the Role of Life Experiences." *American Journal of Psychiatry,* 1986, *143* (9), 1077–1087.

Salem, R. B. "Recommendations for Monitoring Lithium Therapy." *Drug Intelligence Clinical Pharmacy,* 1983, *17,* 346–350.

Schlesinger, H. J., and Hoizman, P. S. "The Therapeutic Aspects of the Hospital Milieu. Prescribing an Activities Program." *Bulletin of the Menninger Clinic,* 1970, *34* (1), 1–11.

Schneider, K. *Clinical Psychopathology.* Orlando, Fla.: Grune & Stratton, 1959.

Schwartz, L. S., and others. "A Supportive Care Clinic, Maintaining the Chronic Psychiatric Patient." *Hillside Journal of Clinical Psychiatry,* 1986, *8* (2), 202–208.

Schwing, G. *A Way to the Soul of the Mentally Ill.* New York: International Universities Press, 1954.

Sechehaye, M. A. *Reality Lost and Regained: Autobiography of a Schizophrenic Girl.* Part 1. (G. Rubin-Rabson, trans.) Orlando, Fla.: Grune & Stratton, 1951.

Serban, G., and Thomas, A. "Attitudes and Behaviors of Acute and Chronic Schizophrenic Patients Regarding Ambulatory Treatment." *American Journal of Psychiatry,* 1974, *131* (9), 991–995.

Shapiro, R., and Shader, E. "Selective Review of Results of Previous Follow-up Studies of Schizophrenia and Other Psychosis." In

World Health Organization, *Schizophrenia: An International Pilot Study.* Chichester, England: Wiley, 1979.

Shrala, M. "Psychotherapy of Schizophrenia as Basic Human Experience." *Psychiatria Fennica,* 1972, 155–175.

Shryock, R. H. *The Development of Modern Medicine.* New York: Knopf, 1947.

Spitzer, R. L., and Fleiss, J. L. "A Re-analysis of the Reliability of Psychiatric Diagnosis." *British Journal of Psychiatry,* 1974, *125,* 341–347.

Stevenson, I. "Comments on 'Is Outcome for Schizophrenia Better in Nonindustrial Societies? The Case of Sri Lanka.'" *Journal of Nervous and Mental Disease,* 1979, *167* (3), 159–160.

Straus, E. W. "The Upright Posture." *Psychiatric Quarterly,* 1952, *26,* 529–561.

Strauss, J., and Carpenter, W. "Characteristic Symptoms and Outcome in Schizophrenia." *American Journal of Psychiatry,* 1974a, *30,* 429–434.

Strauss, J., and Carpenter, W. "The Prediction of Outcome in Schizophrenia." *Archives of General Psychiatry,* 1974b, *31,* 37–42.

Stuart, R. L. "Psychoanalysis and Psychoanalytic Psychotherapy." In H. I. Kaplan and A. M. Freedman (eds.), *Comprehensive Textbook of Psychiatry.* Baltimore, Md.: Williams & Wilkens, 1980, 2136.

Sukhovski, A. A. "Clinical Picture and Dynamics of Long-Term Late Remissions in the Outcome of Schizophrenia." *Zhurnal Nevropatologii I Psikhiatrii S. S. Korsakova,* 1976, *76,* 563–568.

Sulser, F. "Mode of Action of Antidepressant Drugs." *Journal of Clinical Psychiatry,* 1983, *44* (5, Sec. 2), 14–20.

Tausk, V. "On the Origin of the 'Influencing Machine' in Schizophrenia." *Psychoanalytic Quarterly,* 1933, *2,* 519–556. Reprinted in R. Fliess (ed.), *The Psychoanalytic Reader,* Vol. 1. New York: International Universities Press, 1946.

Taylor, M. "Schneiderian First-Rank Symptoms and Clinical Prognostic Features in Schizophrenia." *Archives of General Psychiatry,* 1972, *26,* 64–67.

Tischler, G. L. (ed.). *Diagnosis and Classification in Psychiatry: A*

Critical Appraisal of DSM-III. New York: Cambridge University Press, 1987.

Tooth, G. "Studies in Mental Illness in the Gold Coast." *Colonial Research Publication, 6.* London: Her Majesty's Stationery Office, 1950.

Torrey, E. F. "Management of Schizophrenic Outpatients." *Psychiatric Clinics of North America,* 1986, *9* (1), 143–151.

Tsuang, M. T., and Woolson, R. F. "Excess Mortality in Schizophrenia and Affective Disorders. Do Suicides and Accidental Deaths Solely Account for This Excess?" *Archives of General Psychiatry,* 1978, *35,* 1181–1185.

Valliant, G. "Prospective Prediction of Schizophrenic Remission." *Archives of General Psychiatry,* 1964, *11,* 509–518.

Van Praag, H. M., and Korff, J. "The Dopamine Hypothesis of Schizophrenia. Some Direct Observations." In H. M. Van Pragg (ed.), *On the Origin of Schizophrenic Psychoses.* Amsterdam: De Erven Bohn BV, 1974, 81–98.

Vonnegut, M. "Why I Want to Bite R. D. Laing." *Harpers,* Apr. 1974, pp. 90–93.

Wagemaker, H., and Cade, R. "The Use of Hemodialysis in Chronic Schizophrenia." *American Journal of Psychiatry,* 1977, *134,* 684–685.

Waxler, N. E. "Culture and Mental Illness. A Social Labeling Perspective." *Journal of Nervous and Mental Disease,* 1974, *159,* 379–395.

Waxler, N. E. "Is Outcome for Schizophrenia Better in Nonindustrial Societies? The Case of Sri Lanka." *Journal of Nervous and Mental Disease,* 1979, *167* (3), 144–157.

White, K., and Simpson, G. "Treatment-Resistant Depression." *Psychiatric Annals,* 1987, *17,* 274–278.

Wijesinghe, C. P., Dissanayake, S.A.W., and Dassanayake, P.L.V.N. "Psychiatric Morbidity in an Urban Population in Sri Lanka." Department of Psychiatry, University of Sri Lanka, Colombo, 1975.

Will, O. "Psychotherapeutics and the Schizophrenic Reaction." *Journal of Nervous and Mental Disease,* 1958, *126,* 109–140.

Winokur, G. "Diagnostic Stability Over Time in Schizophrenia,

Mania, and Depression." *New England Journal of Medicine,* 1974, *290,* 1026–1032.

World Health Organization. *Report of Study Group on Schizophrenia.* Geneva: World Health Organization, 1957.

World Health Organization. *Schizophrenia: An International Follow-up Study.* Sussex, England: Wiley, 1979.

Zilboorg, G. "Ambulatory Schizophrenias." *Psychiatry,* 1941, *4,* 149–155.

Zusman, J. "Some Explanations of the Changing Appearance of Psychotic Patients: Antecedents of the Social Breakdown Syndrome Concept." *International Journal of Psychiatry,* 1967, *3,* 216–247.

Index

A

Acute intervention, hospitalization for, 141–156
Acute schizophrenia, absence of, 64
Adapin, 173
Affective psychotic disorder: diagnosis of, 64; and level of function, 19, 36
Age of onset: aspects of, 8–17; and behavioral episodes, 12–13; in composite case, 78–79; and diagnostic subgroups, 68–69; and environment, 8, 13, 16; and length of first crisis, 13–15; and life history, 9–10; and medical episodes, 12; and nature of first crisis, 11–14; and premorbid personality, 14–16; summary on, 16–17; and time of first crisis, 10–11
Aging patient: aspects of remission in, 72–77; in composite case, 84–85; pattern for, 72–73; remission in, 23–24, 36, 72–77, 215–216; response to medication by, 74–75; sociocultural changes for, 75–76; summary on, 76–77

Aliphatic phenothiazines, 165, 166, 167
Allen, C. K., 33, 149, 153n, 156
Allen, R. E., 156
Allen Lacing Technique, 33, 149
Alprazolam (Xanax), 181, 182
Amantadine (Symmetrel), 166, 169
American Psychiatric Association: Committee on Peer Review of, 164, 174; Task Force on Laboratory Tests in Psychiatry of, 175
Amitriptyline (Elavil), 173, 175, 176
Amoxapine (Asendin), 173, 174–175
Andrews, G., 16
Andrews, S., 16
Anglo-American study, 55
Anscombe, R., 160
Anticholinergic effects: and antidepressants, 174, 176; and antipsychotics, 166, 169
Antidepressants: aspects of using, 172–178; in case presentation, 213; classification of, 173; dosages of, 175–176, 178; effectiveness of, 177; serum levels of, 175–176; side effects of, 173–174, 176, 177–178; target symptoms for, 172; uses of, 184